THE JUDICIAL
DEVELOPMENT
OF PRESIDENTIAL
WAR POWERS

THE JUDICIAL
DEVELOPMENT
OF PRESIDENTIAL
WAR POWERS

Martin S. Sheffer

Westport, Connecticut
London

Library of Congress Cataloging-in-Publication Data

Sheffer, Martin S.
    The judicial development of presidential war powers / Martin S.
  Sheffer.
      p. cm.
    Includes bibliographical references and index.
    ISBN 0–275–96435–3 (alk. paper)
    1. War and emergency powers—United States—Cases. 2. Executive
  power—United States—Cases. I. Title.
  KF5060.A68S53   1999
  342.73′062—dc21   98–38287

British Library Cataloguing in Publication Data is available.

Library of Congress Catalog Card Number: 98–38287
ISBN: 0–275–96435–3

First published in 1999

Praeger Publishers, 88 Post Road West, Westport, CT 06881
An imprint of Greenwood Publishing Group, Inc.

Printed in the United States of America

The paper used in this book complies with the
Permanent Paper Standard issued by the National
Information Standards Organization (Z39.48–1984).

10 9 8 7 6 5 4 3 2 1

Copyright Acknowledgments

The author and publisher gratefully acknowledge permission for use of excerpts from the following:

Rossiter, Clinton L. *Constitutional Dictatorship: Crisis Government in the Modern Democracies.* Copyright © 1948 by Princeton University Press. Renewed © 1976. Reprinted by permission of Princeton University Press.

The Supreme Court in the American System of Government by Robert H. Jackson. Copyright © 1955 by William Eldred Jackson and G. Bowdoin Craighill. Reprinted by permission of Harvard University Press.

"The Suspension of Habeas Corpus During the War of the Rebellion" by S. G. Fisher. Reprinted with permission from *Political Science Quarterly*, 3 (1888): 454–488.

"The Impotence of Reticence" by Philip Kurland. Reprinted with permission from *Duke Law Journal* (1968): 619, 624.

In no part of the Constitution is more wisdom to be found, than in the clause which confides the question of war or peace to the legislature, and not to the executive department. Besides the objection to such a mixture to heterogeneous powers, the trust and the temptation would be too great for any one man; not such as nature may offer as the prodigy of many centuries, but such as may be expected in the ordinary successions of magistracy. War is ... the true nurse of executive aggrandizement. In war, a physical force is to be created; and it is the executive will, which is to direct it. In war, the public treasures are to be unlocked; and it is the executive ... which is to dispense them. In war, the honours and emoluments of office are to be multiplied; and it is the executive patronage under which they are to be enjoyed. It is in war, finally, that laurels are to be gathered; and it is the executive brow they are to encircle. The strongest passions and most dangerous weaknesses of the human breast; ambition, avarice, vanity, and honourable or venial love of fame, are all in conspiracy against the desire and duty of peace. 6 J. Madison, *Writings* 174 (Hunt ed. 1906).

In times of peace the people look most to their representative; but in war to the executive only. 5 T. Jefferson, *Writings* 500 (Ford ed. 1895).

Contents

Preface

The progressive growth in the power and prestige of the American presidency, especially in the areas of war, peace, and foreign affairs, has been perhaps the most notable feature of American constitutional development. Beginning with President Thomas Jefferson's use of the navy against the Barbary pirates in 1801, debate has raged over the limitations on presidential authority to commit troops to hostilities without prior congressional authorization.[1] Notwithstanding the constant question of what, if any, unilateral war power the President actually possesses, American chief executives have consistently used military force without seeking congressional approval prior to such action. This steady aggrandizement of power has been dramatically expanded by twentieth-century chief executives, resulting in the concentration of almost unilateral warmaking power in the hands of the President. The use of this unilateral power during the war in Southeast Asia called attention to the danger present in the concentration of such a degree of power,[2] and recent military actions have failed to make the possession and use of such unilateral power less suspect. The accumulation of unilateral power by the President has greatly intensified the ongoing debate concerning presidential war powers, and it is this development that prompted the writing of this casebook.

This book deals with one of the continuing constitutional problems confronting the Republic: the legal development of presidential war powers, potential constitutional dictatorship, and a wartime constitution. One must constantly remember that executive-legislative conflicts regarding questions of emergency, war, and peace, although raising many constitutional controversies, rarely find their way to the judiciary and, when they do, are rarely decided according to proper constitutional interpretation. For the most part, they are resolved (if resolved at all) through political settlements agreed to by Congress and the President. The momentous decision to commit the Nation's blood and deplete its treasury is left almost entirely to nonjudicial officials.[3]

The problem faced by lawyers who must somehow justify the oftentimes extraconstitutional use of presidential power is the very cryptic language presented by Article II itself. There simply is no express language available which can be employed in the specific situations raised in the pages that follow. Consequently, these lawyers, whether in government or in academia, resort to several different techniques to find a basis in the fundamental law for the presidential actions taken or proposed: (1) the generalities of Article II have been read expansively to cover specific actions;[4] or (2) a theory of inherent powers (usually based on past presidential performance not struck down by the courts) is said to justify the means.[5] Moreover, these lawyers argue that ends and means are determined only by the President.[6] The end result of this legal legerdemain is that presidential action takes on the characteristics of constitutional power.[7]

Three basic principles are discernible here, both from the constitutional text and from historical practice: (1) the commander-in-chief clause relates to the war powers, and thus is a shared duty and power with Congress; (2) the President is able to exercise his duties as commander-in-chief so as to give himself extraordinary powers, powers that by and large are limited only by the workings of the political process or the President's own commitments to democratic constraints;[8] and (3) this limitation is because the courts, speaking generally, either postpone ruling or uphold, when they do rule, exercises of the power.[9] The commander-in-chief power thus is open-ended and expandable, and limited less by law than by politics. Since foreign affairs are now central to the attention of the President, as the United States moves into ever closer relations with other nations, this power takes on added significance. It is the basis of the use of the armed forces themselves, oftentimes without express approval of Congress, and since the beginnings of the Cold War it is the only express constitutional warrant for paramilitary operations.[10] Furthermore, as commander-in-chief the President labors under the obligation to succeed. Failure can mean both the end of a political career and "bad press" in the future pages of history books, as seen by the instances of Presidents Truman and Johnson in the Korean and Vietnam conflicts, respectively. Power, in other words, carries responsibilities; the American people likely will forget and forgive any action provided it is successful.[11]

In times of declared war, the President acts as a "constitutional dictator". The Constitution is, as Chief Justice Hughes once said, a "fighting Constitution."[12] There is a tacit understanding that nothing, literally nothing, will be permitted to block winning the war. What is necessary, as determined by the chief executive, is done. The President's duty is to ensure the national survival. Legal niceties are given little attention. National survival is the ultimate value. Congress does not interfere with the manner in which the President as commander-in-chief conducts the war; it is a ready ally in almost everything that he personally and institutionally wishes to do. And the courts lie back, seeking to avoid having to rule on questions of the conduct of commander-in-chief (and war) powers, and when they are forced to rule, they usually uphold presidential action. Congress, moreover, has in the past drawn upon its war powers to give the President carte blanche to take actions considered by him vital to the defense of the United States.[13] This is the doctrine of necessity run riot, a reading into the wartime constitution of the theory of *raison d'etat:* "Reason of state is nothing but the doctrine that whatever is required to insure the survival of the state must be done by the individuals responsible for it, no matter how repugnant such an act may be to them in their private capacity as decent and moral men."[14]

An examination of presidential war powers gives rise to several very perplexing constitutional questions, not always answered completely or truthfully, by judicial decisions. Among them are: Who can suspend the writ of habeas corpus? Who can start a war? When the war is over, who can end it? What are the war powers of Congress, and to what extent may they be delegated to the President? How independent of the Supreme Court are courts-martial and presidential military commissions? What are the President's powers in conquered areas? Can private property be seized as part of a war effort? These (and other) questions are presented in the cases that constitute the judicial development of presidential war powers.

The transitional period between peace and the Cold War lasted only a short time in the United States, from the end of World War II until Korea and the fall of Dien Bien Phu. The result was that virtually no abeyance occurred in an already developed tradition of presidential supremacy in times of crisis (this time short of declared war).[15] The United States was to witness during the decades of the 1950s through the 1980s increasingly confident executive demands for discretion and independence, secrecy and privilege, as foreign commitments mounted and as national security turned inward.[16]

Yet, at the same time, dissenting and critical voices were being heard, and as time went by both Congress and the Supreme Court began to listen. It was therefore inevitable, as long as the constitutional structure retained any continuing vitality, that as executive power burgeoned and as Vietnam shaded into Watergate, pressure would increase within Congress for a reexamination of its role and whether it would claim its share of power or abdicate its responsibility. And in a society where judicial activism was becoming a widely accepted norm it was inevitable that there would be strong expectation that presidential power would be weighed in the judicial forum.

The turning point in the President's establishment, and the Nation's acceptance, of prerogative, emergency powers came with the recognition of the President as Burkean trustee rather than as delegate.[17] In *The Federalist,* No. 70, Alexander Hamilton acknowledged Edmund Burke's argument by suggesting that a "vigorous executive" was not only completely consistent with a republican government, but that a strong executive was "essential" to the protection of the community.[18] Hamilton's intention was to legitimize for America the notion of the President as trustee, the one individual in the Nation whose broad perception of the public interest would allow for his involvement in the entire spectrum of public decision making.[19]

The cases that follow recognize, as a minimum, that war and peace are not the same thing and cannot coexist in the same place at the same time. They recognize, too, that there are times in our history when the President acts, and must act, beyond constitutional constraint. Congress may not be in session and the courts may be unable (or unwilling) to intervene. What force at those times restrains the exercise of presidential prerogative power?

This book on the legal development of presidential war powers is designed for the traditional lecture method of teaching, although it is easily adapted for Socratic-method teaching as well.[20] It attempts to show how the Supreme Court—one of the three great independent branches of the government of the United States—in deciding several hundred cases involving the scope of the national war powers, has (along with presidential initiative and congressional authorization and acquiescence) interpreted and changed the President's status as commander-in-chief. Moreover, in light of the book's ultimate audience (undergraduate students in an area of constitutional law) the approach taken is the perspective of the legal historian, an attempt to combine both the logic of *authority* and the logic of *evidence*. The process by which old principles and old phrases are charged with a new content, in the words of Frederick William Maitland, "is from the lawyer's point of view an evolution of the true intent and meaning of the old law, from the historian's point of view it is almost of necessity a process of perversion and misunderstanding."[21] What the lawyer wants is authority and the newer the better; what the historian wants is evidence and the older the better.[22] It is my contention that the two are not necessarily incompatible. Two hundred years as a constitutional, democratic government, while at the same time providing for presidential dictatorship in times of crisis, does not mean that *old* evidence and *new* authority cannot be used to reach and substantiate the same conclusion. Like all casebooks, regardless of the intended audience, the cases presented here are not an exhaustive listing of all the litigation pertaining to the legal development of presidential war powers. On the contrary, the cases included here are only a representative sample which the author believes best point out and substantiate the principle themes of this casebook.

Acknowledgments of gratitude are always necessary in a book of this sort. Unfortunately there is never enough room to mention everyone, so let me specify the four most important. First, to the three eminent scholars in the field who taught me to appreciate the subject of presidential power: the late Robert S. Hirschfield of Hunter College, CUNY, Louis W. Koenig of New York University, and Saul K. Padover of the New School for Social Research. Each showed me the dynamics and possibilities of the institution and made me fully understand that great power alone makes great leadership possible and that presidential greatness directly depends on democratic constraints. Second, to my former students at Old Dominion University and Tuskegee University who helped develop and clarify many of these ideas during classroom discussions and arguments in my American Presidency and Presidential War Powers courses. Third, to the extraordinarily helpful people at Greenwood Publishing for making this possible, particularly Dr. James T. Sabin, Director of Academic Research and Development, and Meg Fergusson, Production Editor. Fourth, and most important, to my family—to whom this book is dedicated—for their encouragement, patience, and help. My wife Lois, an extraordinarily gifted historian and teacher, offered invaluable suggestions; and my son Andrew, a practicing attorney, aided me in the initial research of this book. After hearing me complain and argue for so long about presidential war powers, they convinced me to put many of these thoughts into book form.

NOTES

1. The issue of constitutional authority to declare war, and the question of the legitimacy of an undeclared war, was first raised by the undeclared naval war with France in 1798, and in Bas v. Tingy, 4 U.S. (4 Dall.) 37 (1800), the Supreme Court ruled that a formal declaration of war was not required. "The United States and the French Republic are in a qualified state of hostility. An imperfect war, or a war, as to certain objects, and to a certain extent, exists between the two nations; and this modified warfare is authorized by the constitutional authority of our country. It is a war *quoad hoc* [as regards this particular matter]. As far as Congress tolerated and authorized the war on our part, so far we may proceed to hostile operations." *Id.* at 45. *Accord*, Talbot v. Seeman, 5 U.S. (1 Cr.) 1 (1801); Little v. Barreme, 6 U.S. (2 Cr.) 170 (1804).

2. Among the principle rites of an unpopular war is the inquisition: the investigation of those men and institutions responsible for the decision to fight. Oftentimes the inquisition seeks only scapegoats. But occasionally it is less concerned with fixing blame than with avoiding future problems. Much of the political, legal, and academic debate, the inquiry into the scope of presidential authority to commit American troops to foreign conflict (Korea, Southeast Asia, Labanon, and Kuwait), partakes more of the redemptive than the punitive. Reveley, *Presidential War-Making: Constitutional Prerogative or Usurpation?*, 55 VA.L.REV. 1243 (1969). Unfortunately, as a Nation, we have been far better at fixing blame than at avoiding future problems.

3. C. Rossiter, THE SUPREME COURT AND THE COMMANDER IN CHIEF 2-3 (R. Longaker ed. 1976).

4. A. Miller, PRESIDENTIAL POWER 162 (1977).

5. *Id.*

6. *Id.*

7. *Id.*

8. *Id.* at 163. The use of troops domestically, in helping to enforce judicial decrees, is a classic example of the point.

9. *Id.* at 164.

10. *Id.*

11. *Id.*

12. Home Building & Loan Association v. Blaisdell, 290 U.S. 398, 426 (1934). *See also* his earlier statement, *War Powers under the Constitution,* 43 A.B.A. REPTS. 238 (1917).

13. *See, e.g.,* the Lever Food and Fuel Control Act, 40 Stat. 286 (1917) and the Lend Lease Act, 55 Stat. 31 (1941). In both instances, Congress virtually delegated Article I to the President.

14. C. Friedrich, CONSTITUTIONAL REASON OF STATE: THE SURVIVAL OF THE CONSTITUTIONAL ORDER 4-5 (1957). The doctrine has also been defined as "the fundamental principle of national conduct, [the] State's first law of motion. It tells the statesman what he must do to preserve the health and strength of the State. The State is an organic structure whose full power can only be maintained by allowing it in some way to continue

growing; and *raison d'etat* indicates both the path and the goal for such a growth." F. Meinecke, MACHIAVELLISM: THE DOCTRINE OF RAISON D'ETAT AND ITS PLACE IN MODERN HISTORY 1 (D. Scott trans. 1957).

15. C. Rossiter, *supra* note 3, at 133.

16. *Id.*

17. One of the fundamental rules of civil society, wrote Edmund Burke in 1790 in his REFLECTIONS ON THE REVOLUTION IN FRANCE 64 (Prometheus ed. 1987), "is that no man should be judge in his own cause." Burke argued that in civil society representatives as trustees must be allowed to act independently of the control of not only their constituency but of natural law. When constrained by natural law, representatives were in time of peril, powerless. When representatives acted as delegates (or simply ciphers for the public), Burke believed anarchy and the dominance of faction were the likely result. This notion of the representative (in this case the President as representative of the entire Nation) as trustee opens the floodgates for the exercise of prerogative power in a republic. D. Franklin, EXTRAORDINARY MEASURES 43-44 (1991).

18. "There is an idea, which is not without its advocates, that a vigorous executive is inconsistent with the genius of republican government. The enlightened well-wishers to this species of government must at least hope that the supposition is destitute of foundation; since they can never admit its truth, without at the same time admitting the condemnation of their own principles. *Energy in the executive is a leading character in the definition of good government.* It is essential to the protection of the community against foreign attacks; it is not less essential to the steady administration of the laws; to the protection of property against those irregular and high-handed combinations which sometimes interrupt the ordinary course of justice; to the security of liberty against the enterprises and assaults of ambition, of faction, and of anarchy....There can be no need, however, to multiply arguments or examples of this head. *A feeble execution is but another phrase for a bad execution; and a government ill executed, whatever it may be in theory, must be, in practice, a bad government."* THE FEDERALIST, No. 70, 423 (C. Rossiter ed. 1961) (Hamilton) (emphasis added).

19. D. Franklin, *supra* note 17, at 45.

20. The Socratic method, derived from dialogues attributed to the ancient Greek philosopher, presupposed that one mark of a truly intelligent person is the ability to ask incisive questions. Accordingly, Socratic method teachers do little lecturing and much questioning. Oftentimes students' questions are answered with still more questions, because the primary objective of the classroom dialogue is not to produce the right answer but to develop defensible modes of inquiry. The purpose is to encourage students to find their own answers and their own modes of inquiry by continually questioning not only the logic of the opinions, but the assumptions implicit in those opinions as well. C. Pyle & R. Pious, THE PRESIDENT, CONGRESS, AND THE CONSTITUTION xxvi (1984).

21. 1 COLLECTED PAPERS 490 (H. Fisher ed. 1911).

22. *Id.*

Introduction

Look for another source

In *The Federalist*, No. 23, Alexander Hamilton, writing about the concept of crisis government and the need for undefined power in the national government, declared that the war powers "ought to exist without limitation, because it is impossible to foresee or define the extent and variety of the means which may be necessary to satisfy them."[1] Hamilton then continued, "The circumstances that endanger the safety of nations are infinite, and for that reason no constitutional shackles can wisely be imposed on the power to which the care of it is committed. This power ought to be coextensive with all the possible combinations of such circumstances; and ought to be under the direction of the same councils which are appointed to preside over the common defence."[2]

The period of civil war permanently transformed our understanding of the war powers. Abraham Lincoln's imaginative combining of the commander-in-chief,[3] take care,[4] and executive power[5] clauses into a notion of presidential war power independent of legislative authority (where ends justified means), laid to rest the earlier, limited meaning of commander-in-chief.[6] Lincoln's assertion of this independent, virtually unlimited war power—the Hamiltonian and prerogative[7] theories—was within two years legitimized and sanctioned by the Supreme Court.[8] This transformation set the stage for the modern presidential office as well as creating the notion of constitutional dictatorship in the United States and beginning the development of the wartime constitution.

The Constitution says that the President shall be commander-in-chief of the armed forces when called into the actual service of the United States. At the same time the Congress is vested with the authority to declare war. Does it follow, then, that any presidentially initiated military engagement violates the Constitution? If so, does that mean that all the conflicts America entered without congressional declarations violate the Constitution? But perhaps formal declaration is not necessary so long as there is congressional authorization. Is that always necessary? Larger questions are involved as well. Is the President merely the servant of Congress, or does he possess powers independent of Congress? Are there circumstances in which his powers might be even greater than those of the Congress? What happens when and if the President and Congress have conflicting views?

Edward S. Corwin began his definitive study of the American presidency[9] by telling us that both legislative and judicial powers denote fairly definable functions of government as well as fairly constant methods for their discharge.[10] Executive power, on the other hand, "is still indefinite as to *function* and retains, particularly when exercised by a single individual, much of its original plasticity as to method."[11] He then went on to say that this indefinable executive power is most spontaneously responsive to emergency conditions.[12] He should have added, had he possessed the power to see the future, that it is a power most subject to abuse.

A first reading of the Constitution would give the reader little inkling of the vast amount of presidential power contained there; certainly nothing approximating "the very delicate, plenary and exclusive power of the President as the sole organ of the federal government in the field of international relations."[13] The powers vested in the President by virtue of Articles I and II are few and seem modest, far fewer and more modest than those bestowed upon Congress. What the Constitution says and does not say, therefore, does not determine exclusively what the President can and cannot do. In other words, the structure of the federal government, the facts and realities of national and international life, the practice of diplomacy, the level of acceptance by the American people, as well as the language of the Constitution, have afforded Presidents unique temptations and unique opportunities to acquire unique powers.[14]

Regarding the intentions of the Framers and presidential power, we can be certain only of some things. First, the presidency was never intended to be a weak institution. Second, the President's role was not simply limited to be that of carrying out the will of Congress. Third, the men who made Article II the most loosely drawn section in the Constitution understood fully, unlike many of their modern counterparts, the distinction between the words *declare* and *make,* for purposes of the war power. Fourth, the philosophers of balanced and strong government and executive prerogative (Aristotle, Niccolo Machiavelli, Thomas Hobbes, James Harrington, John Locke, William Blackstone, David Hume, and Baron de Montesquieu) were extremely influential among the delegates at Philadelphia. Finally, presidential power was not considered incompatible with limited government In the end, the balanced constitution of Locke, Blackstone, and Montesquieu prevailed because, among other reasons, the Framers found it most compatible with their interpretation of republican principles. The idea of a divided initiative in the matter of legislation, coupled with a broad range of autonomous executive power, was created and designed, according to Corwin, "to produce the monarchy of George III with the corruption left out."[15] Presidential power and limited government, at least in theory, were not mutually exclusive principles of governance.[16]

Similar to the problem of presidential power in general (where the solution is not to destroy presidential power but only to constitutionalize its use), the same approach holds true for the war power. The Nation would be ill served in returning entirely to the original intention of the Framers and allowing only Congress to formally determine war and peace. Certainly the televised debate over the military enforcement of United Nations Security Council Resolution No. 678 (the 1991 war with Iraq) is a case in point: with few notable exceptions the quality of the argument was flawed with historical and political inaccuracies on both sides of the aisle, and members showed far more concern in shamefully playing to the galleries and the television audience than in arriving at an intelligent and unemotional conclusion. The war power, in the hands of the President, must exist in order to protect the Nation, but, like all power, it must be doubly chained so as to allow its full protective capacity to function while simultaneously preventing its exercise by the President from doing too much mischief.[17]

Earlier in the development of the Republic, generally that period from Abraham Lincoln through Franklin D. Roosevelt, Presidents would act illegally and then depend on Congress to ratify their actions after the fact.[18] Beginning with Harry Truman and Korea, and continuing through the Indochina war (embracing Vietnam, Laos, Thailand, and Cambodia), the claim was made that the President possessed the power to initiate war without the consent of Congress.[19] In facing two such potentially dangerous choices, the lesser of the two evils (at best) would always be for the President to act illegally and then to look to Congress for ratification of his actions. If Congress should refuse to ratify, then the President's actions stand before the public starkly for what they are—illegal actions forbidden by the Constitution. Such a course of action would be far more preferable than allowing the President to claim an emergency power to act against the law for the good of the Nation, or, what is even worse, claim the exclusive right to determine what is good for the Nation.

Over the years, executive assertions of authority to employ military and paramilitary force have fallen into certain recognizable patterns.[20] One has been to claim that Congress somehow *delegated* authority for the actions of the President.[21] Oftentimes the legislation cited was rather general in nature—for example, the *posse comitatus* legislation initially enacted during the 1792 session of the first Congress[22] or the Habeas Corpus Act of 1863 (enacted after Lincoln had already suspended the Great Writ).[23] A second technique has been to justify the actions in terms of some specific grant of presidential power,[24] such as the commander-in-chief clause. Usually the authority granted is said to give the President some independent power immune from any congressional efforts to limit it. Third, if the claim to a specific grant of authority seems unpersuasive, the President may resort to the executive power mentioned in the first sentence of Article II.[25] Lincoln was among the first to lay hold of this clause, and he argued that it constituted a positive grant of affirmative power that allows the President to do anything necessary and proper (the executive equivalent of Article I, section 8, clause 18) to achieve and promote the national interest.

In each of the foregoing instances, the focus has been on a particular provision of the Constitution, however vague and open-ended it might be. An alternative approach, first suggested by Hamilton in *The Federalist,* No. 23, was to look upon the war powers as an aggregate of all powers granted to the Nation by the Constitution, and all power necessary and proper for carrying out the legitimate objects of the Nation.[26] Lincoln, of course, took this theory one step further when he conceived of the war powers (a resulting power consisting of the executive power, duty to take care, and commander-in-chief clauses) as an aggregation of constitutionally granted powers that, during a wartime emergency, belonged to the President as supreme military commander.[27] Aggregation took the focus off means and put it on ends, which could then be used to justify the means and break the bounds of strict construction.[28]

The next stage of argumentation was to break free from the Constitution entirely. This approach was first advanced by the Supreme Court in *Pennallow v. Doane,*[29] where the power to conduct war was characterized as a matter of national sovereignty and therefore not specifically dependent upon any of the affirmative provisions of the Constitution.[30] Justice Sutherland later developed this theory more fully in *Curtiss-Wright*[31] and encouraged the assumption that because the President spoke for the United States in foreign affairs, he must be, de facto, the sovereign.[32]

Finally, there was the larger claim of an extraconstitutional prerogative power, which may be derived from Locke, George III, Blackstone, international law, and the concomitants of national sovereignty.[33] This claim has taken many forms, from the absolute prerogative of Stuart kings (based on the law of God), to the Locke-Jefferson theory of emergency powers (based on the hope of popular acceptance), to the Hamilton-Nixon theory of inherent national security powers (rooted in secrecy).[34] In each of these instances, the end is always said to justify the means—no matter how questionable the means.

Of equal importance to the historic shift in presidential justifications of the war powers was the startling change in the way academic experts, journalists, and statesmen viewed the situation. In the 1950s and early 1960s, scholars and writers on the presidency (along with experienced statesmen) were saying that the President should have a great deal of leeway in foreign affairs, particularly regarding the use of military force. They usually added that this was what the Framers wanted and the way things have worked since the early days of the Republic.[35] But between 1966 and 1970, something strange happened. Most of these scholars, journalists, and statesmen reversed their views. In the space of four years, presidential experts were arguing that the President did not possess unilateral war-making powers, never had possessed them, never was intended to possess them, and never should possess them.[36]

What caused this astonishing reversal? One reason may have been the kind of men who occupied the White House between the close of 1963 and the autumn of 1974. Lyndon Johnson and Richard Nixon exercised prerogative presidential power at a time when the claimed emergency could never be justified by the factual situation. They were "active-negative personalities,"[37] and generally disliked by scholars and journalists. This was particularly the case with Nixon. By far the most important reason for this change of heart, however, was Vietnam. Many of these people had supported the war in its early stages, but, as the war continued to escalate with no noticeable results except an increase in violence and death, the scholars simply turned against it.[38]

The vast majority of scholars who once supported the war, and had now turned against it, wondered if the prerogative presidency they had been promoting for so long might have helped bring it on. They went back to the old texts and began to read them differently. Now, it turned out, some of the precedents could really be interpreted as instances of Presidents deferring to Congress.[39] Now, too, it seemed that the Framers had left no doubt that the Congress must authorize even the *making* of wars. As for the Supreme Court, its decisions were really meant to limit, not enlarge, presidential claims to unilateral power.[40] And so it went—all the evidence that had been cited in support of presidential war powers underwent a change, and it *now* proved (according to the scholars) just the opposite.[41] All of this made one wonder, however, about the "validity" of history as a guide to judicial decision making.

Without raising the obvious question of whether the scholars, journalists, and statesmen (this second-time around) were guilty of "rewriting American history according to their own specifications" and foisting off "their current political prejudices as eternal American verities,"[42] one conclusion can at least be reached: scholars are human beings, and their reading of what the Framers thought may have been influenced to a degree by what they wished the Framers had thought. It was precisely for this reason, and the potentially dangerous consequences that may flow from rewriting history so conveniently, that Karl L. Popper wrote more than fifty years ago: "We may like to have good rulers, but historical experience shows us that we are not likely to get them. That is why it is of such importance to design institutions which will prevent even bad rulers from causing too much mischief."[43]

The problem, then, and the central theme of the cases and comments that follow, is how can we "chain the dog of war" without simultaneously endangering the Republic? Hopefully, no experienced observer would suggest at this late date that the President be omitted entirely from the decision of why, how, when, and where this Nation goes to war. To do so, judging from the lessons of history, would be both foolish and dangerous. Yet the usual objection one hears that a war-type emergency requires a quick decision by one man is basically invalid. No President acts without consultation. If he has time to summon the Joint Chiefs, the National Security Council, and his chief advisors, he can summon the leaders of Congress. Nor need the final decision be unilateral. Any belligerent action not clearly enough in the national interest to evoke unanimous or strong majority decision by the Congress simply ought not to be undertaken. In a political system based on separation of powers and checks and balances, the people in this Nation must operate under the principle of preparing for the worst, as well as we can, though we should always try to obtain the best. It is simply madness to base all our political efforts upon the faint hope that we shall be successful in obtaining excellent, or even competent, rulers. I suggest this principle not on the basis of some notion of the intrinsic goodness or righteousness of majority rule,[44] but rather because of the inherent baseness of tyranny.[45] In other words, separation of powers and checks and balances exists in the

United States not to guarantee our liberty so much as to aid us in avoiding and resisting tyranny. Democracy, at least as understood by the Framers, meant— and should still mean—that democratic institutions are a really effective safe- guard against domestic, internal tyranny.[46]

One final point: the cases and comments that follow will look at these varied issues and the political and judicial responses to them. It is hoped that this material will come to grips with why the Nation has developed a wartime constitution, how it has been maintained, and what (if anything) can be or should be done about it. If the President does not possess the constitutional authority to initiate war, yet that very authority is necessary to preserve the Nation, does it mean that the Constitution is defective in not allowing the government the proper means of protecting itself? This question, asked about Lincoln's sometimes dictatorial actions during the Civil War,[47] fails to take into account the inescapable fact that war and peace are not the same thing and cannot coexist in the same place at the same time. Institutions of free govern- ment cannot operate normally in abnormal times.[48] Occasionally, the Constitu- tion must be suspended so that it might not be permanently destroyed. If this means that some form of constitutional dictatorship is inevitable, in order for the Nation to survive and then continue as a democracy after the emergency is over, so be it. We gain very little by attempting to turn the clock back two hundred years by invoking the "true" intentions of the Framers (whatever they may actually be). Rather we would be far better served as a Nation by recognizing the inevitability of the concept that dictatorship and democracy are not mutually exclusive and attempting to constitutionalize presidential war and emergency powers by wrapping them in democratic constraints. Moreover, as the cases will show, the Supreme Court should never, as Justice Jackson warned in his *Korematsu* dissent,[50] distort the Constitution to justify unjustifiable behavior.

In *The Federalist,* No. 8, Hamilton wrote with great perception that the war powers would someday become the most dangerous in the whole catalogue of powers.

Safety from external danger is the most powerful director of national conduct. Even the ardent love of liberty will, after a time, give way to its dictates. The violent destruction of life and property incident to war, the continual effort and alarm attendant on a state of continual danger, will compel nations the most attached to liberty to resort for repose and security to institutions which have a tendency to destroy their civil and political rights. To be more safe, they at length become willing to run the risk of being less free.[51]

Almost two hundred years later, Clinton Rossiter brought Hamilton's analysis up to date when he suggested, "We have placed a shocking amount of military power in the President's keeping, but where else, we may ask, could it possibly have been placed?"[52] What it boils down to is that the only way for Congress to play an important role in decisions about war and peace—and at the same time hopefully exert some degree of control over the presidential initiative to *make* war—is to insist upon it, and then to do so. The record to date gives little indication that Congress will defend either its constitutional prerogatives or its statutory powers under the War Powers Resolution[53] or the National Emergencies Act.[54] And if Congress will not stand up for itself, is there any reason to suppose that the President, the Supreme Court, or the people of the United States will stand up for it?

NOTES

1. THE FEDERALIST, No. 23, 153 (C. Rossiter ed. 1961) (Hamilton).
2. *Id.*
3. U.S. Const. art. II, sec. 2.
4. *Id.,* sec. 3.
5. *Id.,* sec. 1.
6. In THE FEDERALIST, No. 69, 417-19, Hamilton had written: "In this respect his authority would be nominally the same with that of the King of Great Britain, but in substance much inferior to it. It would amount to nothing more than the supreme command and direction of the military and naval forces, as first General and Admiral of the Confederacy; while that of the British King extends to the *declaring* of war and to the *raising* and *regulating* of fleets and armies, all which, by the Constitution under consideration, would appertain to the legislature." (Emphasis in the original). As late as 1850, the commander-in-chief clause continued to receive a sometimes limited interpretation by the Supreme Court: "His [the President's] duty and his power are purely military. As commander-in-chief, he is authorized to direct the movements of the naval and military forces placed by law at his command, and to employ them in the manner he may deem most effectual to harass and conquer and subdue the enemy. He may invade the hostile country, and subject it to the sovereignty and authority of the United States. But his conquests do not enlarge the boundaries of the Union, nor extend the operation of our institutions and laws beyond the limits before assigned to them by the legislative power....In the distribution of political power between the great departments of government, there is such a wide difference between the power conferred on the President of the United States, and the authority and sovereignty which belongs to the English Crown, that it would be altogether unsafe to reason from any supposed resemblance between them, either as regards conquest in war, or any other subject where the rights and powers of the executive arm of the government are brought into question." Fleming v. Page, 50 U.S. (9 How.) 278, 279-80 (1850) (Taney, C.J.).
7. *See generally* J. Locke, TWO TREATISES OF GOVERNMENT, ch. 14, sec. 160, 422 (P. Laslett ed. 1960). Locke defined prerogative as the "power to act according to discretion for the public good, without the prescription of the law and sometimes even against it."
8. The Prize Cases, 67 U.S. (2 Bl.) 635 (1863). The habeas corpus question (a principle issue in Lincoln's exercise of the war powers) was settled somewhat less obviously. Congress, by the act of Mar. 3, 1863, authorized the President to suspend the Great Writ during the rebellion. 12 Stat. 755. But by the act of Sept. 15, 1863, the President exercised this authority and suspended the Writ with respect to persons held as prisoners of war, spies, aiders and abettors of the enemy, and so on. 13 Stat. 734. Earlier (1861), of course, Congress passed legislation "approving, legalizing, and making valid all the acts, proclamations, and orders of the President, etc., as if they had been issued and done under the previous express authority and direction of the Congress of the United States." 12 Stat. 326.
9. E. Corwin, THE PRESIDENT: OFFICE AND POWERS (4th ed. 1957). The original edition was published in 1940.
10. *Id.* at 3.
11. *Id.* (Emphasis in the original).
12. *Id.*

13. United States v. Curtiss-Wright Export Corp., 299 U.S. 304, 316 (1936) (Sutherland, J.).

14. L. Henkin, FOREIGN AFFAIRS AND THE CONSTITUTION 37 (1975).

15. E. Corwin, *supra* note 9, at 5. Even Jefferson, the strict constructionist, accepted this view once in office: "A strict observance of the written laws is doubtless one of the high duties of a good citizen, but it is not the *highest.* The laws of necessity, of self-preservation, of saving our country when in danger, are of a higher obligation....To lose our country by a scrupulous adherence to written law, would be to lose the law itself, with life, liberty, property and all those who are enjoying them with us; thus absurdly sacrificing the end to the means." Quoted in G. McKenna, A GUIDE TO THE CONSTITU-TION: A DELICATE BALANCE 42 (1984) (emphasis in the original).

16. *See especially* Sheffer, *Presidential Power and Limited Government,* 21 PRES. STUD. Q. 471 (1991) for a more fully drawn picture of the Framers' intentions. Hopefully it sheds some light on what the Framers thought without being influenced by what the author wished the Framers thought.

17. The notion of "doubly chaining" power comes from John Adams and his idea of balance: "The aristocrat is a monster to be chained, yet so chained as not to be hurt, for he is a most useful and necessary animal in his place. Nothing can be done without him....Bind Aristocracy then with a double cord. Shut him up in a cage, from which however he may be let out to do good but never to do mischief." Quoted in Rossiter, *The Legacy of John Adams,* 46 THE YALE REV. 540 (1957).

18. F. Wormuth & E. Firmage, TO CHAIN THE DOG OF WAR ix (2d ed. 1989).

19. *Id.* Since World War II, no President has lacked the capacity to intervene militarily (or paramilitarily) in the affairs of lesser nations. Most have exercised this power, on their own initiative, without the formal concurrence of Congress, in situations that do not pose a direct and immediate threat to the security of the United States. The list is a long one, but the following can at least be suggested: Korea, the CIA-backed coup in Guatamala, the CIA-backed bombing Indonesa, the CIA-backed invasion of Cuba, the Cuban missile crisis and blockade, the invasion of the Dominican Republic, the Vietnam adventure, the secret war in Laos, the Cambodian incursion, the Cambodian bombing, the *Mayaguez* incident, and the CIA-backed attempts to overthrow the government of Nicaragua. C. Pyle & R. Pious, THE PRESIDENT, CONGRESS, AND THE CONSTITU-TION 288 (1984).

20. Our armed forces have been used more than two hundred times without declarations of war and, in many of these instances, without congressional authorization as well. Omitting major military engagements, such as Korea and Vietnam, many of these involved small operations: antiterrorist actions, protection of American lives and property in civil disturbances, evacuations of Americans and third-party nationals, participation in international policing or peace-keeping efforts, covert operations designed to destabilize or overthrow foreign governments, airlifts or sealifts of supplies to neutrals or friendly nations involved in hostilities, convoying ships of neutral or friendly nations, convoying in disputed waters to assert freedom of navigation, and the imposition of blockades and quarantines. *See especially* F. Wormuth & E. Firmage, *supra* note 18, at 135-63.

21. C. Pyle & R. Pious, *supra* note 19, at 288.

22. 1 Stat. 264. *See also* the act of 1795 (1 Stat. 424); the act of 1807 (2 Stat. 443); and the act of 1861 (12 Stat. 282). In short, presidential power to employ the military in the enforcement of the laws of the United States has undergone enlargement from the first, thanks in part to presidential initiative, in part to congressional legislation. E. Corwin, *supra* note 9, at 133.

23. 12 Stat. 755. President Lincoln regarded the act, authorizing him to suspend the

Great Writ, merely as declaratory. *See especially* Sheffer, *Presidential Power to Suspend Habeas Corpus: The Taney-Bates Dialogue and Ex Parte Merryman,* 11 OKLA. CITY U.L. REV. 1-30 (Spring 1986).

24. C. Pyle & R. Pious, *supra* note 19, at 288.

25. *Id.* at 289.

26. *Id. See* notes 1 and 2 and the specific textual material.

27. *Id.*

28. *Id.*

29. 3 U.S. (3 Dall.) 54 (1795).

30. C. Pyle & R. Pious, *supra* note 19, at 289.

31. United States v. Curtiss-Wright Export Corp., 299 U.S. 304 (1936).

32. Twentieth-century presidents have particularly invoked this notion—for example, Theodore Roosevelt, Woodrow Wilson, Franklin Roosevelt, Harry Truman, John Kennedy, Richard Nixon, Ronald Reagan, and George Bush.

33. C. Pyle & R. Pious, *supra* note 19, at 289.

34. *Id.*

35. *See, e.g.,* Corwin, *Who Has the Power to Make War?,* N.Y. Times Mag., July 31, 1949; Schlesinger, *Letter* to the N.Y. Times Mag., Jan. 14, 1951; as well as numerous written statements and public speeches made during this period by James Reston, George Kennan, Dean Acheson, and Senators William J, Fullbright, Arthur Vandenberg, and Wayne Morse. *Contra,* R. Taft, A FOREIGN POLICY FOR AMERICANS (1951). The academic debate over the original intention of the Framers occurred because of the Coudert Resolution (a sense of Congress resolution prohibiting the sending of American troops abroad without prior congressional authorization.

36. By 1966 Schlesinger was counseling that "something must be done to assure the Congress a more authoritative and continuing voice in fundamental decisions in foreign policy"; A. Schlesinger & A. de Grazia, CONGRESS AND THE PRESIDENCY 28 (1967). *See also* THE BITTER HERITAGE (1967); *Eyeless in Indochina,* N.Y. Rev. of Books, Oct. 21, 1971; *Presidential War,* N.Y. Times Mag., Jan. 7, 1973. Commager, meanwhile, had also altered his view, for he told the Senate in 1967 that there should be a reconsideration of executive-legislative relationships in the conduct of foreign relations—*see* Changing American Attitudes Towards Foreign Policy, hearings before the Senate Comm. on Foreign Relations, 90th Cong., 1st Sess., 21 (1967). *See also* Commager's testimony in War Powers Legislation, hearings before the Senate Comm. on Foreign Relations, 92d Cong., 1st Sess., 7-74 (1971). Schlesinger in 1973 stated that the "idea of prerogative was *not* part of presidential power as defined in the Constitution," although it "remained in the back of [the Framers'] minds"; THE IMPERIAL PRESIDENCY 9 (1973) (emphasis in the original).

37. J. Barber, PRESIDENTIAL CHARACTER (4th ed. 1992). Barber defines "active-negative" as follows: "The contradiction here is between relatively intense effort and relatively low emotional reward for that effort. The activity has a compulsive quality, as if the man were trying to make up for something or to escape from anxiety into hard work. He seems ambitious, striving upward, power-seeking. His stance toward the environment is aggressive and he has a persistent problem in managing his aggressive feelings. His self-image is vague and discontinuous. Life is a hard struggle to achieve and hold power, hampered by the condemnations of a perfectionistic conscience. Active-negative types pour energy into the political system, but it is an energy distorted from within." *Id.* at 9.

38. G. McKenna, *supra* note 15, at 39.

39. In essence, the scholars carried their twentieth century intellectual baggage back two hundred years and became influenced by what they wished the Framers had thought.

See especially A. Schlesinger, *supra* note 36, at 13-105 and F. Wormuth & E. Firmage, *supra* note 18, at 1-106.

40. Without comment, I leave it entirely to the reader to determine how Durand v. Hollins, 8 F.Cas. 111 (1860) (No. 4186), The Prize Cases, 67 U.S. (2 Bl.) 635 (1863), In re Neagle, 135 U.S. 1 (1890), In re Debs, 158 U.S. 564 (1895), United States v. Curtiss-Wright Export Corp., 299 U.S. 304 (1936), United States v. Belmont, 301 U.S. 324 (1937), Ex parte Quirin, 317 U.S. 1 (1942), and Korematsu v. United States, 323 U.S. 214 (1944), can ever be interpreted as decisions intending to limit presidential power.

41. G. McKenna, *supra* note 15, at 39.

42. Schlesinger, *Presidential Powers,* N.Y. Times, Jan. 9, 1951, at 28. Schlesinger this language in 1951 to charge Taft and others with rewriting history. By 1970 the charge could be leveled at him.

43. K. Popper, THE OPEN SOCIETY AND ITS ENEMIES (2 vols., 5th ed. 1966), quoted in A. Miller, SOCIAL CHANGE AND FUNDAMENTAL LAW 268 (1979). The original edition of Popper's work was published in 1944.

44. Popper, in his discussion of the paradoxes of freedom raises the following question: what if it is the will of the people that they should not rule, but a tyrant instead? The free man may exercise his absolute freedom, first by defying the laws and ultimately by defying freedom itself and by clamoring for a tyrant. Popper then tells us, "This is not just a far-fetched possibility; it has happened a number of times; and every time it has happened, it has put in a hopeless intellectual position all those democrats who adopt, as the ultimate basis of their political creed, the principle of the majority rule or a similar form of the principle of sovereignty. On the one hand, the principle they have adopted demands from them that they should oppose any but the majority rule, and therefore the new tyranny; on the other hand, the same principle demands from them that they should accept any decision reached by the majority, and thus the rule of the new tyrant. The inconsistency of their theory must, of course, paralyze their actions. Those of us democrats who demand the institutional control of the rulers by the ruled, and especially the right of dismissing the government by a majority vote, must therefore base these demands upon better grounds than a self-contradictory theory of sovereignty." 1 K. Popper, *supra* note 42, at 123.

45. *Id.* at 125.

46. *Id.* at 126-27.

47. S. Fisher, *The Suspension of Habeas Corpus during the War of the Rebellion,* 3 POL.SCI.Q. 457 (1888). Raising the same question in more modern language, Clinton Rossiter answered it by arguing that a "democratic constitutional government beset by a severe national emergency can be strong enough to maintain its own existence without at the same time being so strong as to subvert the liberties of the people it has been instituted to defend. C. Rossiter, CONSTITUTIONAL DICTATORSHIP: CRISIS GOVERNMENT IN THE MODERN DEMOCRACIES 3 (1948).

48. C. Rossiter, *supra* note 47, at 8.

49. *Id.*

50. "It is said that if the military commander had reasonable military grounds for promulgating the order, they are constitutional and become law, and the Court is required to enforce it....But if we cannot confine military expedients by the Constitution, neither would I distort the Constitution to approve all that the military may deem expedient....A military order, however unconstitutional, is not apt to last longer than the military emergency....But once a judicial opinion rationalizes such an order to show that it conforms to the Constitution, or rather rationalizes the Constitution to show that the Constitution sanctions such an order, the Court for all time has validated [a principle of unconstitutional behavior]. The principle then lies about like a loaded weapon ready for

the hand of any authority that can bring forward a plausible claim of an urgent need. Every repetition imbeds that principle more deeply in our law and thinking and expands it to new purposes.....*A military commander may overstep the bounds of constitutionality, and it is an incident. But if we review and approve, that passing incident becomes the doctrine of the Constitution. There is has a generative power of its own, and all that it creates will be in its own image."* Korematsu v. United States, 323 U.S. 214, 244-46 (1944) (Jackson, J. dissenting) (emphasis added).

51. *The Federalist,* No. 8 at 67 (Hamilton).

52. C. Rossiter, THE AMERICAN PRESIDENCY 11 (3d ed. 1987).

53. Pub.L. No. 93-148, 87 Stat, 555 (1973).

54. Pub.L. No. 94-412, 90 Stat. 1255 (1976). One of the principle issues raised by the Iran-Contra Affair was the failure of President Reagan to report to Congress about covert actions, in direct violation of the Intelligence Oversight Act, 94 Stat. 1981 (1980). The other major issue was the attempt by executive officials to use private and foreign funds to finance activities prohibited by Congress, in direct violation of the Boland Amendment, 98 Stat. 1935 (1984). A further attempt by Congress to regain some control over the imperial presidency involved revision of the Intelligence Oversight Act by requiring specific procedure for reporting covert actions and the use of funds. 105 Stat. 441 (1991).

The problem continues to be, of course, the inability of Congress to establish some degree of control over presidential initiative, and if the initiative cannot be controlled neither can presidential power. What Congress fails to take into account is that by its unwillingness to properly fight the President and strictly enforce the limitations imposed upon him, it has given the executive branch what the Framers feared the most: the joining together of the power of the sword with the power of the purse. L. Fisher & N. Devins, POLITICAL DYNAMICS OF CONSTITUTIONAL LAW 189 (1992).

1

The Early Period

Martin v. Mott, **25 U.S. (12 Wheat.) 19; 6 L.Ed. 537 (1827)**

In August 1814, the governor of the state of New York, in compliance with a request from the President of the United States, ordered certain companies of militia to assemble in the city of New York for the purpose of entering the service of the United States. The President acted in accordance with a federal statute empowering him to call the militia wherever there shall be danger of invasion. Mott, a private in one of the companies called, refused to comply with the order of the governor. In 1818 a court-martial imposed on him a fine of $96, and when he refused to pay he was sentenced to twelve months imprisonment. Martin, a deputy United States marshal, seized certain goods of Mott, which Mott sought to recover by action of replevin.

Basic Question: Can the President, under the laws of the United States, call forth the militia of the states when no invasion has taken place?

Opinion of the Court by Justice Story:
For the more clear and exact considerations of the subject, it may be necessary to refer to the Constitution of the United States, and some of the provisions of the act of 1795. The [C]onstitution declares that Congress shall have power "to provide for calling forth the militia, to execute the laws of the Union, suppress insurrections, and repel invasions"; and also "to provide for organizing, arming and disciplining the militia, and for governing such part of them as may be employed in the service of the United States." In pursuance of this authority, the act of 1795 has provided, "that whenever the United States shall be invaded or be in imminent danger of invasion from any foreign nation or Indian tribe, it shall be lawful for the President of the United States to call forth such number of the militia of the state or states most convenient to the place of danger, of scene of action, as he may judge necessary to repel such invasion

and to issue his order for that purpose to such officer or officers of this militia as he shall think proper."...In our opinion ... the power to provide for repelling invasions includes the power to provide against the attempt and danger of invasion, as the necessary and proper means to effectuate the object. One of the best means to repel invasion is to provide the requisite force for action before the invader himself has reached the soil.

The power thus confided by Congress to the President is doubtless of a very high and delicate nature. A free people are naturally jealous of the exercise of military power; and the power to call the militia into actual service is certainly felt to be one of no ordinary magnitude. But it is not a power which can be executed without a correspondent responsibility. It is, in its terms, a limited power, confined to cases of actual invasion, or of imminent danger of invasion. If it be a limited power, the question arises, by whom is the exigency to be judged of and decided? Is the President the sole and exclusive judge whether the exigency has arisen, or is it to be considered as an open question, upon which every officer to whom the orders of the President are addressed, may decide for himself, and equally open to be contested by every militiaman who shall refuse to obey the orders of the President? We are all of opinion that the authority to decide whether the exigency has arisen, belongs exclusively to the President, and that his decision is conclusive upon all other persons. We think that this construction necessarily results from the nature of the power itself, and from the manifest object contemplated by the act of Congress. The power itself is to be exercised upon sudden emergencies, upon great occasions of state, and under circumstances which may be vital to the existence of the Union. A prompt and unhesitating obedience to orders is indispensable to the complete attainment of the object. The service is a military service, and the command of a military nature; and in such cases every delay, and every obstacle to an efficient and immediate compliance, necessarily tend to jeopardize the public interests. While subordinate officers or soldiers are pausing to consider whether they ought to obey, or are scrupulously weighing the evidence of the facts upon which the commander-in-chief exercises the right to demand their services, the hostile enterprise may be accomplished without the means of resistance....

If we look at the language of the act of 1795, every conclusion drawn from the nature of the power itself is strongly fortified. The words are "whenever the United States shall be invaded, or be in imminent danger of invasion, etc., it shall be lawful for the President, etc., to call forth such number of the militia, etc., as he may judge necessary to repel such invasion." The power itself is confined to the Executive of the Union, to him who is, by the Constitution, "the commander-in- chief of the militia, when called into the actual service of the United States," whose duty it is to "take care that the laws be faithfully executed," and whose responsibility for an honest discharge of his official obligations is secured by the highest sanctions. He is necessarily constituted the judge of the existence of the exigency in the first instance, and is bound to act according to his belief of the facts. If he does so act, and decides to call forth the militia, his orders for this purpose are in strict conformity with the provisions of the law; and it would seem to follow as a necessary consequence, that every act done by a subordinate officer, in obedience to such orders, is equally justifiable. The law contemplates that, under such circumstances, orders shall be given to carry the power into effect; and it cannot therefore be a correct inference that any other person has a just right to disobey them. The law does not provide for any appeal from the judgment of the President, or for any right to subordinate officers to review his decision, and in effect defeat it. Whenever a statute gives a discretionary power to any person, to be exercised by him upon his own opinion of certain facts, it is a sound rule of construction that the statute constitutes him the sole and exclusive judge of the existence of those facts. And, in the present case, we are all of opinion that such is the true construction of the act of 1795. It is no answer that such a power may be abused, for there is no power which is not susceptible of abuse. The remedy for this, as well as for all other official misconduct, if it should occur, is to be found in the Constitution itself. In a free government the danger must be remote, since in addition to the high qualities which the Executive must be presumed to possess, of public virtue and honest devotion to the public interests, the frequency of elections, and the watchfulness of the representatives of the nation, carry with them all the checks which can be useful to guard against usurpation or wanton tyranny....

But it is now contended,... that notwithstanding the judgment of the President is conclusive as to the existence of the exigency, and may be given in evidence as conclusive proof thereof, yet that the avowry is fatally defective, because it omits to aver that the fact did exist. The argument is, that the power confided to the President is a limited power, and can be exercised only in the cases pointed out in the statute, and therefore it is necessary to aver the facts which bring the exercise within the purview of the statute. In short, the same principles are sought to be applied to the delegation and exercise of this power entrusted to the Executive of the nation for great political purposes, as might be applied to the humblest officer in the government, acting upon the most narrow and special authority. It is the opinion of the Court that this objection cannot be maintained. When the President exercises an authority confided to him by law, the presumption is, that it is exercised in pursuance of law, the presumption is, that it is exercised in obedience of law. Every public officer is presumed to act in obedience to his duty, until the contrary is shown; and a fortiori, this presumption ought to be favorably applied to the chief magistrate of the Union. It is not necessarily to aver that threat which he may rightfully do was so done. If the fact of the existence of the exigency were averred, it would be traversable, and of course might be passed upon by a jury; and thus the legality of the orders of the President would depend, not on his own judgment of the facts, but upon the finding of those facts upon the proofs submitted to jury. This view of the objection is precisely the same which was acted upon by the Supreme Court of New York in the case already referred to, and, in the opinion of this Court, with entire legal correctness....

The next objection is, that it does not sufficiently appear in the avowry that the court-martial was a lawfully constituted court-martial, having jurisdiction of the offense at the time of passing its sentence against the original plaintiff.

Various grounds have been assigned in support of this objection. In the first place, it is said that the original plaintiff was never employed in the service of the United States, but refused to enter that service, and that, consequently, he was not liable to the rules and articles of war, or to be tried for the offense by any court-martial organized under the authority of the United States. The case of *Houston v. Moore*,... affords a conclusive answer to this suggestion. It was decided in that case, that although a militiaman, who refused to obey the orders of the President calling him into the public service, was not, in the sense of the act of 1795, "employed in the service of the United States" so as to be subject to the rules and articles of war, yet that he was liable to be tried for the offense under the 5th section of the same act, by a court-martial called under the authority of the United States. The great doubt in that case was, whether the delinquent was liable to be tried for the offense by a court-martial organized under state authority....

Another objection to the proceedings of the court-martial is, that they took place, and the sentence was given, three years and more after the war was concluded, and in a time of profound peace. But the opinion of this Court is, that a court-martial regularly called under the act of 1795, does not expire with the end of a war then existing, nor is its jurisdiction to try these offenses in any shape dependent upon the fact of war or peace. The act of 1795 is not confined in its operation to cases of refusal to obey orders of the President in times of public war. On the contrary, that act authorizes the President to call forth the militia to suppress insurrections, and to enforce the laws of the United States, in times of peace. And courts-martial are under the 5th section of the act, entitled to take cognizance of, and to punish delinquencies in such cases, as well as in cases where the object is to repel invasion in times of war. It would be a strained construction of the act, to limit the authority of the court to the mere time of the existence of the particular exigency, when it might be thereby unable to take cognizance of, and decide upon a single offense. It is sufficient for us to say that there is no such limitation in the act itself....

Of the remaining causes of special demurrer, some are properly matters of defense before the court-martial, and its sentence being a subject within its jurisdiction is conclusive; and others turn upon niceties of pleading, to which no separate answers are deemed necessary. In general, it may be said of them, that the Court [does] not deem them well-founded objections to the avowry.

Upon the whole, it is the opinion of the Court that the judgment of the court for the trial of impeachments, and the correction of errors ought to be reversed, and that the cause be remanded to the same court, with directions to cause a judgment to be entered upon the pleadings in favor of the avowant.

Note: For the first time the Court recognizes, implicitly, that the President's initiative does not require any prior congressional or judicial authorization before it can be used. And if the War Powers Resolution of 1973 does not specifically overturn a judicial decision such as this one, how can it be relied upon as a viable limitation of presidential discretion?

Luther v. Borden, 48 U.S. (7 How.) 1; 12 L.Ed. 581 (1849)

In 1841 the people of the state of Rhode Island were still operating under the old colonial charter with a few minor revisions, using it as their state constitution. This constitution strictly limited the right to vote. Led by a man named Thomas Dorr, the people at various mass meetings throughout the state instituted a new constitution whereby suffrage was greatly increased. The state government claimed that this was an insurrection and appealed to the President to declare martial law. However, no federal forces were used. Members of the state militia led by Borden forced their way into the house of Martin Luther, a Dorr adherent, who sued for trespass. Luther moved to Massachusetts in order to legalize a suit on the basis of diversity of citizenship.

Basic Question: Can the Court decide as to the guaranty of a republican form of a state's government in accordance with Article IV, Section 4?

Opinion of the Court by Chief Justice Taney:

The evidence offered by the plaintiff and the defendants is stated at large in the record; and the questions decided by the Circuit Court, and brought up by the writ of error, are not such as commonly arise in an action of trespass. The existence and authority of the government under which the defendants acted was called into question; and the plaintiff insists, that, before the acts complained of were committed, that government had been replaced and annulled by the people of Rhode Island, and that the plaintiff was engaged in supporting the lawful authority of the State, and the defendants themselves were in arms against it....

It is this opinion of the Circuit Court that we are now called upon to review. It is set forth more at large in the exception, but is in substance as above stated; and the question presented is certainly a very serious one. For, if this Court is authorized to enter upon this inquiry as proposed by the plaintiff and it should be decided that the charter government had no legal existence during the period of time above mentioned—if it had been annulled by the adoption of the opposing government—then the laws passed by its Legislature during that time were nullities; its taxes wrongfully collected; its salaries and compensations to its officers illegally paid; its public accounts improperly settled; and the judgments and sentences of its courts in civil and criminal cases null and void, and the officers who carried their decisions into operation answerable as trespassers, if not in some cases as criminals.

When the decision of this Court might lead to such results, it becomes its duty to examine very carefully its own powers before it undertakes to exercise jurisdiction....

Upon what ground could the Circuit Court of the United States which tried this case have departed from this rule, and disregarded and overruled the decisions of the courts of Rhode Island? Undoubtedly the courts of the United States have certain powers under the Constitution and laws of the United States which do not belong to the State courts. But the power of determining that a State government has been lawfully established, which the courts of the State disown and repudiate, is not one of them. Upon such a question the courts of the United States are bound to follow the decisions of the State tribunals, and must therefore regard the charter government as the lawful and established government during the time of this contest....

Moreover, the Constitution of the United States, as far as it has provided for an emergency of this kind, and authorized the general government to interfere in the domestic concerns of a State, has treated the subject as political in its nature, and placed the power in the hands of that department.

The fourth section of the fourth article of the Constitution of the United States provides that the United States shall guarantee to every State in the Union a republican form of government, and shall protect each of them against invasion; and on the application of the Legislature or of the executive (when the Legislature cannot be convened) against domestic violence.

Under this article of the Constitution it rests with Congress to decide what government is the established one in a State. For as the United States guarantees to each State a republican government, Congress must necessarily decide what government is established in the State before it can determine whether it is republican or not. And when the senators and representatives of a State are admitted into the councils of the Union, the authority of the government under which they are appointed, as well as its republican character, is recognized by the proper constitutional authority. And its decision is binding on every other department of the government, and could not be questioned in a judicial tribunal. It is true that the contest in this case did not last long enough to bring the matter to this issue; and as no senators or representatives were elected under the authority of the government of which Mr. Dorr was the head, Congress was not called upon to decide the controversy. Yet the right to decide is placed there, and not in the courts.

So, too, as relates to the clause in the above mentioned article of the Constitution, providing for cases of domestic violence. It rested with Congress, too, to determine upon the means proper to be adopted to fulfill this guarantee. They might, if they had deemed it most advisable to do so, have placed it in the power of a court to decide when a contingency had happened which required the federal government to interfere. But Congress thought otherwise, and no doubt wisely; and by the Act of 1795, provided, that, "in case of an insurrection in any State against the government thereof it shall be lawful for the President of the United States, on application of the Legislature of such State or of the executive (when the Legislature cannot be convened), to call forth such number of the militia of any other State or States, as may be applied for, as he may judge sufficient to suppress such insurrection."

By this act, the power of deciding whether the exigency had arisen upon which the government of the United States is bound to interfere, is given to the President. He is to act upon the application of the Legislature or of the executive, and consequently he must determine what body of men constitute the Legislature, and who is the governor, before he can act. The fact that both parties claim the right to the government cannot alter the case, for both cannot be entitled to it. If there is an armed conflict, like the one of which we are speaking, it is a case of domestic violence, and one of the parties must be in insurrection against the lawful government. And the President must, of necessity, decide which is the government, and which party is unlawfully arrayed against it, before he can perform the duty imposed upon him by the act of Congress.

After the President has acted and called out the militia, is a circuit court of the United States authorized to inquire whether his decision was right? Could the court, while the parties were actually contending in arms for the possession of the government, call witnesses before it and inquire which party represented a majority of the people? If it could, then it would become the duty of the court (provided it came to the conclusion that the President had decided incorrectly) to discharge those who were arrested or detained by the troops in the service of the United States or the government, which the President was endeavoring to maintain. If the judicial power extends so far, the guarantee contained in the Constitution of the United States is a guarantee of anarchy, and not of order. Yet if this right does not reside in the courts when the conflict is raging, if the judicial power is at that time bound to follow the decision of the political, it must be equally bound when the contest is over. It cannot, when peace is restored, punish as offenses and crimes the acts which it before recognized, and was bound to recognize, as lawful. [**Ed. note:** This extraordinarily truthful statement has never been followed by the Supreme Court—as the cases that follow will attest.]

It is true that in this case the militia were not called out by the President. But upon the application of the governor under the charter government, the President recognized him as the executive power of the State, and took measures to call out the militia to support his authority if it should be found necessary for the general government to interfere; and it is admitted in the argument, that it was the knowledge of this decision that put an end to the armed opposition to the charter government, and prevented any further efforts to establish by force the proposed constitution. The interference of the President, therefore, by announcing his determination, was as effectual as if the militia had been assembled under his orders. And it should be equally authoritative. For certainly no court of the United States, with a knowledge of this decision, would have been justified in recognizing the opposing party as the lawful government; or in treating as wrongdoers or insurgents the officers of the government which the President had recognized, and was prepared to support by an armed force. In the case of foreign nations, the government acknowledged by the President is always recognized in the courts of justice. And this principle has been applied by the act of Congress to the sovereign States of the Union....

A question very similar to this arose in the case of *Martin v. Mott*,...The same principle applies to the case now before the court. Undoubtedly, if the President in exercising this power shall fall into error, or invade the rights of the people of the State, it would be in the power of Congress to apply the proper remedy. But the courts must administer the law as they find it.

The remaining question is whether the defendants, acting under military orders issued under the authority of the government, were justified in breaking and entering the plaintiff's house. In relation to the act of the Legislature declaring martial law, it is not necessary in the case before us to inquire to what extent, nor under what circumstances, that power may be exercised by a State. Unquestionably a military government, established as the permanent government of the State, would not be a republican government, and it would be the duty of Congress to overthrow it. But the law of Rhode Island evidently contemplated no such government. It was intended merely for the crisis, and to meet the peril in which the existing government was placed by the armed resistance to its authority. It was so understood and construed by the State authorities. And, unquestionably, a State may use its military power to put down an armed insurrection, too strong to be controlled by the civil authority. The power is essential to the existence of every government, essential to the preservation of order and free institutions, and is as necessary to the States of this Union as to any other government. The State itself must determine what degree of force the crisis demands. And if the government of Rhode Island deemed the armed opposition so formidable, and so ramified throughout the State, as to require the use of its military force and the declaration of martial law, we see no ground upon which this court can question its authority. It was a state of war; and the established government resorted to the rights and usages of war to maintain itself, and to overcome the unlawful opposition. And in that state of things the officers engaged in its military service might lawfully arrest anyone, who, from the information before them, they had reasonable grounds to believe was engaged in the insurrection; and might order a house to be forcibly entered and searched, when there were reasonable grounds for supposing he might be there concealed. Without the power to do this, martial law and the military array of the government would be mere parade, and rather encourage attack than repel it. No more force, however, can be used than is necessary to accomplish the object. And if the power is exercised for the purposes of opposition, or any injury willfully done to person or property, the party by whom, or by whose order, it is committed would undoubtedly be answerable....

Much of the argument on the part of the plaintiff turned upon political rights and political questions, upon which the Court has been urged to express an opinion. We decline doing so. The high power has been conferred on this Court of passing judgment upon the acts of the State sovereignties, and of the legislative and executive branches of the federal government, and of determining whether they are beyond the limits of power marked out for them respectively by the Constitution of the United States. This tribunal, therefore, should be the last to overstep the boundaries which limit its own jurisdiction. And while it should always be ready to meet any question confided to it by the Constitution, it is equally its duty not to pass beyond its appropriate sphere of action, and to take care not to involve itself in discussions which properly belong to other forums. No one, we believe, has ever doubted the proposition, that, according to the institutions of this country, the sovereignty in every State resides in the people of the State, and that they may alter and change their form of government at their own pleasure. But whether they have changed it or not by abolishing an old government, and establishing a new one in its place, is a question to be settled by the political power. And when that power had decided, the courts are bound to take notice of its decision, and to follow it.

The judgment of the Circuit Court must therefore be affirmed.

Note: When the President decides to use military force to preserve the peace, neither the decision itself nor the methods employed are open to question in the courts of the United States. In such instances, his discretion must control, and the courts cannot intervene and grant relief.

The doctrine of political questions was first formulated by Chief Justice Marshall in *Foster v. Neilson,* 27 U.S. (2 Pet.) 253 (1829). The question at issue was the validity of a grant made by the Spanish government in 1804 of land lying to the east of the Mississippi River, but underlying this question was the broader one whether the region belonged in 1804 to Spain or the United States; and on this point the Court held that its judgment was concluded by the action of "the political departments," the President and Congress, in claiming the land for the United States.

Fleming v. Page, 50 U.S. (9 How.) 603; 12 L.Ed. 276 (1850)

During the nineteenth and early twentieth centuries it was widely assumed that there were certain inherent limitations on what government could do. These were derived from the vision of political morality in both domestic and international relations. The objectives of the United States, and hence the scope of its governmental powers, were supposed to be different from the objectives of those corrupt European regimes that abused their people at home and engaged in bloody conquests abroad.

The owners of the schooner *Catherine* sought to reclaim duties that they had been forced to pay on cargo shipped out of the Mexican port of Tampico while that port was occupied by the United States during the Mexican War. The U.S. tax collector argued that the conquest of Mexico pursuant to a congressional declaration (acknowledgment) of war made Tampico an American port within the meaning of the tax laws.

Basic Question: Can the President, as commander-in-chief, annex territory to the United States by virtue of military conquest?

Opinion of the Court by Chief Justice Taney:

The question certified by the Circuit Court turns upon the construction of the Act of Congress of July 30, 1846. The duties levied upon the cargo of the schooner Catherine were the duties imposed by this law upon goods imported from a foreign country. And if at the time of this shipment Tampico was not a foreign port within the meaning of the Act of Congress, then the duties were illegally charged, and, having been paid under protest, the plaintiffs would be entitled to recover in this action the amount exacted by the collector.

The port of Tampico, at which the goods were shipped, and the Mexican State of Tamaulipas, in which it is situated, were undoubtedly at the time of the shipment subject to the sovereignty and dominion of the United States. The Mexican authorities had been driven out, or had submitted to our army and navy; and the country was in the exclusive and firm possession of the United States and governed by its military authorities, acting under the orders of the President. But it does not follow that it was a part of the United States, or that it ceased to be a foreign country, in the sense in which these words are used in the acts of Congress.

The country in question had been conquered in war. But the genius and character of our institutions are peaceful, and the power to declare war was not conferred upon Congress for the purposes of aggression or aggrandizement, but to enable the general government to vindicate by arms, if it should become necessary, its own rights and the rights of its citizens.

A war, therefore, declared by Congress, can never be presumed to be waged for the purpose of conquests or the acquisition of territory; nor does the law declaring the war imply an authority of the President to enlarge the limits of the United States by subjugating the enemy's country. The United States, it is true, may extend its boundaries by conquest or treaty, and may demand the cession of territory as the condition of peace, in order to indemnify its citizens for the injuries they have suffered, or to reimburse the government for the expense of the war. But this can be done only by the treaty-making power or the legislative authority, and is not a part of the power conferred upon the President by the declaration of war. His duty and his power are purely military. As commander-in-chief, he is authorized to direct the movements of the naval and military forces placed by law at his command, and to employ them in the manner he may deem most effectual to harass and conquer and subdue the enemy. He may invade the hostile country, and subject it to the sovereignty and authority of the United States. But his conquests do not enlarge the boundaries of this Union, nor extend the operation of our institutions and laws beyond the limits before assigned to them by the legislative power.

It is true, that, when Tampico had been captured, and the State of Tamaulipas subjugated, other nations were bound to regard the country, while our possession continued, as the territory of the United States, and to respect it as such....As regarded all other nations, it was a part of the United States, and belonged to them as exclusively as the territory included in our established boundaries.

But yet it was not a part of this Union. For every nation which acquires territory by treaty or conquest holds it according to its own institutions and laws. And the relation in which the port of Tampico stood in the United States while it was occupied by their arms did not depend upon the laws of nations, but upon our own Constitution and acts of Congress. The power of the President under which Tampico and the State of Tamaulipas were conquered and held in subjection was simply that of a military commander prosecuting a war waged against a public enemy by the authority of his government....While it was occupied by our troops,... the inhabitants [of Tampico] were still foreigners and enemies, and owed to the United States nothing more than the submission and obedience, sometimes called temporary allegiance, which is due from a conquered enemy, when he surrenders to a force which he is unable to resist. But the boundaries of the United States, as they existed when war was declared against Mexico, were not extended by the conquest; ... [and] Tampico was, therefore, a foreign port when the shipment was made....

Neither is it necessary to examine the English decisions which have been referred to by counsel. It is true that most of the States have adopted the principles of English jurisprudence, so far as it concerns private and individual rights. And when such rights are in question, we habitually refer to the English decisions, not only with respect, but in many cases as authoritative. But in the distribution of political power between the great departments of government, there is such a wide difference between the power conferred on the President of the United States, and the authority and sovereignty which belongs to the English Crown, that it would be altogether unsafe to reason from any supposed resemblance between them, either as regards conquest in war, or any other subject where the rights and powers of the executive arm of the government are brought into question. Our own Constitution and form of government must be our only guide. And we are entirely satisfied that, under the Constitution and laws of the United States, Tampico was a foreign port, within the meaning of the Act of 1846, when these goods were shipped, and that the cargoes were liable to the duty charged upon them. And we shall certify accordingly to the Circuit Court.

Note: The holding suggests that the President's powers as commander-in-chief are confined to the purely military aspects of military command. Hamilton, for the very political reason of ratification, had argued the same point in The Federalist, No. 69, and so had Story in his Commentaries. Nevertheless, the decision must be considered as a classic example of judicial myopia, one in a series of judicial decisions usually rendered after hostilities have been completed—which purport to limit the President but which in fact do not do so. [A. Miller, <u>Presidential Power</u> 166 (1977).]

Durand v. Hollins, 8 F.Cas. 111 (C.C.D.Pa. 1860) (No. 4186)

This was an action of trespass, brought to recover damages for the destruction by the defendant (naval Captain George N. Hollins) of property at San Juan del Norte, Nicaragua, otherwise called Greytown, on July 13, 1854. Upon direct authorization by President Pierce, who likened the local inhabitants to a "piratical resort of outlaws or a camp of savages," the naval vessel of war, the U.S.S. *Cynne,* bombarded Greytown in retaliation for a mob assault on the American counsel, despite the fact that Greytown was nominally under a British protectorate. After the bombardment a naval landing party torched the entire town, except for the property owned by Cornelius Vanderbilt (the Accessory Transit Company). No lives were lost. Captain Hollins was later sued by Calvin Durand, an American citizen whose property was destroyed during the bombardment.

Basic Question: Can the President, without prior congressional authorization, use military force abroad?

Opinion of the Circuit Court by Justice Nelson:

The executive power, under the Constitution, is vested in the President of the United States. He is commander-in-chief of the army and navy,... and has imposed upon him the duty to "take care that the laws are faithfully executed."...

As the executive head of the nation, the President is made the only legitimate organ of the general government, to open and carry on correspondence or negotiations with foreign nations, in matters concerning the interests of the country or of its citizens. It is to him, also, the citizens abroad must look for protection of person and of property, and for the faithful execution of the laws existing and intended for their protection. For this purpose, the whole executive power of the country is placed in his hands, under the Constitution, and the laws passed in pursuance thereof; and different departments of government have been organized through which this power may be most conveniently executed, whether by negotiation or by force—a department of state and a department of the navy.

Now, as it respects the interposition of the executive abroad, for the protection of the lives or property of the citizen, the duty must, of necessity, rest in the discretion of the President. Acts of lawless violence, or of threatened violence to the citizen or his property, cannot be anticipated and provided for; and the protection, to be effectual or of any avail, may, not infrequently, require the most prompt and decided action. Under our system of government, the citizen abroad is as much entitled to protection as the citizen at home. The great object and duty of government is the protection of the lives, liberty, and property of the people composing it, whether abroad or at home; and any government failing in the accomplishment of the object, or the performance of the duty, is not worth preserving.

I have said, that the interposition of the President abroad, for the protection of the citizen, must necessarily rest in his discretion; and it is quite clear that, in all cases where a public act or order rests in executive discretion neither he nor his authorized agent is personally civilly responsible for the consequences. As was observed by Chief Justice Marshall, in *Marbury v. Madison,...*: "By the Constitution of the United States, the President is invested with certain important political powers, in the exercise of which he is to use his own discretion, and is accountable only to this country in his political character, and to his own conscience. To aid him in the performance of these duties, he is authorized to appoint certain officers, who act by his authority, and in conformity with his orders. In such cases, their acts are his acts, and, whatever opinion may be entertained of the manner in which executive discretion may be used, still there exists, and can exist, no power to control that discretion. The subjects are political. They respect the nation, not individual rights, and being entrusted to the executive, the decision of the executive is conclusive." This is a sound principle, and governs the present case. The question whether it was the duty of the President to interpose for the protection of the citizens at Greytown against an irresponsible and marauding community that had established itself there, was a public political question, in which the government, as well as the citizens whose interests were involved, was concerned, and which belonged to the executive to determine; and his decision is final and conclusive, and justified the defendant in the execution of his orders given through the secretary of the navy.

Judgment for defendant.

Note: The circuit court explicitly states that the President's *initiative* is subject to his own conscience and the needs of the nation (*i.e.,* the law of necessity). Here, essentially, is the legal justification for the commitment of combat troops to Vietnam. Moreover, what Justice Nelson's opinion recognizes here, and what had been recognized since 1817 when the American military occupied Amelia Island off the coast of Georgia and burned pirate settlements, is what international law acknowledges as the protection of the rights of persons and property: if the military action is not excessive it is not an act of war or a legitimate cause for warlike retort by the country suffering it. [E. Corwin, The President: Office and Powers 198 (4th ed. 1957).]

2

Lincoln as Commander-in-Chief

Ex Parte Merryman, **17 F.Cas. 144 (C.C.D.Md. 1861) (No. 9487)**

The petitioner, a citizen of Baltimore, Maryland, was arrested by a military officer acting on the authority of his commanding officer. The petitioner was accused of treason against the United States. The Chief Justice of the United States, while on circuit court duty, issued a writ of habeas corpus directing the commanding officer to deliver the prisoner, and this was refused on the grounds that the officer was authorized by the President to suspend the Great Writ.

Basic Question: Can the President suspend the writ of habeas corpus?

Opinion of the Circuit Court by Chief Justice Taney:
    The application in this case for a writ of habeas corpus is made to me under the 14th section of the Judiciary Act of 1789, 1 Stat. 81, which renders effectual for the citizen the constitutional privilege of the writ of habeas corpus. That act gives to the courts of the United States, as well as to each Justice of the Supreme Court, and to every district judge, power to grant writs of habeas corpus for the purpose of an inquiry into the cause of commitment....
    The commander of the fort, General George Cadwalader, by whom he is detained in confinement, in his return to the writ, does not deny any of the facts alleged in the petition. He states that the prisoner was arrested by order of General Keim, of Pennsylvania, and conducted as aforesaid to Fort McHenry, by his order, and placed in his [General Cadwalader's] custody, to be there detained by him as a prisoner.
    A copy of the warrant or order under which the prisoner was arrested was demanded by his counsel, and refused; and it is not alleged in the return, that any specific act, constituting any offense against the laws of the United States, has been charged against him upon oath, but he appears to have been arrested upon general charges of treason and rebellion, without proof, and without giving the names of the witnesses, or specifying the acts which, in the judgment of the

military officer, constituted these crimes. Having the prisoner thus in custody upon these vague and unsupported accusations, he refused to obey the writ of habeas corpus, upon the ground that he is duly authorized by the President to suspend it.

The case, then, is simply this: a military officer, residing in Pennsylvania, issues an order to arrest a citizen of Maryland, upon vague and indefinite charges, without any proof, so far as appears; under this order, his house is entered in the night, he is seized as a prisoner, and conveyed to Fort McHenry, and there kept in close confinement; and when a habeas corpus is served on the commanding officer, requiring him to produce the prisoner before a Justice of the Supreme Court, in order that he may examine into the legality of the imprisonment, the answer of the officer is that he is authorized by the President to suspend the writ of habeas corpus at his discretion, and in the exercise of that discretion, suspends it in this case, and on that ground refuses obedience to the writ.

As the case comes before me, therefore, I understand that the President not only claims the right to suspend the writ of habeas corpus himself, at his discretion, but to delegate that discretionary power to a military officer, and to leave it to him to determine whether he will or will not obey judicial process that may be served upon him. No official notice has been given to the courts of justice, or to the public, by proclamation or otherwise, that the President claimed this power, and had exercised it in the manner stated in the return. And I certainly listened to it with some surprise, for I had supposed it to be one of those points of constitutional law upon which there was no difference of opinion, and that it was admitted on all hands, that the privilege of the writ could not be suspended except by act of Congress....

The clause of the Constitution, which authorizes the suspension of the privilege of the writ of habeas corpus, is in the 9th section of the first article. This article is devoted to the legislative department of the United States, and has not the slightest reference to the executive department....

It is true, that in the cases mentioned, Congress is, of necessity, the judge of whether the public safety does or does not require it; and their judgment is conclusive. But the introduction of these words is a standing admonition to the legislative body of the danger of suspending it, and of the extreme caution they should exercise, before they give the government of the United States such power over the liberty of a citizen.

It is the second article of the Constitution that provides for the organization of the executive department, enumerates the powers conferred on it, and prescribes its duties. And if the high power over the liberty of the citizen now claimed, was intended to be conferred on the President, it would undoubtedly be found in plain words in this article; but there is not a word in it that can furnish the slightest ground to justify the exercise of the power.

[H]is powers in relation to the civil duties and authority necessarily conferred on him, are carefully restricted, as well as those belonging to his military character. He cannot appoint the ordinary officers of government, nor make a treaty with a foreign nation or Indian tribe, without the advice and consent of the Senate, and cannot appoint even inferior officers, unless he is authorized by an act of Congress to do so. He is not empowered to arrest anyone charged with an offense against the United States, and whom he may, from the evidence before him, believe to be guilty; nor can he authorize any officer, civil or military, to exercise this power, for the fifth article of the amendments to the Constitution expressly provides that no person "shall be deprived of life, liberty or property, without due process of law"—that is, judicial process.

Even if the privilege of the writ of habeas corpus were suspended by act of Congress, and a party not subject to the rules and articles of war were afterwards arrested and imprisoned by regular judicial process, he could not be detained in prison, or brought to trial before a military tribunal, for the article in the amendments to the Constitution immediately following the one above referred to (that is, the sixth article) provides, that "in all criminal prosecutions, the accused shall enjoy the right to a speedy and public trial by an impartial jury of the state and district wherein the crime shall have been committed, which district shall have been previously ascertained by law; and to be informed of the nature and cause of the accusation; to be confronted with the witnesses against him; to have compulsory process for obtaining witnesses in his favor; and to have the assistance of counsel for his defense."

The only power, therefore, which the President possesses, where the "life, liberty or property" of a private citizen is concerned, is the power and duty prescribed in the third section of the second article, which requires "that he shall take care that the laws be faithfully executed." He is not authorized to execute them himself, or through agents or officers, civil or military, appointed by himself, but he is to take care that they be faithfully carried into execution, as they are expounded and adjudged by the coordinate branch of the government to which that duty is assigned by the Constitution. It is thus made his duty to come in aid of the judicial authority, if it shall be resisted by a force too strong to be overcome without the assistance of the executive arm; but in exercising this power he acts in subordination to judicial authority, assisting it to execute its process and enforce its judgments.

With such provisions in the Constitution, expressed in language too clear to be misunderstood by any one, I can see no ground whatever for supposing that the President, in any emergency, or in any state of things can authorize the suspension of the privileges of the writ of habeas corpus, or the arrest of a citizen, except in aid of the judicial power. He certainly does not faithfully execute the laws, if he takes upon himself legislative power also, by arresting and imprisoning a person without due process of law.

Nor can any argument be drawn from the nature of sovereignty, or the necessity of government, for self-defense in times of tumult and danger. The government of the United States is one of delegated and limited powers; it derives its existence and authority altogether from the Constitution, and neither of its branches,... can exercise any of the powers of government beyond those specified and granted....

Yet, under these circumstances, a military officer, stationed in Pennsylvania, without giving any information to the district attorney, and without any application to the judicial authorities, assumes to himself the judicial power in the district of Maryland; undertakes to decide what constitutes the crime of treason or rebellion; what evidence (if indeed he required any) is sufficient to support the accusation and justify the commitment; and commits the party, without a hearing, even before himself, to close custody, in a strongly garrisoned fort, to be there held, it would seem, during the pleasure of those who committed him....

These great and fundamental laws, which Congress itself could not suspend, have been disregarded and suspended, like the writ of habeas corpus, by a military order, supported by force of arms. Such is the case now before me, and I can only say that if the authority which the Constitution has confided to the judiciary department and judicial officers, may thus, upon any pretext or under any circumstances, be usurped by the military power, at its discretion, the people of the United States are no longer living under a government of laws, but every citizen holds life, liberty and property at the will and pleasure of the army officer in whose military district he may happen to be found.

In such a case, my duty was too plain to be mistaken. I have exercised all the power which the Constitution and laws confer upon me, but that power has been resisted by a force too strong for me to overcome. It is possible that the officer who has incurred this grave responsibility may have misunderstood his instruction, and exceeded the authority intended to be given him; I shall, there-fore, order all the proceedings in this case, with my opinion, to be filed and recorded in the circuit court of Maryland, and direct the clerk to transmit a copy, under seal, to the President of the United States. It will then remain for that high officer, in fulfillment of his constitutional obligation to "take care that the laws be faithfully executed," to determine what measures he will take to cause the civil process of the United States to be respected and enforced.

Note: The opinion of the Chief Justice fails to discuss the possibility that the provisions of the Constitution may not be equally applicable in time of war as in time of peace; or that other provisions of the Constitution (activated in time of war) may some-how modify or control those provisions contemplated during domestic tranquillity. The principle of the military always being subject to the civil power is a general truth applicable to times of peace, but applicable in its fullest extent only in times of peace. [Parker, Habeas Corpus and Martial Law 12 (2d ed. 1862).] Taney too easily reaches the conclusion that since Congress possesses, under limited circumstances, the authority to suspend the Great Writ, the President can possess no independent power to do so under identical circumstances. He forgets his own contrary opinion in *Luther v. Borden,* where he argues that a President's assessment of an emergency is conclusive and binding on all political branches of government; and a President possesses an independent sphere of power separate from any power delegated by the legislature.

In addition, the Chief Justice speaks only in terms of the President's suspen-sion of the writ of habeas corpus. But was Lincoln's order of April 27 an actual suspension of the writ, so that it cannot issue, or was it an exercise of presidential emergency power permitting subordinates to disregard the writ when issued, as well as any related judicial proceedings? If suspension is inter-preted as an act of discontinuance, as Taney does, then only the legislature possesses the authority (through specific enactment) forbidding the writ to issue. If, on the other hand, the suspension that is restricted is only the authority to hold the person arrested against the operation of the writ, then the actual suspension requires no legislative act and can come about through circumstances that make suspension absolutely necessary. [*Id.* at 22.] Taney's major error is to interpret Article I, section 9, clause 2 as a grant of power rather than a limited restriction upon a power already in existence. [*Id.* at 23.] Contrary to the assumption of the Chief Justice there is nothing in the Constitution that suggests what governmental institution may invoke the clause or under what circum-stances it may be invoked, save for the two specifics of invasion and rebellion.

The *Prize Cases,* 67 U.S. (2 Bl.) 635; 17 L.Ed. 459 (1863)

By proclamations of April 15, 19, and 27, 1861, President Lincoln established a blockade of southern ports. These cases were brought to recover damages suffered by ships carrying cargoes to the Confederate States during the blockade. The blockade itself was declared before Congress had a chance to assemble and take action on the matter. These ships had been raided and seized by naval ships of the United States.

Basic Question: Did a state of war exist at the time this blockade was instituted that would justify a resort to these means of subduing the hostile force?

Opinion of the Court by Justice Grier:
There are certain propositions of law which must, necessarily, affect the ultimate decision of these cases and many others, which it will be proper to discuss and decide before we notice the special facts peculiar to each.

They are, 1st. Had the President a right to institute a blockade of ports in possession of persons in armed rebellion against the government, on the principles of international law, as known and acknowledged among civilized States? 2d. Was the property of persons domiciled or residing within those States a proper subject of capture on the seas as "enemies' property?"

That a blockade de facto actually existed, and was formally declared and notified by the President on the 27th and 30th of April, 1861, is an admitted fact in these cases. That the President, as the Executive Chief of the Government and Commander-in-Chief of the Army and Navy, was the proper person to make such notification, has not been, and cannot be disputed. Let us inquire whether, at the time this blockade was instituted, a state of war existed which would justify a resort to these means of subduing the hostile force. War has been well defined to be, "That state in which a nation prosecutes its right by force." The parties belligerent in a public war are independent nations. But it is not necessary, to constitute war, that both parties should be acknowledged as independent nations or sovereign States. A war may exist where one of the belligerents claims sovereign rights as against the other.

Insurrection against a government may or may not culminate in an organized rebellion, but a civil war always begins by insurrection against the lawful authority of the government. A civil war is never solemnly declared; it become such by its accidents—the number, power, and organization of the persons who originate and carry it on. When the party in rebellion occupy and hold in a hostile manner a certain portion of territory; have declared their independence; have cast off their allegiance; have organized armies; have commenced hostilities against their former Sovereign, the world acknowledges them as belligerents, and the contest a war. They claim to be in arms to establish their liberty and independence, in order to become a sovereign State, while the sovereign party treats them as insurgents and rebels who owe allegiance, and who should be punished with death for their treason....

As a civil war is never publicly proclaimed, *eo nomine* against insurgents, its actual existence is a fact in our domestic history which the Court is bound to notice and to know. The true test of is existence,.... may be thus summarily stated: "When the regular course of justice is interrupted by revolt, rebellion or insurrection, so that the courts of justice cannot be kept open, civil war exists and hostilities may be prosecuted on the same footing as if those opposing the government were foreign enemies invading the land."

By the Constitution, Congress alone has the power to declare a national or foreign war. It cannot declare war against a State or any number of States, by virtue of any clause in the Constitution. The Constitution confers on the President the whole executive power. He is bound to take care that the laws be faithfully executed. He is Commander-in-Chief of the Army and Navy of the United States, and of the militia of the several States when called into the actual service of the United States. He has no power to initiate or declare war either against a foreign nation or a domestic State. But by the Acts of Congress of ... 1795 ... and 1807,... he is authorized to call out the militia and use the military and naval forces of the United States in case of invasion by foreign nations, and to suppress insurrection against the government of a State or of the United States.

If a war be made by invasion of a foreign nation, the President is not only authorized but bound to resist force, by force. He does not initiate the war, but is bound to accept the challenge without waiting for any special legislative authority. And whether the hostile party be a foreign invader, or States organized in rebellion, it is none the less a war, although the declaration of it be "unilateral."...

This greatest of civil wars was not gradually developed by popular commotion, tumultuous assemblies, or local unorganized insurrections....The President was bound to meet it in the shape it presented itself, without waiting for Congress to baptize it with a name; and no name given to it by him or them could change the fact. It is none the less a civil war, with belligerent parties in hostile array, because it may be called an "insurrection" by one side, and the insurgents be considered as rebels or traitors. It is not necessary that the independence of the revolted province or State be acknowledged in order to constitute it a party belligerent in a war according to the law of nations. Foreign nations acknowledge it as war by a declaration of neutrality. The condition of neutrality cannot exist unless there be two belligerent parties....

Whether the President in fulfilling his duties, as Commander-in-Chief, in suppressing an insurrection, has met with such armed hostile resistance, and a civil war of such alarming proportions as will compel him to accord to them the character of belligerents, is a question to be decided by him, and this Court must be governed by the decisions and acts of the Political Department of the government to which this power was entrusted. "He must determine what degree of force the crisis demands." The proclamation of blockade is, itself, official and conclusive evidence to the court that a state of war existed which demanded and authorized a recourse to such a measure, under the circumstances peculiar to the case....[W]e are of the opinion that the President had the right, *jure belli*, to institute a blockade of ports in possession of the States in rebellion which neutrals are bound to regard.

All persons residing within this territory whose property may be used to increase the revenues of the hostile power are, in this contest, liable to be treated as enemies, though not foreigners. They have cast off their allegiance and made war on their government, and are none the less enemies because they are traitors....Whether the property be liable to capture as "enemies property" does not in any manner depend on the personal allegiance of the owner. It is illegal traffic that stamps it as "enemies property." It is of no consequence whether it belongs to an ally or a citizen....

The produce of the soil of the hostile territory, as well as other property engaged in the commerce of the hostile power, as the source of its wealth and

strength, are always regarded as legitimate prize, without regard to the domicile of the owner, and much more so if he reside and trade within their territory....
Judgments affirmed [except as to certain property in one of the cases].

Note: The President regarded secession as rebellion or insurrection rather than war and believed that he had inherent power as chief executive and commander-in-chief to ensure that the law of the United States was obeyed throughout the Union. Lincoln clung to the theory despite the conflict's magnitude and duration, acting independently throughout the crisis period. He had declared the existence of the emergency, he had taken initial measures to meet it, and he continued to prosecute it to a successful conclusion. The problem of determining what the nature of the conflict was and where the power to meet it resided arose in this case and demonstrated the difficulties that confront the Court under crisis conditions. At issue was the propriety of treating as "enemy property" four neutral ships that had been captured by the navy under the President's blockade proclamations. To uphold this seizure of prizes the Court would have had to accept the validity of the presidential proclamations, and since a blockade was tantamount to recognition of belligerent status under international law, this would mean that the United States and the Confederacy were at war. [R. Hirschfield, The Constitution and the Court 136 (1962).] Such a ruling would not only have embarrassed and endangered the government by providing foreign nations with grounds for establishing relations with the rebels, it also would have implied that the President could institute war measures without a congressional declaration as required by the Constitution. [*Id.*] On the other hand, if the Court stood firmly by the letter of the basic law and invalidated the seizures because there had been no declaration of war by Congress, the whole conduct of the government (that is, of the President) during the initial period of crisis would stand condemned. [*Id.*]

It is this dilemma that the Court is called upon to resolve in this case, and the decision handed down is arguably the most important one in the development of the wartime constitution and the beginning of constitutional dictatorship in the United States. It justifies Lincoln's rather extraordinary conception of constitutional power: insistence on an absolute separation of powers and the belief that all necessary powers of government devolve upon the President. It is Locke's notion of prerogative power taken to its ultimate conclusion. In sustaining Lincoln's actions, the Court legitimizes his argument that *he alone possesses the power to determine* (1) the existence of the emergency, (2) what measures are needed to successfully meet that emergency, and (3) when the emergency is over and the government actions taken no longer needed. In essence, the decision sustains the notion that during an emergency the law of necessity supersedes the law of the Constitution, *i.e.,* during time of war the laws are silent (*inter armes silent leges*). [*Id.* at 146-47.] In other words (and something the Supreme Court would quickly forget as soon as the emergency is over), war and peace are not the same thing and cannot coexist at the same time in the same place.

Ex Parte Vallandigham, 68 U.S. (1 Wall.) 234; 17 L.Ed. 589 (1864)

Along with his 1862 proclamation Lincoln had ordered that persons engaged in disloyal activities be tried by military commission. Clement Vallandigham, a well-known "copperhead," was arrested for making an antiwar speech, tried, found guilty, and sentenced to imprisonment for the war's duration by such a commission. His petition for a writ of habeas corpus was refused by the circuit court, and he was forced to take the case directly to the Supreme Court, which agreed to review the sentence. The petitioner argued that the military commission had no jurisdiction in this case because, as a civilian in an area where the courts were open and functioning, he was entitled to the normal guarantees of due process of law. Furthermore, he contended that the charge on which he was tried—"committing acts for the benefit of the enemy"—was unknown to the Constitution and the laws of the United States. This was a direct challenge to what the Court had legitimized in The *Prize Cases.*

Basic Question: Does the Supreme Court, under its Article III powers, have the jurisdiction to issue writs of habeas corpus, certiorari, and review the proceedings of a military commission?

Opinion of the Court by Justice Wayne:

It has been urged in support of the motion for the writ of certiorari, and against the jurisdiction of a military commission to try the petitioner, that the latter was prohibited by the 30th section of the Act of March 30, 12 Stat. 736, for enrolling and calling out the national forces, as the crimes punishable in it by the sentences of a court-martial or military commission, applied only to persons who are in the military service of the United States and subject to the Articles of War....

It is affirmed in the 13th paragraph of the 1st section of [the instructions for the government of the armies of the United States] that military jurisdiction is of two kinds. First, that which is conferred and defined by statute; second, that which is derived from the common law of war....

In the armies of the United States, the first is exercised by courts-martial while cases which do not come within the "rules and regulation of war," or the jurisdiction conferred by statute or court-martial, are tried by military commissions.

These jurisdictions are applicable, not only to war with foreign nations, but to a rebellion, when a part of a country wages war against its legitimate government, seeking to throw off all allegiance to it, to set up a government of its own.

Our first remark upon the motion for a certiorari is, that there is no analogy between the power given by the Constitution and law of the United States to the Supreme Court, and the other inferior courts of the United States and to the judges of them, to issue such processes, and the prerogative power by which it is done in England. The purposes for which the writ is issued are alike, but there is no similitude in the origin of the power to do it. In England, the Court of King's Bench has a superintendence over all courts of an inferior criminal jurisdiction, and may, by the plenitude of its power, award a certiorari to have any indictment removed and brought before it; and where such certiorari is allowable, it is awarded at the instance of the King, because every indictment is at the suit of the King, and he has the prerogative of suing in whatever court he pleases. The courts of the United States derive authority to issue such a writ from the Constitution and the legislation of Congress....

The appellate powers of the Supreme Court, as granted by the Constitution, are limited and regulated by the Acts of Congress, and must be exercised subject to the exceptions and regulations made by Congress....In other words, the petition before us we think not to be within the letter or spirit of the grants of appellate jurisdiction to the Supreme Court. It is not, in law or equity, within the meaning of those terms as used in the 3d article of the Constitution. Nor is a military commission a court within the meaning of the 14th section of the Judiciary Act of 1789. That Act is denominated to be one to establish the judicial courts of the United States, and the 14th section declares that all the "before mentioned courts" of the United States shall have power to issue writs of *scire facias, habeas corpus,* and all other writs not specially provided for by statute, which may be necessary for the exercise of their respective jurisdictions, agreeably to the principles and usages of law. The words in the section, "the before mentioned" courts, can only have reference to such courts as were established in the preceding part of the Act, and excludes the idea that a court of military commission can be one of them.

Whatever may be the force of Vallandigham's protest, that he was not triable by a court of military commission, it is certain that his petition cannot be brought within the 14th section of the Act; and further, that the court cannot, without disregarding its frequent decisions and interpretation of the Constitution in respect to its judicial power, originate a writ of certiorari to review or pronounce any opinion upon the proceedings of a military commission....

In the case *Ex parte Milburn,...* Chief Justice Marshall said, as the jurisdiction of the court is appellate, it must first be shown that it has the power to award a habeas corpus. *In re Kaine,...* the court denied the motion, saying that the court's jurisdiction to award the writ was appellative, and that the case had not been so presented to it, and for the same cause refused to issue a writ of certiorari, which, in the course of the argument, was prayed for. In *Ex parte Metzher,...* it was determined that a writ of certiorari could not be allowed to examine a commitment by a district judge, under the Treaty between the United States and France, for the reason that the judge exercised a special authority, and that no provision had been made for the revision of his judgment. So does a court of military commission exercise a special authority. In the case before us, it was urged that the decision in [the *Metzger*] case had been made upon the ground that the proceeding of the district judge was not judicial in its character, but that the proceedings of the military commission were so; and further, it was said that the ruling in that case had been over-ruled by a majority of the judges in *Raines'* case. There is a misapprehension of the report of the latter case, and as to the judicial character of the proceedings of the military commission, we cite what was said by this Court in the case of *United States v. Ferreira,...*

"The powers conferred by Congress upon the district judge and the secretary are judicial in their nature, for judgment and discretion must be exercised by both of them, but it is not judicial in either case, in the sense in which judicial power is granted to the courts of the United States." Nor can it be said that the authority to be exercised by a military commission is judicial in that sense. It involves a discretion to examine, to decide and sentence, but there is no original jurisdiction in the Supreme Court to issue a writ of *habeas corpus ad subjiciendum* to review or reverse its proceedings, or the writ of certiorari to revise the proceedings of a military commission. And as to the President's action in such matters, and those acting in them under his authority, we refer to the opinions expressed by this Court in the cases of *Martin v. Mott,...* and *Dynes v. Hoover,...*

For the reasons given, our judgment is, that the writ of certiorari prayed for to revise and review the proceedings of the Military Commission, by which Clement L. Vallandigham was tried, sentenced and imprisoned, must be denied, and so do we order accordingly.

Note: The validity of the President's institution of martial rule was thus challenged, but the Court avoided the issue. The action by the judiciary would set the precedent for all future litigation during periods of emergency. Adopting the government's technical argument as their own opinion, the justices found that the failure of the circuit court to act in this matter constituted a fatal flaw in the proceedings. Under both their original jurisdiction (derived from the Constitution) and their appellate jurisdiction (derived from the Judiciary Act of 1789), they could review only the proceedings of a court, and a military commission was not such a body. As a result, the executive retained the power to dispense justice in those areas which he had designated as theaters of military operations, and on no occasion during the war did the Supreme Court attempt to subordinate military to civil authority or to rebuke the President for relying on martial rule rather than on procedures established by the Constitution or by congressional acts.

Ex Parte Milligan, 71 U.S. (4 Wall.) 2; 18 L.Ed. 281 (1866)

Of all the arbitrary practices in which Lincoln found it imperative to engage, certainly the most dubious and judicially assailable was the trial of civilians by military commission. It was one thing for him to proclaim a blockade of the South, suspend the writ of habeas corpus along the nation's most important line of communications, raise the limits of the regular forces in the absence of Congress, or even issue the Emancipation Proclamation while denying that Congress had any such power. It was quite another, certainly in a country that could trace its legal history back through the Petition of Right, to authorize military trial of disaffected civilians in areas where the civil courts were open and functioning. Yet this is precisely what Lincoln did in his proclamation of 1862. One year later he issued a second proclamation suspending the privilege of the writ, and this time cited as authority the Habeas Corpus Act of 1863. He did not mention the subject of military commissions, and it is extremely important to note that Congress did not mention them in the 1863 statute. Whatever military trials of civilians took place during the war found their authority in the President's position as commander-in-chief.

Nevertheless, there is no case on the records of the Supreme Court or other federal courts in which this practice was impugned in the course of the war. There are three reasons for this fact: first, because trials of this nature in areas where the regular courts were functioning were extremely rare, since the normal method of dealing with persons suspected of treasonable activity was arrest without warrant, detention without trial, and release without punishment; second, because most federal courts went out of their way to avoid a brush with the military authorities; and third, because the Supreme Court itself put a damper on attempts to challenge the constitutionality of these controversial trials by military commission with its decision in the *Vallandigham* case.

Lambdin P. Milligan, a "Son of Liberty" who had done a great deal more than merely give speeches in defiance of Lincoln and the Union, was arrested October 5, 1864, at his home in Indiana, tried by a military commission established under presidential authority, and sentenced to be hanged for disloyal activities. This sentence was approved by President Andrew Johnson. At the time of his arrest and trial the circuit court in Indianapolis was open for business and fully prepared to take cognizance of his case under the procedure outlined in the 1863 statute. Sections 2 and 3 of the law provided that lists of prisoners arrested upon the authority of the President were to be furnished by the Secretaries of State and War to the circuit and district court judges. If grand juries returned no indictments against them, they were to be discharged by judicial order upon taking an oath of allegiance and entering into recognizance for good behavior. Where such lists were not furnished, a judge could discharge a prisoner on a writ of habeas corpus if satisfied of his loyalty. (This procedure had been completely ignored in Milligan's case). On May 10, 1865, just prior to execution, a writ of habeas corpus was issued by the circuit court in Indianapolis, and on a division of opinion the case was brought before the Supreme Court. Later that same day the sentence of hanging was stayed and then commuted to life imprisonment by President Johnson.

Basic Question: Did the military commission have the jurisdiction, legally, to place Milligan on trial?

Opinion of the Court by Justice Davis:

During the late wicked Rebellion the temper of the times did not allow that calmness in deliberation and discussion so necessary to a correct conclusion of a purely judicial question. Then, considerations of safety were mingled with the exercise of power, and feelings and interests prevailed which are happily terminated. Now that the public safety is assured, this question, as well as all others, can be discussed and decided without passion or the admixture of any element not required to form a legal judgment. We approach the investigation of this case fully sensible of the magnitude of the inquiry and the necessity of full and cautious deliberation.

...Milligan, not a resident of one of the rebellious states, or a prisoner of war, but a citizen of Indiana for twenty years past, and never in the military or naval service, is, while at his home, arrested by the military power of the United States, imprisoned and, on certain criminal charges preferred against him, tried, convicted, and sentenced to be hanged by a military commander of the military district of Indiana. Had this tribunal the legal power and authority to try and punish this man?

No graver question was ever considered by this Court, nor one which more nearly concerns the birthright of every American citizen when charged with crime, to be tried and punished according to law. The power of punishment is alone through the means which the laws have provided for that purpose, and if they are ineffectual, there is an immunity from punishment, no matter how great an offender the individual may be, or how much his crimes may have shocked the sense of justice of the country, or endangered its safety. By the protection of the law human rights are secured; withdraw that protection, and they are at the mercy of wicked rulers, or the clamor of an excited people. If there was law to justify this military trial, it is not our province to interfere; if there was not, it is our duty to declare the nullity of the whole proceedings. The decision of this question does not depend on argument or judicial precedents, numerous and highly illustrative as they are. These precedents inform us of the extent of the struggle to preserve liberty and to relieve those in civil life from military trials. The Founders of our government were familiar with the history of that struggle; and secured in a written Constitution every right which the people had wrested from power during a contest of ages. By that Constitution and the laws authorized by it, this question must be determined....

Time has proven the discernment of our ancestors; for even these provisions, expressed in such plain English words, that it would seem the ingenuity of man could not evade them, are now, after the lapse of more than seventy years, sought to be avoided. Those great and good men foresaw that troublous times would arise, when rulers and people would become restive under restraint, and seek by sharp and decisive measures to accomplish ends deemed just and proper; and that the principles of constitutional liberty would be in peril, unless established by irrepealable law. The history of the world had taught them that what was done in the past might be attempted in the future. The Constitution of the United States is a law for rulers and people, equally in war and in peace, and covers with the shield of its protection all classes of men, at all times, and under all circumstances. No doctrine, involving more pernicious consequences, was ever invented by the wit of man than that any of its provisions can be suspended during any of the great exigencies of government. Such a doctrine leads directly to anarchy or despotism, but the theory of necessity on which it is based is false; for the government, within the Constitution, has all the powers granted to it which are necessary to preserve its existence, as has been happily proved by the result of the great effort to throw off its just authority.

Every trial involves the exercise of judicial power; and from what source did the Military Commission that tried him derive their authority? Certainly no part of the judicial power of the country was conferred on them; because the Constitution expressly vests it "in one Supreme Court and such inferior courts as the Congress may from time to time ordain and establish," and it is not pretended that the commission was a court ordained and established by Congress. They cannot justify on the mandate of the President; because he is controlled by law, and has his appropriate sphere of duty, which is to execute, not to make, the laws; and there is "no unwritten criminal code in which resort can be had as a source of jurisdiction."

But it is said that the jurisdiction is complete under the "laws and usages of war." It can serve no useful purpose to inquire what those laws and usages are, whence they originated, where found, and on whom they operate; they can never be applied to citizens in states which have upheld the authority of the government, and where the courts are open and their process unobstructed. This Court has judicial knowledge that in Indiana the Federal authority was always unopposed, and its courts always open to hear criminal accusations and redress grievances; and no usage of war could sanction a military trial there for any offense whatever of a citizen in civil life, in nowise connected with the military service. Congress could grant no such power; and to the honor of our national legislature be it said, it has never been provoked by the state of the country even to attempt its exercise. One of the plainest constitutional provisions was, therefore, infringed when Milligan was tried by a court not ordained and established by Congress, and not composed of judges appointed during good behavior.

It is claimed that martial law covers with its broad mantle the proceedings of this Military Commission. The proposition is this: That in a time of war the commander of an armed force (if in his opinion the exigencies of the country demand it, and of which he is to judge), has the power, within the lines of his military district, to suspend all civil rights and their remedies, and subject citizens as well as soldiers to the rule of his will; and in the exercise of his lawful authority cannot be restrained, except by his superior officer or the President of the United States....

The statement of this proposition shows its importance; for, if true, republican government is a failure, and there is an end of liberty regulated by law. Martial law, established on such a basis, destroys every guaranty of the Constitution, and effectually renders the "military independent of and superior to the civil power"—the attempt to do which by the [British] King was deemed by our fathers such an offense, that they assigned it to the world as one of the causes which impelled them to declare their independence. Civil liberty and this kind of martial law cannot endure together; the antagonism is irreconcilable and, in the conflict, one or the other must perish....

It will be borne in mind that this is not a question of the power to proclaim martial law, when war exists in a community and the courts and civil authorities are overthrown. Nor is it a question what rule a military commander, at the head of his army, can impose on States in rebellion to cripple their resources and quell the insurrection. The jurisdiction claimed is much more extensive. The necessities of the service, during the late Rebellion, required that the loyal states should be placed within the limits of certain military districts and commanders appointed in them; and, it is urged, that this, in a military sense, constituted them the theater of military operations; and, as in this case, Indiana had been and was again threatened with invasion by the enemy, the occasion was furnished to establish martial law. The conclusion does not follow from the premises. If armies were collected in Indiana, they were to be employed in another locality, where the laws were obstructed and the national authority disputed. On her soil there was no hostile foot; if once invaded, that invasion was at an end, and with it all pretext for martial law. Martial law cannot arise from a threatened invasion. The necessity must be actual and present; the invasion real, such as effectually closes the courts and deposes the civil administration....

It follows, from what has been said on this subject, that there are occasions when martial rule can be properly applied. If, in foreign invasion or civil war, the courts are actually closed, and it is impossible to administer criminal justice according to law, then, on the theater of actual military operations, where war really prevails, there is a necessity to furnish a substitute for the civil authority, thus overthrown, to preserve the safety of the army and society; and as no power is left but the military, it is allowed to govern by martial rule until the laws can have their free course. A necessity creates the rule, so it limits its duration; for, if this government is continued after the courts are reinstated, it is a gross usurpation of power. Martial rule can never exist where the courts are open, and in the proper and unobstructed exercise of their jurisdiction....

If the military trial of Milligan was contrary to law, then he was entitled, on the facts stated in his petition, to be discharged from custody by the terms of the act of Congress of March 3d, 1863....Milligan avers he was a citizen of Indiana, not in the military or naval service, and was detained in close confinement, by order of the President,...If these averments were true (and their truth is conceded for the purpose of this case), the court was required to liberate him on taking certain oaths prescribed by the law, and entering into recognizance for his good behavior.

But it is insisted that Milligan was a prisoner of war, and, therefore, excluded from the privileges of the statute. It is not easy to see how he can be treated as a prisoner of war, when he lived in Indiana for the past twenty years, was arrested there, and had not been, during the late troubles, a resident of any of the states in rebellion. If in Indiana he conspired with bad men to assist the enemy, he is punishable for it in the courts of Indiana; but, when tried for the offense, he cannot plead the rights of war; for he was not engaged in legal acts of hostility against the government, and only such persons, when captured, are prisoners of war. If he cannot enjoy the immunities attaching to the character of a prisoner of war, how can he be subject to their pains and penalties?...

Note: As a restraint on a President beset by martial crisis the decision was then, and now, of practically no value whatsoever. It cannot be emphasized too strongly that the decision in this case, following the close of the rebellion by a full year, altered not in the slightest degree the extraordinary methods through which that rebellion had been suppressed, and did nothing more than deliver from jail a handful of individuals who in any event would have probably gained their freedom in short order. [C. Rossiter, The Supreme Court and the Commander in Chief 34 (Longaker ed. 1976).] And upon all Presidents who have come after, the decision has had precious little demonstrable effect. No President seems to have given it the slightest thought in determining the scope and form of his martial powers, and that in any case Davis so overstated his point as to render his observations wholly meaningless for a constitutional government faced with the reality of the 20th century. [*Id.* at 35.] The Constitution of the United States *does not cover* "with the shield of its protection all classes of men, at all times and under all circumstances," and there is nothing to be gained by insisting that it does. [*Id.*]

It is simply not true that "martial law cannot arise from a threatened invasion," or that "martial rule can never exist where the courts are open." These statements do not present an accurate definition of the allowable limits of the martial powers of President and Congress in the face of foreign threats or internal disorder. Nor was Davis's dictum on the specific power of Congress in this matter any more accurate. And, however eloquent and quotable his words on the untouchability of the Constitution in time of actual crisis, they do not now, and did not then, express the realities of American constitutional law. *Ex parte Milligan* was an exhibition of judicial self-hypnosis of which no defender of the Court could possibility be proud. [*Id.* at 37.] It is not always easy to see the alleged decisive difference between *Ex parte Vallandigham* and *Ex parte Milligan*. The decision in the former has a hollow ring, which makes the echo of the latter even more hollow. If the Court had been at all anxious to test the President's reading of his powers—if, for example, Davis had really believed that the Constitution meant what it said about trial by jury—it would have been no trouble at all to alter Vallandigham's petition from one for certiorari to one for a writ of habeas corpus, returnable before one of the justices, if not the Court itself. [*Id.*] In sum, *Ex parte Milligan* is sound doctrine in forbidding the presidential establishment of military commissions for the trial of civilians in areas where the civil courts are open—but it is little else. Its general observations on the limits of the war powers are no more valid today than they were in 1866. Here again the law of the Constitution is what Lincoln did in the crisis, not what the Court said after the crisis was over and the President dead. [*Id.* at 39.]

Remember not to put too much faith in a precedent created for normal times, when the times are abnormal and the national interest is at stake.

3

Age of Industrial Disorder through Wilson

In Re Neagle (Cunningham v. Neagle), **135 U.S. 1; 34 L.Ed. 55 (1890)**

David Neagle, a United States marshal, had been assigned by the Attorney General as bodyguard for Justice Stephen Field when he was sitting as Circuit Judge in California. Field was attacked by one David S. Terry; Neagle killed Terry in defense of Field. Neagle was then arrested by the California authorities and held on a charge of murder. The case reached the Supreme Court on Neagle's application for a writ of habeas corpus. Under the terms of section 753 of the Revised Statutes, a writ of habeas corpus could be issued, *inter alia,* only for a person who "is in custody for [an] act done or omitted in pursuance of a law of the United States."

Basic Questions: Could the President, without congressional action, issue an executive order through the Attorney General to authorize Neagle to protect Justice Field? Was the order of the Attorney General, acting under the authority of the President, "a law of the United States" pursuant to the statute?

Opinion of the Court by Justice Miller:

We have no doubt that Mr. Justice Field when attacked by Terry was engaged in the discharge of his duties as Circuit Justice of the Ninth Circuit, and was entitled to all the protection under those circumstances which the law could give him.

It is urged, however, that there exists no statute authorizing any such protection as that which Neagle was instructed to give Judge Field in the present case, and indeed no protection whatever against a vindictive or malicious assault growing out of the faithful discharge of his official duties; and that the language of section 753 of the Revised Statutes, that the party seeking the benefits of the writ of habeas corpus must in this connection show that he is "in custody for an act done or omitted in pursuance of a law of the United States," makes it necessary that upon this occasion it should be shown that the act for which Neagle is imprisoned was done by virtue of an act of Congress. It is not supposed that any special act of Congress exists which authorizes the marshals or deputy marshals of the United States in express terms to accompany the judges of the Supreme Court through their circuits, and act as a bodyguard to them, to defend them against malicious assaults against their persons. But we are of [the] opinion that this view of the statute is an unwarranted restriction of the meaning of a law designed to extend in a liberal manner the benefit of the writ of habeas corpus to persons imprisoned for the performance of their duty. And we are satisfied that if it was the duty of Neagle, under the circumstances, a duty which could only arise under the laws of the United States, to defend Mr. Justice Field from a murderous attack upon him, he brings himself within the meaning of the section we have recited. This view of the subject is confirmed by the alternative provision, that he must be in custody "for an act done or omitted in pursuance of a law of the United States or of an order, process, or decree of a court or judge thereof, or is in custody in violation of the Constitution or of a law or treaty of the United States."

In the view we take of the Constitution of the United States, any obligation fairly and properly inferable from the general scope of his duties under the laws of the United States is "a law" within the meaning of this phrase. It would be a great reproach to the system of government of the United States, declared to be within its sphere sovereign and supreme, if there is to be found within the domain of its powers no means of protecting the judges, in the conscientious and faithful discharge of their duties, from the malice and hatred of those upon whom their judgments may operate unfavorably....

Where, then, are we to look for the protection which we have shown Judge Field was entitled to when engaged in the discharge of his official duties? Not to the courts of the United States; be-cause, as has been more than once said in this Court, in the division of the powers of government between the three great departments, executive, legislative and judicial, the judicial is the weakest for the purposes of self-protection and for the enforcement of the powers which it exercises. The ministerial officers through whom its commands must be executed are marshals of the United States, and belong emphatically to the executive department of the government....

The Constitution, Section 3, Article 2, declares that the President "shall take care that the laws be faithfully executed," and he is provided with the means of fulfilling this obligation by his authority to commission all the officers of the United States, and, by and with the advice and consent of the Senate, to appoint the most important of them and to fill vacancies. He is declared to be commander-in-chief of the army and navy of the United States. The duties which are thus imposed upon him he is further enabled to perform by the recognition of the Constitution, and the creation by acts of Congress, of executive departments,... the heads of which are familiarly called cabinet ministers. These aid him in the performance of the great duties of his office, and represent him in a thousand acts to which it can hardly be supposed his personal attention is called, and thus he is enabled to fulfill the duty of his great department, expressed in the phrase that "he shall take care that the laws be faithfully executed."

Is this duty limited to the enforcement of acts of Congress or of treaties of the United States according to their express terms, or does it include the rights, duties and obligations growing out of the Constitution itself, our international relations, and all the protection implied by the nature of the government under the Constitution?...

We cannot doubt the power of the President to take measures for the protection of a judge of one of the courts of the United States, who, while in the discharge of the duties of his office, is threatened with a personal attack which may probably result in his death, and we think it clear that where this protection is to be afforded through the civil power, the Department of Justice is the proper one to set in motion the necessary means of protection. The correspondence already recited in this opinion between the marshal of the Northern District of California, and the Attorney General, and the district attorney of the United States for that district, although prescribing no very specific mode of affording this protection by the Attorney General, is sufficient, we think, to warrant the marshal in taking the steps which he did take, in making the provisions which he did make, for the protection and defense of Mr. Justice Field.

But there is positive law investing the marshals and their deputies with powers which not only justify what Marshal Neagle did in this matter, but which imposed it upon him as a duty. In chapter 14, title 13, of the Revised Statutes of the United States,... section 788 declares: "The marshals and their deputies in such state may have, by law, in executing the laws of the United States as the sheriffs and their deputies in such state may have, by law, in executing the laws thereof." If, therefore, a sheriff of the state of California was authorized to do in regard to the laws of California what Neagle did, that is, if he was authorized to keep the peace, to protect a judge from assault and murder, then Neagle was authorized to do the same thing in reference to the laws of the United States. ...That there is a peace of the United States; that a man assaulting a judge of the United States while in the discharge of his duties violates that peace; that in such case the marshal of the United States stands in the same relation to the peace of the United States which the sheriff of the county does to the peace of the state of California, are questions too clear to need argument to prove them. That it would be the duty of a sheriff, if one had been present at this assault by Terry upon Judge Field, to prevent this breach of the peace, to prevent this assault, to prevent the murder which was contemplated by it, cannot be doubted. And if, in performing his duty, it became necessary, for the protection of Judge Field or of himself, to kill Terry, in a case where, like this, it was evidently a question of the choice of who should be killed, the assailant and violator of the law and disturber of the peace, or the unoffending man who was in his power, there can be no question of the authority of the sheriff to have killed Terry. So the marshal of the United States, charged with the duty of protecting and guarding the judge of the United States court against this special assault upon his person and his life, being present at the critical moment, when prompt action was necessary, found it to be his duty—a duty which he had no liberty to refuse to perform—to take the steps which resulted in Terry's death. This duty was imposed on him by the section of the Revised Statutes which we have recited, in connection with the powers conferred by the state of California upon its peace officers, which become, by this statute, in proper cases, transferred as duties to the marshals of the United States....

If the duty of the United States to protect its officers from violence, even to death, in discharge of the duties which its laws impose upon them, be established, and Congress has made the writ of habeas corpus one of the means by which this protection is made efficient, and if the facts of this case show that the prisoner was acting both under the authority of law, and the directions of his superior officers of the Department of Justice, we can see no reason why this writ should not be made to serve its purpose in the present case....

The result of which we have arrived upon this examination is, that in the protection of the person and the life of Mr. Justice Field while in the discharge of his official duties, Neagle was authorized to resist the attack of Terry upon him; that Neagle was correct in the belief that without prompt action on his part the assault of Terry upon the judge would have ended in the death of the latter; that such being his well-founded belief, he was justified in taking the life of Terry, as the only means of preventing the death of the man who was intended to be his victim; that in taking the life of Terry, under the circumstances, he was acting under the authority of the laws of the United States, and was justified in so doing; and that he is not liable to answer to the courts of California on account of his part in that transaction. We therefore affirm the judgment of the Circuit Court authorizing his discharge from the custody of the sheriff of San Joaquin County.

Note: No particular problem exists when executive orders are based squarely on express statutory terms. In that connection, the President is similar to any administrative agency—even though the question of whether the Administrative Procedure Act, 5 U.S.C.A. 551, applies to him is unsettled. [A. Miller, Presidential Power 88 (1977).] When, however, executive orders find no express warrant in the statutes and only inferential warrant in the Constitution, problems can and do arise.

It has been suggested that the *Neagle* opinion can be read to mean that the President's power under the "take care" clause is analogous to that expressly given to Congress in the implied powers clause of Article I, section 8, clause 18 of the Constitution: "The President's authority in this respect should include the power to take all measures, not prohibited by the Constitution or statute, 'which shall be necessary and proper for carrying into execution' the laws of the United States or for the protection of federal rights, privileges, and immunities." [2 B. Schwartz, A Commentary on the Constitution of the United States 63 (1963).] But that latitudinarian view, while somewhat accurate, overstates the case regarding the *Neagle* decision. Even though the Court said in *Neagle* that "there is a peace of the United States" violated by the assault on the judge, the "take care" clause is *not* here analogous to the "necessary and proper" clause relating to Congress. It would become so when combined with additional judicial decisions. [A. Miller, 90.]

Of specific interest, at this point, is the fact that an order of the Attorney General (which may be said to be that of the President) was held to be "a law of the United States"—a direct, express holding that the President does have lawmaking powers. An implied obligation of the President to protect federal officials became a law to whose execution he must faithfully execute. [*Id.* at 90-91.]

In Re Debs, 158 U.S. 564; 39 L.Ed. 1092 (1895)

In July 1894, the Cleveland Administration used the labor injunction to help break the Pullman strike, one of the most important labor actions in American history. In May 1894, the Pullman Car Company, because of the prevailing business depression, imposed a 20 percent wage cut on its employees. At the same time it maintained the existing level of executive salaries and company dividends. Several thousand Pullman workers, organized with the American Railway Union, thereupon went out on strike. Under the leadership of Eugene V. Debs, the union presently resorted to a secondary boycott by refusing to move trains hauling Pullman cars. The strikers and their sympathizers shortly engaged in mob violence to block rail traffic. The result was the physical obstruction of interstate commerce and blockage of the mails in Chicago and elsewhere in the nation.

To deal with this crisis the Cleveland Administration employed an antistrike strategy. The basis of it was injunctions issued by federal courts which provided a justification for executive intervention in support of judicial authority. The day after the injunction was issued further rioting occurred, at which point President Grover Cleveland decided to interfere in the strike. Over the protest of Illinois governor John Altgeld, he dispatched federal troops to Chicago and assigned five thousand deputy marshals sworn in for the occasion. Debs and his fellow union leaders, ignoring the court order, were arrested for conspiring to obstruct the mails and interfere with interstate commerce. Debs was tried and convicted in federal district court, and the court invoked the Sherman Act as authority for the injunction and for the convictions (on the ground that the strikers had engaged in a conspiracy in restraint of trade within the meaning of the law). The court disregarded the objection that in enacting the antitrust law Congress had presumably been aiming at corporate trusts and not at labor unions. Debs and his associates sought a writ of habeas corpus from the United States Supreme Court.

Basic Question: Was this injunction, for violation of which Debs had been jailed for contempt of court, granted with jurisdiction?

Opinion of the Court by Justice Brewer:

The case presented by the bill is this: The United States, finding that the interstate transportation of persons and property, as well as the carriage of the mails, is forcibly obstructed, and that a combination and conspiracy exists to subject the control of such transportation to the will of the conspirators, applied to one of their courts, sitting as a court of equity, for an injunction to restrain such obstruction and prevent carrying into effect such conspiracy. Two questions of importance are presented: First. Are the relations of the general government to interstate commerce and the transportation of the mails such as authorize a direct interference to prevent a forcible obstruction thereof? Second. If authority exists, as authority in governmental affairs implies both power and duty, has a court of equity jurisdiction to issue an injunction in aid of the performance of such duty?

What are the relations of the general government to interstate commerce and the transportation of the mails? They are those of direct supervision, control, and management. While under the dual system which prevails with us the powers of government are distributed between the state and the nation, and while the latter is properly styled a government of enumerated powers, yet within the limits of such enumeration it has all the attributes of sovereignty, and, in the exercise of those enumerated powers, acts directly upon the citizen, and not, through the intermediate agency of the state.

"The government of the Union, then, is, emphatically and truly, a government of the people. In form and in substance it emanates from them. Its powers are granted by them, and are to be exercised directly on them, and for their benefit."

"No trace is to be found in the Constitution of an intention to create a dependence of the government of the Union on those of the states, for the execution of the great powers assigned to it. Its means are adequate to its ends, and on those means alone was it expected to rely for the accomplishment of its ends. To impose on it the necessity of resorting to means which it cannot control, which another government may furnish or withhold, would render its course precarious, the result of its measures uncertain, and create a dependence on other governments, which might disappoint its most important designs, and is incompatible with the language of the Constitution."...

"Both the states and the United States existed before the Constitution. The people, through that instrument, established a more perfect union by substituting a national government, acting, with ample power, directly upon the citizens, instead of the confederate government, which acted with powers, greatly restricted, only upon the states."...

"We hold it to be an incontrovertible principle that the government of the United States may, by means of physical force, exercise through its official agents, execute on every foot of American soil the powers and functions that belong to it. This necessarily involves the power to command obedience to its laws, and hence the power to keep the peace to that extent."

Among the powers expressly given to the national government are the control of interstate commerce and the creation and management of a post-office system for the nation. Article I, section 8, of the Constitution provides that "the Congress shall have power: ... Third, to regulate commerce with foreign nations and among the several states, and with the Indian tribes.... Seventh, to establish post offices and post roads."

Congress has exercised the power granted in respect to interstate commerce in a variety of legislative acts....

Under the power vested in Congress to establish post-offices and post roads, Congress has, by a mass of legislation, established the great post-office system of the country, with all its detail of organization, its machinery for the transaction of business, defining what shall be carried and what not, and the prices of carriage, and also prescribing penalties for all offenses against it....

As, under the Constitution, power over interstate commerce and the transportation of the mails is vested in the national government, and Congress, by virtue of such grant, has assumed actual and direct control, it follows that the national government may prevent any unlawful and forcible interference therewith. But how shall this be accomplished? Doubtless, it is within the competency of Congress to prescribe by legislation that any interferences with these matters shall be offenses against the United States, and prosecuted and punished by indictments in the proper courts. But is that the only remedy? Have the vast interests of the nation in interstate commerce, and in the transportation of the mails, no other protection than lies in the possible punishment of those who interfere with it? To ask the question is to answer it. By Article III, section 2, clause 3, of the federal Constitution, it is provided: "The trial of all crimes except in cases of impeachment shall be by jury; and such trial shall be held in the state where the said crime shall have been committed." If all the inhabitants of a state, or even a great body of them, should combine to obstruct interstate commerce or the transportation of the mails, prosecutions for such offenses had in such a community would be doomed in advance to failure. And if the certainty of such failure was known, and the national government had no other way to enforce the freedom of interstate commerce and the transportation of the mails than by prosecution and punishment of interference therewith, the whole interests of the nation in these respects would be at the absolute mercy of a portion of the inhabitants of that single state.

But there is no such impotency in the national government. The entire strength of the nation may be used to enforce in any part of the land the full and free exercise of all national powers and the security of all rights entrusted by the Constitution to its care. The strong arm of the national government may be put forth to brush away all obstructions to the freedom of interstate commerce or the transportation of the mails. If the emergency arises, the army of the nation, and all its militia, are at the service of the nation, to compel obedience to its laws.

But, passing to the second question, is there no other alternative than the use of force on the part of the executive authorities whenever obstructions arise to the freedom of interstate commerce or the transportation of the mails? Is the army the only instrument by which rights of the public can be enforced, and the peace of the nation preserved? Grant that any public nuisance may be forcibly abated, either at the instance of the authorities, or by any individual suffering private damage therefrom. The existence of this right of forcible abatement is not inconsistent with, nor does it destroy, the right of appeal, in an orderly way, to the courts for a judicial determination, and an exercise of their powers, by writ of injunction and otherwise, to accomplish the same result....

So, in the case before us, the right to use force does not exclude the right of appeal to the courts for a judicial determination, and for the exercise of all their powers of prevention. Indeed, it is more to the praise than the blame of the government that, instead of determining for itself questions of right and wrong on the part of these petitioners and their associates, and enforcing that determination by the club of the policeman and the bayonet of the soldier, it submitted all those questions to the peaceful determination of judicial tribunals, and invoked their consideration and judgment as to the measure of its rights and powers, and the correlative obligations of those against whom it made complaint. And it is equally to the credit of the latter that the judgment of those tribunals was by the great body of them respected, and the troubles which threatened so much disaster terminated.

Neither can it be doubted that the government has such an interest in the subject-matter as enables it to appear as party plaintiff in this suit. It is said that equity only interferes for the protection of property, and that the government has no property interest. A sufficient reply is that the United States have a property in the mails, the protection of which was one of the purposes of this bill....

Every government, entrusted by the very terms of its being with powers and duties to be exercised and discharged for the general welfare, has a right to apply to its own courts for any proper assistance in the exercise of the one and the discharge of the other....[W]hile it is not the province of the government to interfere in any mere matter of private controversy between individuals, or to use its great powers to enforce the rights of one against another, yet, whenever the wrongs complained of are such as affect the public at large, and are in respect of matters which by the *Constitution are entrusted to the care of the nation, and concerning which the nation owes the duty to all the citizens of securing to them their common rights, then the mere fact that the government has no pecuniary interest in the controversy is not sufficient to exclude it from the courts, or prevent it from taking measures therein to fully discharge those constitutional duties.* [Emphasis added.]

The petition for the writ of habeas corpus is denied.

Note: The central principle is one of inherent powers—the capacity of the chief executive to execute not only the laws passed by Congress but, in legal theory, the President's *own* law, and of even going so far as setting aside the law in order to meet perceived emergencies. [A. Miller, Presidential Power 117-18 (1977).] This, in general, means that there is a doctrine of constitutional reason of state *(raison d'etat)* or, to employ the more familiar term of Locke, of presidential prerogative. The President has a rather open-ended authority to use such means as are necessary to execute the laws and, further, that the term *laws* is itself sufficiently flexible to cover far more than merely the statutes of Congress.

Taken in conjunction with the doctrine of the *Neagle* case that "there is a peace of the United States," the *Debs* ruling, gives to the President powers belonging to the United States—that is, to the national government as a whole. [E. Corwin, The President: Office and Powers 152 (4th ed. 1957).] In other words, the Court in *Neagle, Debs,* and *Ex parte Siebold,* 100 U.S. 371 (1879), followed the Hamilton-Lincoln approach of postulating certain general, aggregate powers of the United States and then, in the absence of specific legislation to the contrary, attributed those powers to the President. [C. Rossiter, The Supreme Court and the Commander in Chief 197-98 (Longaker ed. 1976).]

The claimed emergency power to use troops in domestic situations was considered an exception to the norm, an exertion of executive power in the face of extraordinary events. In theory, troops were to be used only in the event of severe disruption, in order to return the system to a state of orderly functioning. But domestic pressures during the age of industrial disorder helped bring about subtle changes in the use of troops in the domestic sphere and, as a result, an interpretive broadening of presidential powers. Apart from any autonomous presidential power to use troops to protect "the peace of the United States," the Court has had no difficulty finding a firm statutory basis for presidential use of force domestically has existed since the early days of the Republic; and there seems to be little doubt that the existing statutes (U.S.C., Title 10, sections 331-34) authorize the use of inherent presidential power, if they do not strictly confine it.

Moyer v. Peabody, **212 U.S. 78; 53 L.Ed. 410 (1909)**

During a labor dispute in Colorado the governor (James Peabody) had declared a county to be in a state of insurrection and proclaimed martial law and authorized the use of troops to put down violence. He further ordered that the plaintiff (Charles Moyer) should be arrested as a leader of the outbreak, and should be detained [the detention lasting from March 30 to June 15, 1904] until he could be discharged with safety, and that then he should be delivered to the civil authorities, to be dealt with according to law. Peabody's imprisonment was without probable cause and he was denied access to the courts of the state, although they were open during the time of the emergency.

Basic Question: Is the executive's determination of the factual situation binding upon the courts as a limit on judicial review?

Opinion of the Court by Justice Holmes:

This is an action brought by the plaintiff in error against the former governor of the state of Colorado, the former adjutant general of the national guard of the same state, and a captain of the company of the national guard, for an imprisonment of the plaintiff by them while in office. The complaint was dismissed on demurrer, and the case comes here on a certificate that the demurrer was sustained solely on the ground that there was no justification in the circuit court.

The complaint alleges that the imprisonment was continued from the morning of March 30, 1904, to the afternoon of June 15, and that the defendants justified under the Constitution of Colorado, making the governor commander in chief of the state forces, and giving him power to call them out to execute laws, suppress insurrection, and repel invasion. It alleges that his imprisonment was without probable cause, that no complaint was filed against the plaintiff, and that (in that sense) he was prevented from having access to the courts of the state, although they were open during the whole time; but it sets our proceedings on habeas corpus, instituted by him before the supreme court of the state, in which that court refused to admit him to bail and ultimately discharged the writ....

The plaintiff's position, stated in a few words, is that the action of the governor, sanctioned to the extent that it was by the decision of the supreme court, was the action of the state and therefore within the 14th Amendment; but that, if that action was unconstitutional, the governor got no protection from personal liability for his unconstitutional interference with the plaintiff's rights. It is admitted, as it must be, that the governor's declaration that a state of insurrection existed is conclusive of that fact. It seems to be admitted also that the arrest alone would not necessarily have given a right to bring this suit....But it is said that a detention for so many days, alleged to be without probable cause, at a time when the courts were open, without an attempt to bring the plaintiff before them, makes a case on which he has a right to have a jury pass.

We shall not consider all of the questions that the facts suggest, but shall confine ourselves to stating what we regard as a sufficient answer to the complaint, without implying that there are not others equally good. Of course, the plaintiff's position is that he has been deprived of his liberty without due process. But it is familiar that what is due process of law depends on circumstances. It varies with the subject-matter and the necessities of the situation. Thus, summary proceedings suffice for taxes, and executive decisions for exclusion from the country....What, then, are the circumstances of this case? By agreement the record of the proceedings upon habeas corpus was made part of the complaint. The facts that we are to assume are that a state of insurrection existed and that the governor, without sufficient reason, but in good faith, in the course of putting the insurrection down, held the plaintiff until he thought that he safely could release him.

It would seem to be admitted by the plaintiff that he was president of the Western Federation of Miners, and that, whoever was to blame, trouble was apprehended with the members of that organization. We mention these facts not as material, but simply to put in more definite form the nature of the occasion on which the governor felt called upon to act. In such a situation we must assume that he had a right, under the state Constitution and laws, to call out troops, as was held by the supreme court of the state. The Constitution is supplemented by an act providing that "when an invasion of or insurrection in the state is made or threatened, the governor shall order the nation guard to repel or suppress the same."....That means that he shall make the ordinary use of the soldiers to that end; that he may kill persons who resist, and, of course, that he may use the milder measure of seizing the bodies of those whom he considers to stand in the way of restoring peace. Such arrests are not necessarily for punishment, but are by the way of precaution, to prevent the exercise of hostile power. So long as such arrests are made in good faith and in the honest belief that they are needed in order to head the insurrection off, the governor is the final judge and cannot be subjected to an action after he is out of office, on the ground that he had not reasonable ground for his belief....

No doubt there are cases where the expert on the spot may be called upon to justify his conduct later in court, notwithstanding the fact that he had sole command at the time and acted to the best of his knowledge. This is the position of the captain of a ship. But, even in that case, great weight is given to his determination, and the matter is to be judged on the facts as they appeared then, and not merely in the light of the event....When it comes to a decision by the head of the state upon a matter involving its life, the ordinary rights of individuals must yield to what he deems the necessities of the moment. Public danger warrants the substitution of executive process for judicial process....As no one would deny that there was immunity for ordering a company to fire upon a mob in insurrection, and that a state law authorizing the governor to deprive citizens of life under such circumstances was consistent with the 14th Amendment, we are of [the] opinion that the same is true of a law authorizing by implication what was done in this case. As we have said already, it is unnecessary to consider whether there are other reasons why the circuit court was right in its conclusion. It is enough that, in our opinion, the declaration does not disclose a "suit authorized by law to be brought to redress the deprivation of any right secured by the Constitution of the United States."...

Note: Apart from any autonomous presidential power to use troops to protect "the peace of the United States," which reputedly is found in a broad interpretation of the Constitution in such cases as *Neagle, Debs,* and *Siebold,* a firm statutory basis for presidential use of force domestically has existed since the early days of the Republic. Whether the statutes prohibit any independent exercise of power by the President is an unsettled question. There is no doubt, however, that the statutes authorize the use of presidential power, if they do not strictly confine it. *Moyer,* in following prior precedent, concluded that the governor's determination of necessity as well as the means used to restore order were conclusive on the courts; and the judiciary would not intervene as long as the action was taken in good faith. In other words, Holmes's majority opinion brushed aside as immaterial the facts that the Court previously treated as absolutely crucial in *Milligan.*

The doctrine prevailed until the mid-1930s, when the Court, in *Sterling v. Constantin,* 287 U.S. 378 (1932), responding to the use of troops by the governor of Texas to control the production of oil and the purported violence arising from the production controls, concluded that the governor has absolute discretion to declare an emergency and to determine the exigency for the use of troops. *But the Court declared that the measures taken were themselves reviewable;* and the Court determined that the measures taken were not directly related to quelling disorder. [C. Rossiter, The Supreme Court and the Commander in Chief 206 (Longaker ed. 1976).]

Sterling was an important step forward, for it did away with the apparent absolutism of *Moyer,* while declaring more broadly that the use of military force in domestic situations could not escape constitutional limitations and judicial review. Also decided along similar lines was *Scheur v. Rhodes,* 416 U.S. 232 (1974), one of several cases emerging from the Kent State tragedy in 1971 when students were killed by national guard troops dispatched by the governor of Ohio. In considering the technical legal issues that had been presented to it, the Court put an important gloss on *Sterling* when it held that, while a declaration of emergency by the executive is entitled to great weight, it is not conclusive and the measures used cannot be free from judicial review. [*Id.* at 207.]

Be advised, once again, to read these somewhat limiting decisions narrowly.

United States v. Midwest Oil Co., 236 U.S. 459; 59 L.Ed. 673 (1915)

No appropriations of public land may be made for any purpose except by authority of Congress. However, the long-continued practice of withdrawing from the public domain by executive orders (i.e., for the purpose of creating Indian reservations or prevent mineral depletion) has raised an implied delegation of authority from Congress to take such action.

President William H. Taft withdrew by proclamation a large area of land in California in which oil had been discovered, and then requested that Congress ratify his action. Congress did pass a statute in June 1910, but it gave the President authority only to make *future* withdrawals. The Midwest Oil Company entered the land illegally, extracted oil, and the government then brought a bill in equity to recover the land and to obtain an accounting of the oil extracted. The case turned on the validity of the withdrawal proclamation. (Additional facts are contained in the Court's opinion).

Basic Question: May congressional acquiescence in an executive practice over an extended period render impossible (nonjusticiable) a legal challenge to the assertion of the presidential authority implicit in the practice, on the ground that the passage of time has transformed a legal question into a mere "political" question?

Opinion of the Court by Justice Lamar:
All public lands containing petroleum or other mineral oils and chiefly valuable therefore, have been declared by Congress to be "free and open to occupation, exploration, and purchase by citizens of the United States ... under regulations prescribed by law." Act of February 11, 1897, c.216, 29 Stat. 526; R.S. 2319, 2329.

All these regulations permitted exploration and location without the payment of any sum, and as title could be obtained for a merely nominal amount, many persons availed themselves of the provisions of the statute. Large areas of California were explored; and petroleum having been found, locations were made, not only by the discoverer but by others on adjoining land. And, as the flow through the well on one lot might exhaust the oil under the adjacent land, the interest of each operator was to extract the oil as soon as possible so as to share what would otherwise be taken by the owners of nearby wells.

The result was that oil was so rapidly extracted that on September 17, 1909, the Director of the Geological Survey made a report to the Secretary of the Interior which, with enclosures, called attention to the fact that, while there was a limited supply of coal on the Pacific coast and the value of oil as a fuel had been fully demonstrated, yet at the rate at which oil lands in California were being patented by private parties it would "be impossible for the people of the United States to continue ownership of oil lands for more than a few months. After that the Government will be obliged to repurchase the very oil that it has practically given away...." In view of the increasing use of fuel by the American Navy there would appear to be an immediate necessity for assuring the conservation of a proper supply of petroleum for the Government's own use ..." and "pending the enactment of adequate legislation on this subject, the filing of claims to oil lands in the State of California should be suspended."

This recommendation was approved by the Secretary of the Interior. Shortly afterwards he brought the matter to the attention of the President [Taft], who, on September 27, 1909, issued the following Proclamation: "Temporary Petroleum Withdrawal No. 5."

"In aid of proposed legislation affecting the use and disposition of the petroleum deposits on the public domain, all public lands in the accompanying lists are hereby temporarily withdrawn from all forms of location, settlement, selection,... entry, or disposal under the mineral or nonmineral public-land laws. All locations or claims existing and valid on this date may proceed to entry in the usual manner after field investigation and examination." The list described an area aggregating 3,041,000 acres in California and Wyoming, though, of course, the order only applied to the public lands therein, the acreage of which is not shown.

On March 27, 1910, six months after the publication of the Proclamation, William T. Henshaw and others entered upon a quarter section of this public land in Wyoming so withdrawn. They made explorations, bored a well, discovered oil and thereafter assigned their interest to the Appellees, who took possession and extracted large quantities of oil. On May 4, 1910, they filed a location certificate.

As the explorations by the original claimants, and the subsequent operation of the well, were both long after the date of the President's Proclamation, the Government filed, in the District Court of the United States for the District of Wyoming, a Bill in Equity against the Midwest Oil Company and the other Appellees, seeking to recover the land and to obtain an accounting for 50,000 barrels of oil alleged to have been illegally extracted. The court sustained the defendant's demurrer and dismissed the bill. Thereupon the Government took the case to the Circuit Court of Appeals for the Eighth Circuit which rendered no decision but certified certain questions to this Court, where an order was subsequently passed directing the entire record to be sent up for consideration.

...On the part of the Government it is urged that the President, as Commander-in-Chief of the Army and Navy, had a power to make the order for the purpose of retaining and preserving a source of supply of fuel for the Navy, instead of allowing the oil land to be taken up for a nominal sum, the Government being then obliged to purchase at a great cost what it had previously owned. It is argued that the President, charged with the care of the public domain, could, by virtue of the executive power vested in him by the Constitution (Art. 2, sec. 1), and also in conformity with the tacit consent of Congress, withdraw, in the public interest, any public land from entry or location by private parties.

The Appellees, on the other hand, insist that there is no dispensing power in the Executive and that he could not suspend a statute or withdraw from entry or location any land which Congress had affirmatively declared should be free and open to acquisition by citizens of the United States. They further insist that the withdrawal order is absolutely void since it appears on its face to be a mere attempt to suspend a statute—supposed to be unwise—in order to allow Congress to pass another more in accordance with what the Executive thought to be in the public interest.

1. We need not consider whether, as an original question, the President could have withdrawn from private acquisition what Congress had made free and open to occupation and purchase. The case can be determined on other grounds and in the light of the legal consequences flowing from a long continued practice to make orders like the one here involved. For the President's proclama-

tion of September 27, 1909, is by no means the first instance in which the Executive, by a special order, has withdrawn land which Congress by general statute, had thrown open to acquisition by citizens....Scores and hundreds of these orders have been made; and treating them as they must be *(Wolsey v. Chapman,* 101 U.S. 769), as the act of the President, an examination of official publications will show that (excluding those made by virtue of special congressional action, *Donnelly v. United States,* 228 U.S. 255) he has during the past 80 years, without express statutory authority—but under the claim of power so to do—made a multitude of Executive Orders which operated to withdraw public land that would otherwise have been open to private acquisition....

They show that prior to the year 1910 there had been issued 99 Executive Orders establishing or enlarging Military Reservations; 109 Executive Orders establishing or enlarging Military Reservations and setting apart land for water, timber, fuel, hay, signal stations, target ranges and rights or way for use in connection with Military Reservations; 44 Executive Orders establishing Bird Reserves.

In the sense that these lands may have been intended for public use, they were reserved for a public purpose. But they were not reserved in pursuance of law or by virtue of any general or special statutory authority. For, it is to be specially noted that there was no act of Congress providing for Bird Reserves or for these Indian Reservations. There was no law for the establishment of these Military Reservations or defining their size or location. There was no statute empowering the President to withdraw any of these lands from settlement or to reserve them for any of the purposes indicated.

But when it appeared that the public interest would be served by withdrawing or reserving parts of the public domain, nothing was more natural than to retain what the Government already owned. And in making such orders, which were thus useful to the public, no private interest was injured. For prior to the initiation of some right given by law the citizen had no enforceable interest in the public statute and no private right in land which was the property of the people. The President was in a position to know when the public interest required particular portions of the people's lands to be withdrawn from entry or location; his action inflicted no wrong upon any private citizen, and being subject to disaffirmance by Congress, could occasion no harm to the interest of the public at large. On the contrary it uniformly and repeatedly acquiesced in the practice and, as shown by these records, there had been, prior to 1910, at least 252 Executive Orders making reservations for useful, though non-statutory purposes.

The right of the President to make reservations—and thus withdraw land from private acquisition—was especially recognized in *Grisar v. McDowell,* 6 Wall. 364, 381, where ... it was said that "from an early period in the history of the Government it has been the practice of the President to order, from time to time, as the exigencies of the public service required, parcels of land belonging to the United States to be reserved from sale and set apart for public uses."...

2. It may be argued that while these facts and rulings prove a usage they do not establish its validity. But government is a practical affair intended for practical men. Both officers, law-makers and citizens naturally adjust themselves to any long-continued action of the Executive Department—on the presumption that unauthorized acts would not have been allowed to be often repeated as to crystallize into a regular practice. That presumption is not reasoning in a circle but the basis of a wise and quieting rule that in determining the meaning of a statute or the existence of a power, weight shall be given to the usage itself—

even when the validity of the practice is the subject of investigation....

3. These decisions do not, of course, mean that private rights could be created by an officer withdrawing for a railroad more than had been authorized by Congress in the land grant act. *Southern Pacific v. Bell,* 183 U.S. 685; *Brandon v. Ard,* 211 U.S. 21. Nor do these decisions mean that the Executive can by his course of action create a power. But they do clearly indicate that the long-continued practice, known to and acquiesced in by Congress, would raise a presumption that the withdrawals had been made in pursuance of its consent or of a recognized administrative power of the Executive in the management of the public lands. This is particularly true in view of the fact that the land is property of the United States and that the land laws are not of a legislative character in the highest sense of the term (Art. 4, sec. 3) "but savor somewhat of mere rules prescribed by an owner of property for its disposal." *Butte City Water Co. v. Baker,* 196 U.S. 126.

These rules or laws for the disposal of public land are necessarily general in their nature. Emergencies may occur, or conditions may so change as to require that the agent in charge should, in the public interest, withhold the land from sale; and while no such express authority has been granted, there is nothing in the nature of the power exercised which prevents Congress from granting it by implication just as could be done by any other owner of property under similar conditions. The power of the Executive, as agent in charge, to retain that property from sale need not necessarily be expressed in writing....

The case is therefore remanded to the District Court with directions that the decree dismissing the Bill be reversed.

Note: In sustaining the power of the President to order withdrawals from the public domain not only without the sanction of Congress, but even contrary to its legislation, the Court required that such legislation must have been systematically ignored by successive Presidents through a long term of years. [E. Corwin, The President: Office and Powers 156-57 (4th ed. 1957).] In other words, extended *presidential practice, accompanied by congressional silence,* becomes a source of authority for the President. Once again, *Neagle, Debs,* and *Midwest Oil* stand for the proposition of an independent inherent executive power—that an executive action can have the force of law and does not require prior congressional authorization; and, ultimately, the President is recognized as being able to acquire authority from the silences of Congress as well as from its positive enactments, provided only the silences are sufficiently prolonged. [A. Miller, Presidential Power 92 (1977).]

Hamilton v. Kentucky Distilleries, 251 U.S. 146; 64 L.Ed. 194 (1919)

On November 11, 1918, the armistice with Germany was signed. On November 21, Congress passed and the President approved the War-Time Prohibition Act, which provided that alcoholic beverages held in bond should not be moved therefrom except for export. The purpose was to conserve the man power of the nation and to increase the efficiency of war production. The Kentucky Distilleries contended that the act was invalid since hostilities had ceased, thus, bringing an end to the wartime powers. Furthermore, they argued that the government could not enforce such an act since the police power was reserved to the states.

Basic Question: Was the War-Time Prohibition Act valid?

Opinion of the Court by Justice Brandeis:
The armistice with Germany was signed November 11, 1918. Thereafter Congress passed, and on November 21, 1918, the President approved the War-Time Prohibition Act ... which provides as follows: "That after June thirtieth, nineteen hundred and nineteen, until the conclusion of the present war and thereafter until the termination of demobilization, the date of which shall be determined by the President ..., for the purpose of conserving the man power of the Nation, and to increase efficiency in the production of arms, munitions, ships, food, and clothing for the army and navy, it shall be unlawful to sell for beverage purposes any distilled spirits, and during said time no distilled spirits held in bond shall be removed therefrom for beverage purposes except for export...."
On October 10, 1919, the Kentucky Distilleries & Warehouse Company,... brought in the District Court of the United States for the Western District of Kentucky a suit against Hamilton, collector of internal revenue for that district, alleging that the above act was void or had become inoperative, and praying that he be enjoined from interfering, by reason of that act, with the usual process of withdrawal, distribution and sale of the whisky in bond. The case was heard before the District Judge on plaintiff's motion for a preliminary injunction and defendant's motion to dismiss. A decision without opinion was rendered for the plaintiff; and, the defendant declining to plead further, a final decree was entered granting a permanent injunction in accordance with the prayer of the bill....
...Four contentions are made in support of the relief prayed for: (1) That the act was void when enacted because it violated the Fifth Amendment; (2) that it became void before these suits were brought by reason of the passing of the war emergency; (3) that it was abrogated or repealed by the Eighteenth Amendment; (4) that by its own terms it expired before the commencement of these suits....
First. Is the act void because it takes private property for public purposes without compensation in violation of the Fifth Amendment?...
That the United States lacks the police power, and that this was reserved to the states by the Tenth Amendment, is true. But it is none the less true that when the United States exerts any of the powers conferred upon it by the Constitution, no valid objection can be based upon the fact that such exercises may be attended by the same incidents which attended the exercise by a state of its police power, or that it may tend to accomplish a similar purpose....The war power of the United States, like its other powers and like the police power of the

states, is subject to applicable constitutional limitations. (*Ex parte Milligan*, 4 Wall. 2, 121-127, ...); but the Fifth Amendment imposes in this respect no greater limitation upon the national power than does the Fourteenth Amendment upon state power (*In re Kemmler*, 136 U.S. 436, 448 ...). If the nature and conditions of a restriction upon the use or disposition of property is such that a state could, under the police power impose it consistently with the Fourteenth Amendment without making compensation, then the United States may for a permitted purpose impose a like restriction consistently with the Fifth Amendment without making compensation; for prohibition of the liquor traffic is conceded to be an appropriate means of increasing our war efficiency....

Second. Did the Act become void by the passing of the war emergency before the commencement of these suits? It is conceded that the mere cessation of hostilities under the armistice did not abridge or suspend the power of Congress to resort to prohibition of the liquor traffic as a means of increasing our war efficiency, that the support and care of the army and navy during demobilization was within the war emergency, and that, hence, the act was valid when passed. The contention is that between the date of its enactment and the commencement of these suits it had become evident that hostilities would not be resumed, that demobilization had been effected, that thereby the war emergency was removed, and that when the emergency ceased the statute became void....

The present contention may be stated thus: That notwithstanding the act was a proper exercise of the war power of Congress at the date of its approval and contains its own period of limitation—"until the conclusion of the present war and thereafter until the termination of demobilization"—the progress of events since that time had produced so great a change of conditions and there now is so clearly a want of necessity for conserving the man power of the nation, for increased efficiency in the production of arms, munitions, and supplies, that the prohibition of the sale of distilled spirits for beverage purposes can no longer be enforced, because it would be beyond the constitutional authority of Congress in the exercise of the war power to impose such a prohibition under the present circumstances. Assuming that the implied power to enact such a prohibition must depend, not upon the existence of a technical state of war, terminable only with the ratification of a treaty of peace or a proclamation of peace ..., but upon some actual emergency ... arising out of the war or incident to it, still, as was said in *Stewart v. Kahn*, 11 Wall. 493, 507 ...: "The power is not limited to victories in the field and the dispersion of the insurgent forces. It carries with it inherently the power to guard against the immediate renewal of the conflict, and to remedy the evils which have arisen from its rise and progress."

No principle of our constitutional law is more firmly established that that this Court may not, in passing upon the validity of a statute, inquire into the motives of Congress.... Nor may the court inquire into the wisdom of the legislation....Nor may it pass upon the necessity for the exercise of a power possessed, since the possible abuse of a power is not an argument against its existence....

Conceding, then, for the purposes of the present case, that the question of the continued validity of the War-Time Prohibition Act under the changed circumstances depends upon whether it appears that there is no longer any necessity for the prohibition of the sale of distilled spirits for beverage purposes, it remains to be said that on obvious grounds every reasonable intendment must be made in favor of its continuing validity, the prescribed period of limitation not having arrived; that to Congress in the exercise of its powers, not least the war power, upon which the very life of the nation depends, a wide latitude of discretion must be accorded; and that it would require a clear case to justify a court in declaring that such an act, passed for such a purpose, had ceased to have force because the power of Congress no longer continued. In view of facts of public knowledge,... that the treaty of peace had not yet been concluded, that the railways are still under national control by virtue of the war powers, that other war activities have not been brought to a close, and that it cannot even be said that the man power of the nation has been restored to a peace footing, we are unable to conclude that the act has ceased to be valid.

Third. Was the act repealed by the adoption of the Eighteenth Amendment? By the express terms of the amendment the prohibition thereby imposed becomes effective after one year of its ratification....

The Eighteenth Amendment, with its implications, if any, is binding, not only in times of peace, but in war. If there be found by implication a denial to Congress of the right to forbid before its effective date any prohibition of the liquor traffic, that denial must have been operative immediately upon the adoption of the amendment, although at that time demobilization of the army and the navy was far from complete. If the amendment effected such a denial of power, then it would have done so equally, had hostilities continued flagrant or been renewed. Furthermore, the amendment is binding alike upon the United States and the individual states. If it guarantees a year of immunity from interference by the federal government with the liquor traffic, even to the extent of abrogating restrictions existing at the time of its adoption, it is difficult to see why the guaranty does not extend also to immunity from interference by the individual states, with like results also as to then existing state legislation. The contention is clearly unsound.

Fourth. Did the prohibition imposed by the act expire by limitation before the commencement of these suits? The period therein prescribed is "until the con-clusion of the present war and thereafter until the termination of demobilization, the date of which shall be determined and proclaimed by the President of the United States." It is contended both that the war has been concluded and that the demobilization has terminated.

In the absence of specific provisions to the contrary the period of war has been held to extend to the ratification of the treaty of peace or the proclamation of peace.... From the fact that other statutes concerning war activities contain each a specific provision for determining when it shall cease to be operative, and from the alleged absence of such a provision here, it is argued that the term "conclusion of the war" should not be given its ordinary legal meaning; that instead it should be construed as the time when actual hostilities ceased; ... or, more generally, when the actual war emergencies ceased by reason of our complete victory and the disarmament of the enemy, coupled with the demobilization of our army and the closing of war activities; or when the declared purposed of the act of "conserving the man power of the nation, and to increase efficiency in the production of arms, munitions, ships, food, and clothing for the army and navy" shall have been fully satisfied. But there is nothing in the words used to justify such a construction....It was expected that the "conclusion of the war" would precede the termination of demobilization. Congress, therefore, pro-vided that the time when the act ceased to be operative should be fixed by the President's ascertaining and proclaiming the date when demobilization had terminated.

...The "date of which shall be determined and proclaimed by the President" is a phrase so definite as to leave no room for construction. This requirement cannot be satisfied by passing references in messages to Congress, nor by newspaper interviews with high officers of the army or with officials of the War Department....If he [the President] had believed on October 28, 1919, that demobilization had, in an exact sense, terminated, he would doubtless have issued then a proclamation to that effect; for he had manifested a strong conviction that restriction upon the sale of liquor should end. Only by such proclamation could the purpose of Congress be attained, and the serious consequences attending uncertainty be obviated. But in fact demobilization had not terminated at the time of the veto of the act of October 28, 1919, or at the time these suits were begun, and,... it has not yet terminated....

The War-Time Prohibition Act being thus valid and still in force, the decree in No. 589 is reversed, and the case is remanded to the District Court, with direction to dismiss the bill;...

No. 589. Reversed.

Note: The *War Prohibition Cases* [*Hamilton, Clark Distilling Co. v. Western Maryland Ry.,* 242 U.S. 311 (1917), *Ruppert v. Caffey,* 251 U.S. 264 (1919), *United States v. Standard Brewery,* 251 U.S. 210 (1919)] recognized that war endows Congress with an indefinite legislative competence in the promotion of "war efficiency" closely comparable with the power of the states at all times in the promotion of public welfare.

Four justices dissented in *Ruppert,* primarily because they reached the conclusion that bourbon and beer are not the same thing. Justice McReynolds, joined by Justices Day, Van Devanter, and Clarke, argued as follows: "The argument runs: This Court has held in *Hamilton* ... that under a power implied because necessary and proper to carry into execution the above named powers relating to war, in October 1919, Congress could prohibit the sale of intoxicating liquors. In order to make such a prohibition effective the sale of nonintoxicating beer must be forbidden. Wherefore, from the implied power to prohibit intoxicants the further power to prohibit this nonintoxicant must be implied. The query at once arises: If all this be true, why may not the second implied power engender a third under which Congress may forbid the planting of barley or hops, the manufacture of bottles or kegs, etc." 251 U.S. at 305-06. However, it was one thing to acknowledge that the plaintiff in this case had had his interests heavily injured, but quite another thing to compare the plight of Colonel Ruppert with that of Lambdin P. Milligan.

Block v. Hirsh, 256 U.S. 135; 65 L.Ed. 865 (1921)

The facts of the case are contained in the Court's opinion.

Basic Question: Is the Emergency Rent Act constitutional?

Opinion of the Court by Justice Holmes:

This is a proceeding brought by the defendant in error, Hirsh, to recover possession of the cellar and first floor of a building on F Street in Washington which the plaintiff in error, Block, holds over after the expiration of a lease to him. Hirsh bought the building while the lease was running, and on December 15, 1919, notified Block that he should require possession on December 31 when the lease expired. Block declined to surrender the premises, relying upon the Act of October 22, 1919,...

By Section 109 of the act the right of a tenant to occupy any hotel ... is to continue notwithstanding the expiration of this term, at the option of the tenant, subject to regulations by the Commission appointed by the act, so long as he pays the rent and performs the conditions as fixed by the lease or as modified by the Commission. It is provided in the same section that the owner shall have the right of possession "for actual and bona fide occupancy by himself, or his wife, children or dependents ... upon giving thirty days' notice in writing." According to his affidavit Hirsh wanted the premises for his own use, but he did not see fit to give the thirty days' notice because he denied the validity of the act. The statute embodies a scheme or code which it is needless to set forth, but it should be stated that it ends with the declaration in section 122 that the provisions of Title 2 are made necessary by emergencies growing out of the war, resulting in rental conditions in the District [of Columbia] dangerous to the public health and burdensome to public officers, employees and accessories, and thereby embarrassing the Federal Government in the transaction of the public business. As emergency legislation the Title is to end in two years unless sooner repealed.

No doubt it is true that the legislative declaration of facts that are material only as the ground for enacting a rule of law, for instance, that a certain use in a public one, may not be held conclusive by the Courts....But a declaration by a legislature concerning public conditions that by necessity and duty it must know, is entitled at least to great respect. In this instance Congress stated a publicly notorious and almost world-wide fact. That the emergency declared by the statute did exist must be assumed, and the question is whether Congress was incompetent to meet it in the way in which it has been met by most of the civilized countries of the world.

The general proposition to be maintained is that circumstances have clothed the letting of buildings in the District of Columbia with a public interest so great as to justify regulation by law. Plainly circumstances may so change in time or so differ in space as to clothe with such an interest what at other times or in other places would be a matter of purely private concern....

...These cases are enough to establish that a public exigency will justify the legislature in restricting property rights in land to a certain extent without compensation....We do not perceive any reason for denying the justification held good in the foregoing cases to a law limiting the property rights now in question if the public exigency requires that ... Congress has stated the unquestionable embarrassment of Government and danger to the public health in the existing condition of things. The space in Washington is necessarily monopolized in comparatively few hands, and letting portions of it is as much a business as any other. Housing is a necessary of life. All the elements of a public interest justifying some degree of public control are present. The only matter that seems to us open to debate is whether the statute goes too far. For just as there comes a point at which the police power ceases and leaves only that of eminent domain, it may be conceded that regulations of the present sort pressed to a certain height might amount to a taking without due process of law....

Perhaps it would be too strict to deal with this case as concerning only the requirement of thirty days' notice. For although the plaintiff alleged that he wanted the premises for his own use the defendant denied it and might have prevailed upon that issue under the act....The main point against the law is that tenants are allowed to remain in possession at the same rent that they have been paying [rent control], unless modified by the Commission established by the act, and that thus the use of the land and the right of the owner to do what he will with his own and to make what contracts he pleases are cut down. But if the public interest be established the regulation of rates is one of the first forms in which it is asserted, and the validity of such regulation has been settled since *Munn v. Illinois,* 94 U.S. 113....

Assuming that the end in view otherwise justified the means adopted by Congress, we have no concern of course with the question whether those means were the wisest, whether they may not cost more than they come to, or will effect the result desired. It is enough that we are not warranted in saying that legislation that has been resorted to for the same purpose all over the world, is futile or has no reasonable relation to the relief sought....

The statute is objected to on the further ground that landlords and tenants are deprived by it of a trial by jury on the right to possession of the land. If the power of the Commission established by the statute to regulate the relation is established, as we think it is, by what we have said, this objection amounts to little. To regulate the relation and to decide except the facts affecting it are hardly separable. While the act is in force there is little to decide except whether the rent allowed is reasonable, and upon that question the courts are given the last word. A part of the exigency is to secure a speedy and summary administration of the law and we are not prepared to say that the suspension of ordinary remedies was not a reasonable provision of a statute reasonable in its aim and intent. The plaintiff obtained a judgment on the ground that the statute was void, root and branch. That judgment is reversed.

Note: The Emergency Rent Cases [Block, Brown v. Feldman, 256 U.S. 270 (1921)] suggested that the "just compensation" clause of the Fifth Amendment was held to be less restrictive of governmental power in a public emergency and "to tide over a passing trouble" than in normal times. Three years later, in *Chastleton Corp. v. Sinclair,* 264 U.S. 543 (1924), the Court held that the rent control law for the District of Columbia (a 1922 extension of the 1919 law upheld in *Block*) had ceased to operate because the emergency which justified it had come to an end.

The only case in which any part of the vast body of regulatory legislation enacted in World War I was declared unconstitutional was *United States v. Cohen Grocery Co.,* 225 U.S. 81 (1921). Here, the Court invalidated several lines in section 4 of the Lever Act of 1917 as contrary to certain safeguards of the Fifth and Sixth Amendments, especially in that they failed to set up "an ascertainable standard of guilt." This was hardly a blow to presidential power, since the decision was handed down three days before Congress terminated the act and many others by joint resolution (41 Stat. 1359).

Two months after America's entry into World War II, the Supreme Court dealt once again with the Emergency Shipping Fund Act of 1917 in *United States v. Bethlehem Steel Corp.,* 315 U.S. 289 (1942). While upholding the latter's claim in a dispute over a contract, Justice Black's opinion gave the Court's blessing to the use of the war power and economic wartime regulation: "We cannot regard the Government of the United States at war as so powerless that it must seek the organization of a private corporation as a helpless suppliant. The Constitution grants to Congress power 'to raise and support Armies,' 'to provide and maintain a Navy,' and 'to make all laws necessary and proper to carry these powers into execution.' Under this authority Congress can draft men for battle service. Its power to draft business organizations to support the fighting men who risk their lives can be no less." *Id.* at 303.

In short, the lesson of the World War I cases was that the more general principles of constitutional law and theory, those that ordinarily govern the delegation of legislative power, the scope of national power over the ordinary life of the citizen, and the interpretation of the "due process" clause as a restraint on substantive legislative power, became highly malleable, and that even the more specific provisions of the Bill of Rights took on an unaccustomed flexibility. The contrast, therefore, between the Lincolnian "dictatorship" and the Wilsonian was not one of tenderness for customary constitutional restraints; it was one of method. The immediate basis of the former was the "commander-in-chief" clause and strict insistence on the separation of powers principles; the immediate basis of the latter (because of Wilson's proclivity to the British parliamentary system) was the national legislative power and minimization of that principle. [E. Corwin, The President: Office and Powers 237 (4th ed. 1957).] In other words, where Lincoln had broken down the separation of powers by assuming legislative authority on his own initiative, Wilson accomplished the same purpose by fusing the two political branches into a single organ of government under his (executive) domination.

The Supreme Court not only accepted this pattern but welcomed it, since the inclusion of Congress in the crisis regime removed many of the problems that had arisen during the Civil War. For example, the justices were relieved of many of the burdens during the emergency because of the methods adopted to meet it. Thus the fact that war had been declared in the constitutionally prescribed manner relieved them of a problem which the Civil War Court had been forced to resolve. [R. Hirschfield, The Constitution and the Court 148 (1962).] And even though broad economic controls were introduced during this second crisis, the Court was able to avoid many of the problems created thereby because the executive's policies were often effectuated through resort to the extralegal (and nonjusticiable) technique of applying "indirect sanctions" to secure compliance with the President's directives. [*Ibid.*] Finally, insofar as military and foreign policy were concerned, the Court took the first opportunity to point out that both the responsibility and the power for the conduct of such affairs lies in the political departments, and therefore "the propriety of what may be done in the exercise of this political power is not subject to judicial inquiry or decision." [*Oetjen v. Central Leather Co.,* 246 U.S. 297, 302 (1918).]

With no question regarding the constitutionality of the regime's existence to be decided, and with the way in which the executive acquired his power to prosecute the emergency not seriously disputed, the most important matters presented for judicial determination during World War I involved *only* the government's exercise of power in mobilizing the economic resources of the Nation and in circumscribing the liberties of its citizens. [R. Hirschfield, 148-49.] In relation to these very serious problems Civil War precedents were not directly to the point, since the World War I regime operated almost entirely under statutory authority, and therefore the power being tested was the *war power* of the combined political organs of American government rather than the authority of the President alone. But insofar as the judicial attitude toward the exercise of that power was concerned, the second crisis experience did not differ from the first. [*Id.* at 149.] For the Supreme Court again gave the political branches a wide berth and adopted a "theory of relativity" in distinguishing between the wartime and the peacetime Constitution.

As a result of World War I, the extraordinary aspects of wartime government were formalized by giving them an aura of legality and extended by including within the purview of governmental authority all aspects of the Nation's life. Wilson had adapted the Lincolnian conception of emergency rule to the circumstances of modern society, and the Supreme Court had quickly and wholeheartedly accepted the result. The next crisis President would borrow from both of his wartime predecessors in meeting the emergency which confronted him, and the Court would also accept his regime. [*Id.* at 151.]

What would, by the end of the World War I period, become the *war powers of the Nation,* eventually became (during World War II) the *war powers of the President,* regardless of the linguistic label.

Missouri v. Holland, 252 U.S. 416; 64 L.Ed. 641 (1920)

After a federal statute dealing with the problem had been declared unconstitutional three years earlier, Great Britain and the United States signed a treaty in 1916 to save from extinction various species of birds that migrated through both the United States and Canada. In addition to provisions for protecting the birds, the treaty stipulated that both countries would attempt to institute measures necessary to fulfill the purposes of the agreement. In 1918, Congress passed the Migratory Bird Treaty Act which authorized the Secretary of Agriculture to issue regulations concerning the killing, capturing, and selling of those birds named in the treaty. The state of Missouri brought a complaint in federal district court to prevent Holland, a game warden, from enforcing the Act and the Secretary's regulations. Among other objections, Missouri claimed that the statute was unconstitutional by virtue of the Tenth Amendment and that its sovereign right as a state had been violated. The district court held the Migratory Bird Treaty Act constitutional, and Missouri appealed.

Basic Question: Do the treaty and statute interfere invalidly with the rights reserved to the states by the Tenth Amendment?

Opinion of the Court by Justice Holmes:

This is a bill in equity brought by the State of Missouri to prevent a game warden of the United States from attempting to enforce the Migratory Bird Treaty Act of July 3, 1918, ... and the regulations made by the Secretary of Agriculture in pursuance of the same. The ground of the bill is that the statute is an unconstitutional interference with the rights reserved to the States by the Tenth Amendment.

To answer this question it is not enough to refer to the Tenth Amendment, reserving the powers not delegated to the United States, because by Article II, section 2, the power to make treaties is delegated expressly, and by Article VI treaties made under the authority of the United States, along with the Constitution and laws of the United States made in pursuance thereof, are declared the supreme law of the land. If the treaty is valid there can be no dispute about the validity of the statute under Article I, section 8, as a necessary and proper means to execute the powers of the Government. The language of the Constitution as to the supremacy of treaties being general, the question before us is narrowed to an inquiry into the ground upon which the present supposed exception is placed.

It is said that a treaty cannot be valid if it infringes the Constitution, that there are limits, therefore, to the treaty-making power, and that one such limit is that what an act of Congress could not do unaided, in derogation of the powers reserved to the States, a treaty cannot do. An earlier act of Congress that attempted by itself and not in pursuance of a treaty to regulate the killing of migratory birds within the States had been held bad in the District Court. *United States v. Shauver,* 214 Fed.Rep. 154; *United States v. McCullagh,* 221 Fed.Rep. 288. Those decisions were supported by arguments that migratory birds were owned by the States in their sovereign capacity for the benefit of their people, and that under cases like *Geer v. Connecticut,* 161 U.S. 519, this control was one that Congress had no power to displace. The same argument is supposed to apply now with equal force.

Whether the two cases were decided rightly or not they cannot be accepted as a test of the treaty power. Acts of Congress are the supreme law of the land only when made in pursuance of the Constitution, while treaties are declared to be so when made under the authority of the United States. It is open to question whether the authority of the United States means more than the formal acts prescribed to make the convention. We do not mean to imply that there are no qualifications to the treaty-making power; but they must be ascertained in a different way. It is obvious that there may be matters of the sharpest exigency for the national well being that an act of Congress could not deal with but that a treaty followed by such an act could, and it is not lightly to be assumed that, in matters requiring national action, "a power which must belong to and somewhere reside in every civilized government" is not to be found. *Andrews v. Andrews,* 188 U.S. 14, 33. What was said in that case with regard to the powers of the States applies with equal force to the powers of the nation in cases where the States individually are incompetent to act. We are not yet discussing the particular case before us but only are considering the validity of the test proposed. With regard to that we may add that when we are dealing with words that also are a constituent act, like the Constitution of the United States, we must realize that they have called into life a being the development of which could not have been foreseen completely by the most gifted of its begetters. It was enough for them to realize or to hope that they had created an organism; it has taken a century and has cost their successors much sweat and blood to prove that they created a nation. The case before us must be considered in the light of our whole experience and not merely in that of what was said a hundred years ago. The treaty in question does not contravene any prohibitory words to be found in the Constitution. The only question is whether it is forbidden by some invisible radiation from the general terms of the Tenth Amendment. We must consider what this country has become in deciding what that Amendment has reserved.

The State as we have intimated founds its claim of exclusive authority upon an assertion of title to migratory birds, an assertion that is embodied in statute. No doubt it is true that as between a State and its inhabitants the State may regulate the killing and sale of such birds, but it does not follow that its authority is exclusive of paramount powers. To put the claim of the State upon title is to lean upon a slender reed. Wild birds are not in the possession of anyone; the possession is the beginning of ownership. The whole foundation of the State's rights is the presence within their jurisdiction of birds that yesterday had not arrived, tomorrow may be in another State and in a week a thousand miles away. If we are to be accurate we cannot put the case of the State upon higher ground than that the treaty deals with creatures that for the moment are within the state borders, that it must be carried out by officers of the United States within the same territory, and that but for the treaty the State would be free to regulate this subject itself....

Here a national interest of very nearly the first magnitude is involved. It can be protected only by national action in concert with that of another power. The subject-matter is only transitorily within the State and has no permanent habitat therein. But for the treaty and the statute there soon might be no birds for any powers to deal with. We see nothing in the Constitution that compels the Government to sit by while a food supply is cut off and the protectors of our forests and our crops are destroyed. It is not sufficient to rely upon the States. The reliance is vain, and were it otherwise, the question is whether the United

States is forbidden to act. We are of [the] opinion that the treaty and statute must be upheld....

    Decree affirmed.

Note: Is a treaty power broader than, or limited to, the enumerated powers of Congress? In other words, can the President and the Senate accomplish through treaties ends which the President and both houses of Congress could not accomplish by legislation alone? It need hardly be mentioned that the potential under the *Missouri v. Holland* decision has never been realized. Under this decision a treaty need only be made under the authority of the United States. The subject-matter of a treaty need be only in the general realm of matters properly the subject of an international arrangement. By contrast a statute must be made in pursuance of the Constitution. In effect, therefore, and within limits, there can be the results of de facto amendment of the Constitution by means of a treaty that will require or authorize statutory implementation. In the light of the doctrine enunciated in *Belmont* and *Pink*—executive agreements have the same force of law as treaties—can we presume that the same would be true of an executive agreement?

    By the terms of Article VI of the Constitution a properly ratified treaty is part of the supreme law of the land. No state law can prevail against a treaty. On the other hand, a federal statute and a treaty are on the same plane of legality and the one that is later in point of time is the one to be enforced. The only example in our history of a treaty overriding a federal statute enacted earlier is that portrayed in *Cook v. United States,* 388 U.S. 102 (1933).

4

Roosevelt and Total Emergency, I

United States v. Curtiss-Wright Export Corp., 299 U.S. 304; 81 L.Ed. 255 (1936)

In 1934 Congress passed a joint resolution authorizing the President to prohibit the sale of munitions to two South American nations—Paraguay and Bolivia—which were embattled over the disputed land of Chaco, for as long as he believed that such an embargo would contribute to peace. President Franklin D. Roosevelt immediately issued a proclamation ordering an embargo on arms sales to the countries. Subsequently, the Curtiss-Wright Export Corporation was indicted for selling fifty machine guns to Bolivia. In the district court, the corporation contended that the President's actions were illegal because Congress had unconstitutionally delegated legislative powers to the executive. The district court judge agreed and the government appealed directly to the Supreme Court, which reversed the lower court's ruling.

Basic Question: Is this joint resolution of Congress an illegal delegation of legislative power to the President?

Opinion of the Court by Justice Sutherland:
    First. It is contended that by the Joint Resolution (48 Stat. 811) the going into effect and continued operation of the resolution was conditioned (a) upon the President's judgment as to its beneficial effect upon the reestablishment of peace between the countries engaged in armed conflict in the Chaco; (b) upon the making of a proclamation, which was left to his unfettered discretion, thus constituting an attempted substitution of the President's will for that of Congress; (c) upon the making of a proclamation putting an end to the operation of the resolution, which again was left to the President's unfettered discretion; and (d) further, that the extent of its operation in particular cases was subject to limitation and exception by the President, controlled by no standard. In each of these par-

ticulars, appellees urge that Congress abdicated its essential functions and delegated them to the Executive.

Whether, if the Joint Resolution had related solely to internal affairs it would be open to challenge that it constituted an unlawful delegation of legislative power to the Executive, we find it unnecessary to determine. The whole aim of the resolution is to affect a situation entirely external to the United States, and falling within the category of foreign affairs. The determination which we are called to make, therefore, is whether the Joint Resolution, as applied to that situation, is vulnerable to attack under the rule that forbids a delegation of the law-making power. In other words, assuming (but not deciding) that the challenged delegation, if it were confined to internal affairs, would be invalid, may it nevertheless be sustained on the ground that its exclusive aim is to afford a remedy for a hurting condition with foreign territory?

It will contribute to the elucidation of the question if we first consider the differences between the powers of the federal government in respect of foreign or external affairs and those in respect of domestic or internal affairs. That there are differences between them, and that these differences are fundamental, may not be doubted.

The two classes of powers are different, both in respect of their origin and their nature. The broad statement that the federal government can exercise no powers except those specifically enumerated in the Constitution, and such implied powers as are necessary and proper to carry into effect the enumerated powers, is categorically true only in respect of our internal affairs. In that field, the primary purpose of the Constitution was to carve from the general mass of legislative powers then possessed by the states such portions as it was thought desirable to vest in the federal government, leaving those not included in the enumeration still in the states....That this doctrine applies only to powers which the states had, is self evident. And since the states severally never possessed international powers, such powers could not have been carved from the mass of state powers but obviously were transmitted to the United States from some other source. During the colonial period, those powers were possessed exclusively by and were entirely under the control of the Crown. By the Declaration of Independence "the Representatives of the United States of America" declared the United [not the several] Colonies to be free and independent states, and as such to have "full power to levy War, conclude Peace, contract Alliances, establish Commerce and to do all other Acts and Things which independent States may of right do."

As a result of the separation from Great Britain by the colonies, acting as a unit, the powers of external sovereignty passed from the Crown not to the colonies severally, but to the colonies in their collective and corporate capacity as the United States of America. Even before the Declaration, the colonies were a unit in foreign affairs, acting through a common agency—namely the Continental Congress, composed of delegates from the thirteen colonies. That agency exercised the powers of war and peace, raised an army, created a navy, and finally adopted the Declaration of Independence. Rulers come and go; governments end and forms of government change; but sovereignty survives. A political society cannot endure without a supreme will somewhere. Sovereignty is never held in suspense. When, therefore, the external sovereignty of Great Britain in respect of the colonies ceased, it immediately passed to the Union....

[The Constitution invested] the federal government with the powers of external sovereignty did not depend upon the affirmative grants of the Constitution. The powers to declare and wage war, to conclude peace, to make treaties, to maintain diplomatic relations with other sovereignties, if they had never been mentioned in the Constitution, would have vested in the federal government as necessary concomitants of nationality....As a member of the family of nations, the right and power of the United States is that field are equal to the right and power of the other members of the international family. Otherwise, the United States is not completely sovereign. The power to acquire territory by discovery and occupation ..., the power to expel undesirable aliens ..., the power to make such international agreements as do not constitute treaties in the constitutional sense ..., none of which is expressly affirmed by the Constitution, nevertheless exist as inherently inseparable from the conception of nationality....

Not only, as we have shown, is the federal power over external affairs in origin and essential character different from that over internal affairs, but participation in the exercise of the power is significantly limited. In this vast external realm, with its important, complicated, delicate and manifold problems, the President alone has the power to speak or listen as a representative of the nation. He makes treaties with the advice and consent of the Senate; but he alone negotiates. Into the field of negotiation the Senate cannot intrude; and Congress itself is powerless to invade it. As Marshall said in his great argument of March 7, 1800, in the House of Representatives, "The President is the sole organ of the nation in its external relations and its sole representative with foreign nations."

"The President is the constitutional representative of the United States with regard to foreign nations. He manages our concerns with foreign nations and must necessarily be most competent to determine when, how, and upon what subjects negotiation may be urged with the greatest prospect of success. For his conduct he is responsible to the Constitution. The committee considered this responsibility the surest pledge for the faithful discharge of his duty. They think the interference of the Senate in the direction of foreign negotiations calculated to diminish that responsibility and thereby to impair the best security for the national safety. The nature of transactions with foreign nations, moreover, requires caution and unity of design, and their success frequently depends on secrecy and dispatch."...

It is important to bear in mind that we are here dealing not alone with an authority vested in the President by an exertion of legislative power, but with such an authority plus the very delicate, plenary and exclusive power of the President as the sole organ of the federal government in the field of international relations—a power which does not require as a basis for its exercise an act of Congress, but which, of course, like every other governmental power, must be exercised in subordination to the applicable provisions of the Constitution. It is quite apparent that if, in the maintenance of our international relations, embarrassment—perhaps serious embarrassment—is to be avoided and success for our aims achieved, congressional legislation which is to be made effective through negotiation and inquiry within the international field must often accord to the President a degree of discretion and freedom from statutory restriction which would not be admissible were domestic affairs alone involved. Moreover, he, not Congress, has the better opportunity of knowing the conditions which prevail in foreign countries, and especially is this true in time of war. He has his confidential sources of information. He has his agents in the form of diplomatic, consular and other officials. Secrecy in respect of information gathered by them may be highly necessary, and the premature disclosure of it productive of harmful results....

When the President is to be authorized by legislation to act in respect of a matter intended to affect a situation in foreign territory, the legislator properly bears in mind the important consideration that the form of the President's action—or, indeed, whether he shall act at all—may well depend, among other things, upon the nature of the confidential information which he has or may thereafter receive, or upon the effect which his action may have upon foreign relations. This consideration, in connection with what we have already said on the subject, discloses the unwisdom of requiring Congress in this field of governmental power to lay down narrowly definite standards by which the President is to be governed....

...It is enough to summarize by saying that, both upon principle and in accordance with precedent, we conclude there is sufficient warrant for the broad discretion vested in the President to determine whether the enforcement of the statute will have a beneficial effect upon the reestablishment of peace in the affected countries; whether he shall make proclamation to bring the resolution into operation; whether and when the resolution shall cease to operate and to make proclamation accordingly; and to prescribe limitations and exceptions to which the enforcement of the resolution shall be subject....

The judgment of the court below must be reversed and the case remanded for further proceedings in accordance with the foregoing opinion.

Reversed.

Note: The President's powers in foreign affairs flow from being commander-in-chief of the military and from specific powers (shared with the Senate) to make treaties and appoint ambassadors. Numerous other powers have developed in practice, from appointing diplomatic corps and negotiating with foreign governments, to using military forces to implement foreign policy independent of congressional authorization. Congressional legislation and treaties have also expanded presidential power. And Presidents may defend controversial actions as necessary under their obligation to "take care" that the laws are faithfully executed.

A principle justification—which has become known as the "sole organ theory"—for presidential independence in foreign affairs was offered by John Marshall in the House of Representatives in defense of President John Adams's extradition of a fugitive under the Jay Treaty. His broad view of inherent power runs back to Alexander Hamilton's The Federalist, No. 23. The Supreme Court in *Curtiss-Wright* wrote the sole organ theory into constitutional law. In upholding a delegation of power by Congress to the President that the Court would have invalidated had it been in the area of domestic, rather than foreign, affairs, the dicta of Sutherland's opinion recognized a large area of inherent power by the President in the foreign relations area. All this in spite of his dubious reading of history: he maintained that sovereignty—including control over foreign relations—passed directly from the English Crown to the national government, despite the fact that during the postindependence period the original thirteen states each acted on their own in foreign affairs and Article II of the Articles of Confederation recognized the sovereignty of the states.

Curtiss-Wright also exemplifies the Court's deference to the President in foreign affairs in recognition of the fact that Congress, not the judiciary, provides the most effective check. But even though Congress may have formal authority to perform the "checking" function, since 1789 the effective control of the executive in foreign affairs has so eroded congressional authority that the President has become, in Lord Bryce's label, "the practical" sovereign. And this presidential prerogative in foreign affairs—that of administration plus a capacity to set the tone for and establish the directions of international negotiations— takes several forms, not least of which is recognition of other governments. [A. Miller, <u>Presidential Power</u> 135 (1977).] The most significant single factor in the determination of American foreign policy is presidential domination, either personally or through acts of his subordinates. He can govern by fait accompli; he is able to manipulate public opinion and control, in large part, the political milieu in which he must operate. Ultimate formal power may be *shared* with Congress, but far too often members are *co-opted* by the President to become a part of the executive branch. [*Ibid.*]

United States v. Belmont, 301 U.S. 324; 81 L.Ed. 1134 (1937)

Outraged by the triumph of totalitarian communism in Russia, the United States waited until 1933 to recognize the Soviet government. As part of the recognition agreements, the Soviet government agreed not to sue American banks for funds deposited by Russian companies prior to the Russian Revolution. Instead, the Soviet government assigned its claims to those funds (obtained through uncompensated expropriations) to the U.S. government, which then sought to recover them from American bankers. The executors of one of those bankers, August Belmont, resisted on the ground that it was against the public policy of the State of New York, where the funds of the Petrograd Metal Works had been deposited with Belmont, to recognize the legality of a foreign act of expropriation. Had the expropriation and assignments been recognized by a treaty, there would have been no doubt about the validity of the U.S. government's claim to the deposits. But here the assignment was accomplished by an exchange of diplomatic correspondence with Maxim Litvinov, the Soviet foreign minister, to which the Senate had not given its consent. The state courts held for Belmont and against the United States.

Basic Question: May state law bar the operation of a executive agreement?

Opinion of the Court by Justice Sutherland:

We take judicial notice of the fact that coincident with the assignment set forth in the complaint, the President recognized the Soviet government, and normal diplomatic relations were established between that government and the Government of the United States, followed by an exchange of ambassadors. The effect of this was to validate, so far as this country is concerned, all acts of the Soviet Government here involved from the commencement of its existence. The recognition, establishment of diplomatic relations, the assignment, and agreement with respect thereto, were all parts of one transaction, resulting in an international compact between the two governments. That the negotiations, acceptance of the assignment and agreements and understandings in respect thereof were within the competence of the President may not be doubted. Governmental power over internal affairs is distributed between the national government and the several states. Governmental power over external affairs is not distributed, but is vested exclusively in the national government. And in respect of what was done here, the Executive has authority to speak as the sole organ of that government....The assignment and the agreements in connection therewith did not, as in the case of treaties, as that term is used in the treaty making clause of the Constitution (Art. II, Sec. 2), require the advise and consent of the Senate.

A treaty signifies "a compact made between two or more independent nations with a view to the public welfare."...But an international compact, as this was, is not always a treaty which requires the participation of the Senate. There are many such compacts, of which, a protocol, a *modus vivendi*, a postal convention, and agreements like that now under consideration are illustrations....We held that although this might not be a treaty requiring ratification by the Senate, it was a compact negotiated and proclaimed under the authority of the President, and as such was a "treaty" within the meaning of the Circuit Court of Appeals

Act, the construction of which might be reviewed upon direct appeal to this Court.

Plainly, the external powers of the United States are to be exercised without regard to state laws or policies. The supremacy of a treaty in this respect has been recognized from the beginning. Mr. Madison, in the Virginia Convention, said that if a treaty does not supersede existing state laws, as far as they contravene its operation, the treaty would be ineffective....And while this rule in respect of treaties is established by the express language of Cl. 2, Art. VI, of the Constitution, the same rule would result in the case of all international compacts and agreements from the very fact that complete power over international affairs is in the national government and is not and cannot be subject to any curtailment or interference on the part of the several states....In respect of all international negotiations and compacts, and in respect of our foreign relations generally, state lines disappear. As to such purposes the State of New York does not exist. Within the field of its powers, whatever the United States rightfully undertakes, it necessarily has warrant to consummate. And when judicial authority is invoked in aid of such consummation, state constitutions, state laws, and state policies are irrelevant in the inquiry and decision. It is inconceivable that any of them can be interposed as an obstacle to the effective operation of a federal constitutional power....

The public policy of the United States relied upon as a bar to the action is that declared by the Constitution, namely, that private property shall not be taken without just compensation. But the answer is that our Constitution, laws and policies have no extraterritorial operation, unless in respect of our own citizens....What another country has done in the way of taking over property of its nationals, and especially of its corporations, is not a matter for judicial consideration here. Such nationals must look to their own government for any redress to which they may be entitled. So far as the record shows, only the rights of the Russian corporation have been affected by what has been done; and it will be time enough to consider the rights of our nationals when, if ever, by proper judicial proceeding, it shall be made to appear that they are so affected as to entitle them to judicial relief. The substantive right to the moneys, as now disclosed, became vested in the Soviet Government as the successor to the corporation; and this right that government has passed to the United States....

It results that the complaint states a cause of action and that the judgment of the court below to the contrary is erroneous. In so holding, we deal only with the case as now presented and with the parties now before us. We do not consider the status of adverse claims, if there be any, of others not parties to this action. And nothing we have said is to be construed as foreclosing the assertion of any such claim to the fund involved, by intervention or other appropriate proceeding. We decide only that the complaint alleges facts sufficient to constitute a cause of action against the respondents.

Judgment reversed.

Note: Treaties differ from executive agreements in several regards. Treaties require the advise and consent of the Senate, while executive agreements do not. Treaties, unlike executive agreements, may supersede prior conflicting statutes. *United States v. Schooner Peggy,* 5 U.S. (1 Cr.) 103 (1801); *United States v. Capps,* 204 F.2d 655 (4th Cir. 1953), *aff'd on other grounds,* 348 U.S. 296 (1955). Otherwise, officials in the executive branch have considerable latitude in entering into international compacts either by treaty or by executive agreement.

The vast majority of executive agreements are based on statutory authority or treaty language. Although these agreements lack what the Supreme Court calls the "dignity" of a treaty, since they do not require Senate approval, they are nevertheless valid international compacts. *Altman & Co. v. United States,* 224 U.S. 583 (1912). In other words, executive agreements are on the same legal level as treaties. In addition to treaties and statutory authority, the executive branch claims four sources of constitutional authority that allows the President to enter into executive agreements: (1) his duty as chief executive to represent the nation in foreign affairs, (2) his authority to receive ambassadors and other public ministers, (3) his authority as commander- in-chief, and (4) his duty to "take care the laws be faithfully executed." The scope of these unilateral initiatives has rarely been effectively narrowed by judicial and congressional actions, provided that the executive agreement is not inconsistent with legislation enacted by Congress in the exercise of its constitutional authority.

United States v. Pink, 315 U.S. 203; 86 L.Ed. 796 (1942)

Following diplomatic recognition of Soviet Russia in 1933 President Roosevelt negotiated the Litvinov Assignment, under which it was stipulated that instead of each government prosecuting claims for recovery of assets against citizens of the other, the Soviet Union would give title to claims to assets in America to the United States government and vice versa. In *Belmont,* a New York banker, August Belmont, contended that funds deposited in his bank by the Petrgrad Metal Works prior to the Russian Revolution in 1917 were subject to New York laws and thus could not be confiscated by the federal government. Justice Sutherland, relying on his earlier opinion in *Curtiss-Wright,* however, upheld the agreement as a valid international compact that superseded the laws of New York. Subsequently, the federal government sought to recover the assets of the New York branch of the First Russian Insurance Company and sued Louis H. Pink, Superintendent of Insurance for the State of New York. The state supreme court dismissed the government's complaint and a federal court of appeals affirmed, whereupon the government appealed to the Supreme Court.

Basic Question: Do executive agreements have the same legal effect as treaties?

Opinion of the Court by Justice Douglas:

This Court, speaking through ... Justice Sutherland, held that the conduct of foreign relations is committed by the Constitution to the political department of the Federal Government; that the propriety of the exercise of that power is not open to judicial inquiry; and that recognition of a foreign sovereign conclusively binds the courts and "is retroactive and validates all actions and conduct of the government so recognized from the commencement of its existence."...It further held that recognition of the Soviet Government, the establishment of diplomatic relations with it, and the Litvinov Assignment were "all parts of one transaction, resulting in an international compact between the two governments." After stating that, "in respect of what was done here, the Executive had authority to speak as the sole organ" of the national government, it added: "The assignment and the agreements in connection therewith did not, as in the case of treaties, as that term is used in the treaty making clause of the Constitution (Art. II, Sec. 2), require the advise and consent of the Senate." It held that the "external powers of the United States are to be exercised without regard to state laws or policies. The supremacy of a treaty in this respect has been recognized from the beginning." And it added that "all international compacts and agreements" are to be treated with similar dignity for the reason that "complete power over international affairs is in the national government and is not and cannot be subject to any curtailment or interference on the part of the several states."...

The holding in the Belmont case is therefore determinative of the present controversy, unless the stake of foreign creditors in this liquidation proceeding and the provision which New York has provided for their protection call for a different result....

If the President had the power to determine the policy which was to govern the question of recognition, then the Fifth Amendment does not stand in the way of giving full force and effect to the Litvinov Assignment. To be sure, aliens as well as citizens are entitled to the protection of the Fifth Amendment....A State is not precluded, however, by the Fourteenth Amendment from according priority to local creditors as against creditors who are nationals of foreign countries and whose claims arose abroad....By the same token, the Federal Government is not barred by the Fifth Amendment from securing for itself and our nationals priority against such creditors. And it matters not that the procedure adopted by the Federal Government is globular and involves a regrouping of assets. There is no Constitutional reason why this Government need act as the collection agent for national or other countries when it takes steps to protect itself or its own nationals on external debts. There is no reason why it may not, through such devices as the Litvinov Assignment, make itself and its nationals whole from assets here before it permits such assets to go abroad in satisfaction of claims of aliens made elsewhere and not incurred in connection with business conducted in this country. The fact that New York has marshaled the claims of the foreign creditors here involved and authorized their payment does not give them immunity from that general rule.

If the priority had been accorded American claims by treaty with Russia, there would be no doubt as to its validity....The same result obtains here. The powers of the President in the conduct of foreign relations include the power, without consent of the Senate, to determine the public policy of the United States with respect to the Russian nationalization decrees. "What government is to be re-garded here as representative of a foreign sovereign state is a political rather than a judicial question, and is to be determined by the political department of the government....That authority is not limited to a determination of the government to be recognized. It includes the power to determine the policy which is to govern the question of recognition. Objections to the underlying policy as well as objections to recognition are to be addressed to the political department and not to the courts....Power to remove such obstacles to full recognition as settlement of claims of our nationals ... certainly is a modest implied power of the President who is the "sole organ of the federal government in the field of international relations."...Effectiveness in handling the delicate problems of foreign relations requires no less. Unless such a power exists, the power of recognition might be thwarted or seriously diluted. No such obstacle can be placed in the way of rehabilitation of relations between this country and another nation, unless the historic conception of the powers and responsibilities of the President in the conduct of foreign affairs ... is to be drastically revised. It was the judgment of the political department that full recognition of the Soviet Government required the settlement of all outstanding problems including the claims of our nationals. Recognition and the Litvinov Assignment were interdependent. We would usurp the executive function if we held that that decision was not final and conclusive in the courts....

We recently stated in *Hines v. Davidowitz,* 312 U.S. 52, 68 [1941], that the field which affects international relations is "the one aspect of our government that from the first has been most generally conceded imperatively or demanded broad national authority"; and that any state power which may exist "is restricted to the narrowest of limits." There, we are dealing with the question as to whether a state statute regulating aliens survived a similar federal statute. We held that it did not. Here, we are dealing with an exclusive federal function. If state laws and policies did not yield before the exercise of the external powers of the United States, then our foreign policy might be thwarted. These are delicate matters. If state action could defeat or alter our foreign policy, serious consequences might ensue. The nation as a whole would be held to answer if a State created difficulties with a foreign power....

We repeat that there are limitations on the sovereignty of the States. No State can rewrite our foreign policy to conform to its own domestic policies. Power over external affairs is not shared by the States; it is vested in the national government exclusively. It need not be so exercised as to conform to state laws or state policies, whether they be expressed in constitutions, statutes, or judicial decrees. And the policies of the States become wholly irrelevant to judicial inquiry when the United States, acting within its constitutional sphere, seeks enforcement of its foreign policy, in the courts....

We hold that the right to the funds or property in question became vested in the Soviet Government as the successor to the First Russian Insurance Co.; that this right has passed to the United States under the Litvinov Assignment; and that the United States is entitled to the property as against the corporation and the foreign creditors.

The judgment is reversed and the cause is remanded to the Supreme Court of New York for proceedings not inconsistent with this opinion.

Reversed.

Concurring opinion by Justice Frankfurter:

That the President's control of foreign relations includes the settlement of claims is indisputable. Thus, referring to the adhesion of the United States to the Dawes Plan, Secretary of State Hughes reported that "this agreement was negotiated under the long-recognized authority of the President to arrange for the payment of claims in favor of the United States and its nationals. The exercise of this authority has many illustrations, one of which is the Agreement of 1901 for the so-called Boxer Indemnity."...The President's power to negotiate such a settlement is the same whether it is an isolated transaction between this country and a friendly nation, or is part of a complicated negotiation to restore normal relations, as was the case with Russia.

That the power to establish such normal relations with a foreign country belongs to the President is equally indisputable. Recognition of a foreign country is not a theoretical problem or an exercise in abstract symbolism. It is the assertion of national power directed towards safe-guarding and promoting our interests and those of civilization. Recognition of a revolutionary government normally involves the removal of areas of friction. As often as not, areas of friction are removed by the adjustment of claims pressed by this country on behalf of its nationals against a new regime....

The controlling history of the Soviet regime and of this country's relations with it must be read between the lines of the Roosevelt-Litvinov Agreement. One needs to be no expert in Russian law to know that the expropriation decrees intended to sweep the assets of Russian companies taken over by that government into Russia's control no matter where those assets were credited. Equally clear is it that the assignment by Russia meant to give the United States, as part of the comprehensive settlement, everything that Russia claimed under its laws against Russians. It does violence to the course of negotiations between the United States and Russia, and to the scope of the final adjustment, to assume that a settlement thus made on behalf of the United States—to settle both money claims and to soothe feelings—was to be qualified by the variant notions of the courts of the forty-eight states regarding "situs" or "jurisdiction" over intangibles or the survival of extent Russian corporations. In our dealings with the outside world, the United States speaks with one voice and acts as one, unembarrassed by the complications as to domestic issues which are inherent in the distribution of political power between the national government and the individual states.

Note: *Belmont* and *Pink,* particularly when read in light of *Curtiss-Wright,* support a broad and independent presidential authority to enter into executive agreements. They are now regarded in the same legal light as treaties and are considered as part of the supreme law of the land against which state law cannot prevail.

As a result of these holdings, Presidents may circumvent the treaty-making provision—and it is small wonder that executive agreements now outnumber treaties. Many of the most sensitive agreements were not known to Congress until it passed the Case-Nablocki Act of 1972 (86 Stat. 619), requiring notification within sixty days of "any international agreement" (later amended to require notification within twenty days).

One further point: if *Missouri v. Holland,* 252 U.S. 416 (1920), stands for the proposition that there are no substantive limits on the treaty-making power (*i.e.,* treaties create power and are in effect a de facto amendment to the Constitution), and *Curtiss-Wright* stands for the proposition that the President is the "sole organ of foreign affairs" for the United States, and *Belmont* and *Pink* stand for the proposition that treaties and executive agreements are virtually the same, does all of this actually mean that secret, executive agreements can also amend the Constitution? If they can we are truly talking about an *imperial presidency*—*and* both the courts and Congress are largely to blame.

Employers Group of Motor Freight Carriers v. National War Labor Board, 143 F.2d 145 (D.C. Cir. 1944)

Significant as are the strictly martial powers of the President, they are greatly overshadowed by other commander-in-chief powers, which for want of a better label will be called the President's "civil" powers as commander-in-chief. The World War II Court, with seven Roosevelt appointees and a Chief Justice who had supported an emergency approach to economic depression, was well attuned to the language of power and quite prepared to acquiesce in the crisis decisions of the political branches. Like the earlier wartime courts, it raised no constitutional barriers against the exercise of whatever authority the government considered necessary to meet the emergency although in at least one instance that authority was used with flagrant disregard for the right of American citizens. This was "total war" and the government had total power.

Although Roosevelt had followed Woodrow Wilson's lead in establishing his crisis government primarily on statutory delegations of power, the scope of the World War II delegations related to economic affairs was so broad that new issues were raised. As in 1917-19, most of the agencies charged with administering the World War II emergency program were established by the executive. Congress, in 1940, had authorized the creation of an Office for Emergency Management (OEM) within the Executive Office of the President, but before the war's end the President, without specific congressional approval, had created twenty-nine major agencies (plus their manifold alphabetical progeny) under the OEM. These agencies drew on executive power in enforcing their orders, and the "indirect sanctions" again became a major weapon of crisis government. Thus strikes were prevented by placing the Selective Service System under the War Manpower Commission, which issued a "work or fight" order in February 1942. And employer cooperation with government directives was achieved by threats of publicity, deprivation of raw materials, and denial of war contracts. Moreover, President Roosevelt resorted to outright seizure of industrial facilities on twenty-eight occasions between 1942 and 1945, eleven of these coming before passage of the War Labor Disputes Act (57 Stat. 163) which authorized such action; and after V-E Day, President Truman, citing that Act and his power as commander-in-chief, used the seizure method more than forty times.

The facts of the case are contained in the opinion of the circuit court.

Basic Question: Are the "orders" of the National War Labor Board (NWLB) judicially reviewable?

Opinion of the Circuit Court by Judge Edgerton:
This is a suit to annul and enjoin a "directive order" of the National War Labor Board....

The complaint set forth that the plaintiffs and their employees failed to reach an agreement regarding wages and hours; that the Conciliation Service of the United States Department of Labor was also unsuccessful; that the Department referred the dispute to the Board and the Board to its Trucking Commission. In

April 1943, after hearings, the Trucking Commission made findings and issued "the following Directive Order: 1. Employees ... shall receive an increase of $2.75 per week. 2. All work performed in excess of 8 hours in any regular working day shall be paid for at one and a half times the regular straight time rates. 3. Employees not working on the holidays designated ... shall receive 8 hours pay at straight time rates." The Board declined to review this action of the Trucking Commission and declared it final.

The complaint asserts that the Board's findings and order are "unlawful, being violative of applicable statutes, and executive orders of the President of the United States, are arbitrary and capricious, and unsupported by any material evidence of record, have resulted and will continue to result, unless changed and modified, in irreparable injury to the employers affected thereby." More specifically, the complaint asserts that the Board considered supposed wage inequalities that no such inequalities actually existed with the New England area, that no others were pertinent, and that the Board had been forbidden by Executive Order No. 9328 ... to consider inequalities. The complaint also asserts ... that findings of the Board, in other cases, "have been enforced by governmental seizure of the property and business of allegedly noncomplying respondents." It concludes that "obviously plaintiffs must comply" with the Board's directive order, but does not say that they have complied or are complying.

We think the District Court was right in granting the defendants' motion to dismiss the complaint. The Board's order is not reviewable.

It is clear and undisputed that no statute authorizes review of the War Labor Board's orders. As we point out below, the legislative history of the War Labor Disputes Act implies a positive intention that these orders should not be reviewed....Without suggesting that the factors named are in themselves sufficient, the case in which the Supreme Court has sustained suits, not specially authorized by statute, to annul or enjoin alleged administrative action may be classified for present purposes in two groups. Either (1) the administrative action was directly injurious to legally protected interests of the plaintiff or (2) it furnished a basis for probable judicial proceedings against the plaintiff....The present case is of neither sort. Judicial review of administrative action cannot be confined by a formula, and existing categories may be extended if need arises....No money, property, or opportunity has been taken or withheld from the appellants, and no one threatens, and no one could maintain, either judicial or administrative proceedings against the appellants upon the authority of the Board's order. In these circumstances there is no occasion for review of the Board's order....

The grant to the Board, in the War Labor Disputes Act, of authority to "decide" disputes and "provide by order the wages and hours ... which shall be in effect" is not directly relevant here, since the Board's order was issued in April, 1943, and the War Labor Disputes Act was not passed until the following June. There is nothing to suggest that this Act should be given retroactive effect. But even if this Act had been in effect when the order was issued, the quoted language of the Act would not have made the order enforceable or reviewable. This is made clear both by the legislative history of this Act and by decisions of the Supreme Court under the Transportation Act of 1920. It follows that the more limited language of Executive Order 9017, "the Board shall finally determine the dispute," does not make the order enforceable or reviewable....

Executive Order 9370, issued August 16, 1943, which authorizes the Director of Economic Stabilization, when the War Labor Board reports to him that its orders have not been complied with, to direct withdrawal of priorities and government contracts "in order to effectuate compliance," is irrelevant here. The Board has not reported or threatened to report appellants' failure to comply with its order. Moreover the Director has stated in a letter to the Board, correctly we think, that Order 9370 applies only to Board orders issued under the War Labor Disputes Act. The only function of the Price Administrator is connection with the Board's present order was to consider whether the authorized wage increases would probably be required, and the Director approved the "proposed adjustments." It does not appear that either of these officers has threatened or is authorized to take any steps which would tend to require appellants to comply with the Board's order or to penalize them for noncompliance.

Appellants say in effect, though in other terms, that if they do not comply with the order the Board may notify the President of their noncompliance and the President may take possession of their plants and facilities. We have no occasion to decide whether in our opinion this is true. In some instances concerns which had failed to comply with Board orders have ultimately been taken over by Presidential orders. In other instances concerns which had not been the subject of any Board order have been taken over by Presidential orders. If it be true, as appellants suggest, that the President may ultimately take possession of their plants and facilities, that possibility is irrelevant not only because it is speculative but also because it is independent of the Board's order. Neither the broad constitutional power nor the broad statutory power of the President to take and use property in furtherance of the war effort depends upon any action of the War Labor Board. Any action of the Board would be informatory and "at most, advisory." Appellants' demand that we annul and enjoin the Board's order therefore amounts to a demand that we prevent the Board from giving the President advice which appellants contend would be erroneous. A court might as well be asked to prevent the Secretary of State or the Attorney General from giving alleged erroneous advice. The correctness of administrative advice cannot be reviewed by the courts. They have neither the necessary authority nor the necessary qualifications for such work.

Affirmed.

Note: In rejecting the request to enjoin enforcement of a "directive order" by the NWLB, the circuit court found that the directive was merely informatory, at most advisory. In legal theory, then, the NWLB was not an "office" wielding power, but purely an advisory body. The court, in Employers Group, did not confront the actual facts of the NWLB's powers: it did act independently of the President and even though it ostensibly merely advised him, the President without fail took that "advice"—decisions of the Board. [A. Miller, Presidential Power 180 (1977).] Had the court been willing to delve beneath the surface appearances, it would have found that the NWLB had "jurisdiction to settle all labor disputes likely to interrupt work which contributed to the effective prosecution of the war." [Executive Order 9017.] Thus the commander-in-chief powers of the President enabled him, during time of declared war, to alter the formal Constitution and its allocation of powers to create "offices," which heretofore had been considered a congressional power. [*Id.* at 181.] No other case tested FDR's commander-in-chief powers. What Lincoln began in 1861 and Wilson expanded in 1917 took an extraordinary incremental jump after 1941.

But how could the directives of such presidential agencies be enforced?

Steuart & Bros. v. Bowles, 322 U.S. 398; 88 L.Ed. 1350 (1944)

In 1943 the President promulgated Executive Order 9370, by which the Director of Economic Stabilization could issue "directives" requiring government agencies to withdraw any government largess—contracts, benefits, etc.—when it was found that a party was not complying with an order of the NWLB. Steuart & Bros., however, dealt with the Office of Price Administration (OPA), which had been empowered by Congress to issue rationing orders. On it own authority, the OPA imposed "sanctions"—blacklisting companies that violated OPA rationing orders. Petitioner acknowledged the validity of the rationing order of OPA, but argued that the suspension order—the sanction—was invalid because it was a penalty not authorized by Congress. The district court refused to issue the injunction.

Basic Question: Do the powers of the President under Section 2(a)(2) of Title III of the Second War Powers Act to "allocate" materials include the power to issue suspension orders and withhold rationed materials?

Opinion of the Court by Justice Douglas:

...The constitutional authority of Congress to authorize as a war emergency measure the allocation or rationing of materials is not challenged. No question of delegation of authority is present....

The argument, rather, is that the authority to "allocate" materials does not include the power to issue suspension orders; and that no such power will be implied since suspension orders are penalties to which persons will not be subjected unless the statute plainly imposes them....In that connection it is pointed out that Congress provided criminal and civil sanctions for violations of Title III of the Act. By Sec. 2(a)(5) any person who wilfully violates those provisions of the Act or any rule, regulation or order promulgated thereunder is guilty of a misdemeanor and subject to fine and imprisonment. By Sec. 2(a)(6) federal courts have power, among others, to enjoin any violation of those provisions of the Act or any rule, regulation or order thereunder. It is therefore contended that when violations of regulations under the Act are used as the basis for withholding rationed materials from persons, sanctions for law enforcement are created by administrative fiat contrary to the Act in question and contrary to constitutional requirements.

We agree that it is for Congress to prescribe the penalties for the laws which it writes. It would transcend both the judicial and the administrative function to make additions to those which Congress has placed behind a statute....Hence we would have no difficulty in agreeing with petitioner's contention if the issue were whether a suspension order could be used as a means of punishment of an offender. But that statement of the question is a distortion of the issue presented on this record.

The problem of scarcity of materials is often acute and critical in a great war effort such as the present one. Whether the difficulty be transportation or production, there is apt to be an insufficient supply to meet essential civilian needs after military and industrial requirements have been satisfied. Thus without rationing, the fuel tanks of a few would be full; the full tanks of many would be empty. Some localities would have plenty; communities less favorably situated would suffer. Allocation or rationing is designed to eliminate such inequalities and to treat all alike who are similarly situated. The burdens are thus shared equally and limited supplies are utilized for the benefit of the greatest number. But middlemen—wholesalers and retailers—bent on defying the rationing system could raise havoc with it. By disregarding quotas prescribed for each householder and by giving some more than the allotted share they would defeat the objectives of rationing and destroy any program allocation. These middlemen are the chief if not the only conduits between the source of limited supplies and the consumers. From the viewpoint of a rationing system a middleman who distributes the product in violation and disregard of the prescribed quotas is an inefficient and wasteful conduit....But in times of war the national interest cannot wait on individual claims to preference. The waging of war and the control of its attendant economic problems are urgent business. Yet if the President has the power to channel raw materials into the most efficient industrial units and thus save scarce materials from wastage it is difficult to see why the same principle is not applicable to the distribution of fuel oil.

If petitioner established that he was eliminated as a dealer or that his quota was cut down for reasons not relevant to allocation or efficient distribution of fuel oil, quite different considerations would be presented. But we can make no such assumption here. The suspension order rests on findings of serious violations repeatedly made. These violations were obviously germane to the problem of allocation of fuel oil....

None of the findings is challenged here. Taken at their face value, as they must be, they refute the suggestion that the order was based on considerations not relevant to the problem of allocation. They sustain the conclusion that in restricting petitioner's quota the Office of Price administration was doing no more than protecting a community against distribution which measured by rationing standards was inequitable, unfair, and inefficient. If the power to "allocate" did not embrace that power it would be feeble power indeed.

What we have said disposed of the argument that if petitioner has violated Ration Order No. 11 the only recourse of the Government is to proceed under Sec. 2(a)(5) or Sec. 2(a)(6) which provide criminal and civil sanctions. Those remedies are sanctions for the power to "allocate." They hardly subtract from that power. Yet they would be allowed to do just that if it were held that violations by middlemen of the ration orders and regulations could never be the basis of reallocation of fuel oil into more reliable channels of distribution.

It is finally pointed out that Congress has seldom used the licensing power and that that power, when used, has been employed sparingly. Thus one of the sanctions of the Emergency Price Control Act of 1942 ... is the power to revoke licenses for violations of maximum prices or rents. That power may be utilized only in judicial proceedings; and licenses may be suspended only for limited periods. That consideration would be germane to the present problem if Congress had implemented the allocation procedure with a licensing system. Then the question might arise whether revocation of the license rather than the reallocation of materials by administrative action was the appropriate procedure in case of violations. Congress, however, did not adopt the licensing system when it came to rationing. And the failure to do so is hardly a reason for saying that the power to "allocate" is less replete than a reading of the Act fairly permits.

Affirmed.

Note: According to the Court's opinion, the President already had emergency legislative power to establish agencies (*Employers Group*) and, now, had the power to invoke sanctions against violators of orders of those organizations. That means, simply, that necessity—as perceived by the President—either knows no law or make its own law, which then is enforced in the courts.   [A. Miller, Presidential Power 182 (1977).] It exemplified the doctrine of raison *d'etat* in its purest form. For example, a well-known demand of FDR clearly indicated the concept of his commander- in-chief powers in wartime, and also revealed how Congress (generally speaking) willingly complied with the President's demands.   In a message to Congress on September 7, 1942, the President demanded that Congress repeal some provision of the Emergency Price Control Act of 1942 (56 Stat. 23):

I ask the Congress to take this action by the first of October. Inaction on your part by that date will leave me with an inescapable responsibility to the people of this country to see to it that the war effort is no longer imperiled by threat of economic chaos. *In the event that the Congress should fail to act, and act adequately, I shall accept the responsibility, and I will act....*The President has the powers, under the Constitution and under Congressional acts, to take measures necessary to avert a disaster which would interfere with the winning of the war. I have given the most thoughtful consideration to meeting this issue without further reference to the Congress. I have determined, however, on this vital matter to consult with the Congress....The American people can be sure that I shall not hesitate to use every power vested in me to accomplish the defeat of our enemies in any part of the world where our own safety demands such defeat. When the war is won, the powers under which I act automatically revert to the people—to whom they belong. [(Emphasis added). 88 Cong.Rec. 7044.]

In effect, FDR was threatening to suspend the Constitution. [E. Corwin, The President: Office and Powers 252 (4th ed. 1957).] Congress, to be sure, speedily complied with the presidential demand, but there can be little doubt that, if challenged in the courts, the Supreme Court would have acquiesced in what—for lack of a more genteel term—could be called constitutional dictator-ship. The consequence is obvious: the United States has one Constitution for peacetime and another for wartime. The Supreme Court has never expressly stated that, but it is the inescapable inference to be drawn from actions of Lincoln, Wilson, and Roosevelt—and the handful of decisions which have resulted from those extraordinary (extralegal) acts. The hard logic of events create situations in which constitutional niceties have no relevance. What the President wants to do as commander-in-chief will be done—usually with the ready cooperation of Congress and the Court.

One case involving statutorily authorized seizure came before the Court during the war but, unfortunately, did not settle any important constitutional issues.   For example, does "production" include "distribution" within the meaning of the Smith-Connally (War Labor Disputes) Act? Rather the Court upheld in *Montgomery Ward v. United States,* 326 U.S. 690 (1945) the seizure by implication in holding that the case was moot, thus allowing the circuit court decision (upholding the seizure) to stand. [See the decisions at 58 F.Supp. 408 (1945) and 150 F.2d 369 (7t^h Cir. 1945).]

No case involving statutorily unauthorized seizure was reviewed during the war. However, the validity of such action was upheld by implication in a post-war case. The Court, in sustaining a lower court decision which awarded damages to a coal company for losses suffered while its property had been under government control, said that private properties "may be subjected to public operation only for a short time to meet war or emergency needs, and can then be returned to their owners." [*United States v. Peewee Coal Corp.*, 341 U.S. 114 (1951).]

Yakus v. United States, 321 U.S. 414; 88 L.Ed. 834 (1944)

Some of the most important problems raised by the vast scope of the congressional delegations of economic power to the President involved the Emergency Price Control Act of 1942 (56 Stat. 23) and the amendments contained in the Inflation Control Act of 1942 (56 Stat. 765). These statutes gave the price administrator wide discretionary authority to halt inflation and set up an Emergency Court of Appeals with exclusive jurisdiction to determine the validity of orders issued by the OPA. The petitioner was tried and convicted for the willful sale of wholesale cuts of beef prices above the maximum prices prescribed by the price regulations set down by the Price Administrator. Petitioner challenged the statutes as an improper delegation of legislative power, a violation of the Fifth Amendment's "due process" and "just compensation" provisions, and as an unconstitutional incursion on the Court's own authority.

Basic Questions: Do the acts in question involve an unconstitutional delegation to the Price Administrator of the legislative power of Congress to control prices? Can Congress frustrate judicial review by granting federal courts jurisdiction to enforce statutes but at the same time denying them authority to determine the constitutionality of those statutes?

Opinion of the Court by Chief Justice Stone:

That Congress has constitutional authority to prescribe commodity prices as a war emergency measure, and that the Act was adopted by Congress in the exercise of that power, are not questioned here, and need not now be considered save as they have a bearing on the procedural features of the Act later to be considered which are challenged on constitutional grounds....

The Constitution as a continuously operative charter of government does not demand the impossible or the impracticable. It does not require that Congress find for itself every fact upon which it desires to base legislative action or that it make for itself detailed determinations which it has declared to be prerequisite to the application of the legislative policy to particular facts and circumstances impossible for Congress itself properly to investigate. The essentials of the legislative function are the determination of the legislative policy and its formulation and promulgation as a defined and binding rule of conduct—here the rule, with penal sanctions, that prices shall not be greater than those fixed by maximum price regulations which conform to standards and will tend to further the policy which Congress has specified the basic conditions of fact upon whose existence or occurrence, ascertained from relevant data by a designated administrative agency, it directs that its statutory command shall be effective. It is no objection that the determination of facts and the inferences to be drawn from them in the light of the statutory standards and declaration of policy call for the exercise of judgment, and for the formulation of subsidiary administrative policy within the prescribed statutory framework....

Nor does the doctrine of separation of powers deny to Congress power to direct that an administrative officer properly designated for that purpose have ample latitude within which he is to ascertain the conditions which Congress has made prerequisite to the operation of its legislative command. Acting within its constitutional power to fix prices it is for Congress to say whether the data on the basis of which prices are to be fixed are to be confined within a narrow or a broad range. In either case the only concern of courts is to ascertain whether the will of Congress has been obeyed. This depends not upon the breadth of the definition of the facts or conditions which the administrative officer is to find but upon the determination whether the definition sufficiently marks the field within which the Administration is to act so that it may be known whether he has kept within it in compliance with the legislative will....

Under these sections the Administrator may not only alter or set aside the regulation, but he has wide scope for the exercise of his discretionary power to modify or suspend a regulation pending its administrative and judicial review. Hence we cannot assume that petitioners, had they applied to the Administrator, would not have secured all the relief to which they were entitled. The denial of a right to a restraining order or interlocutory injunction to one who has failed to apply for available administrative relief, not shown to be inadequate, is not a denial of due process....

Here, in the exercise of the power to protect the national economy from the disruptive influences of inflation in time of war Congress has seen fit to postpone injunctions restraining the operations of price regulations until their lawfulness could be ascertained by an appropriate and expeditious procedure. In so doing it has done only what a court of equity could have done, in the exercise of its discretion to protect the public interest. What the courts could do Congress can do as the guardian of the public interest of the nation in time of war. The legislative formulation of what could otherwise be a rule of judicial discretion is not a denial of due process or a usurpation of judicial functions....

Our decisions leave no doubt that when justified by compelling public interest the legislature may authorize summary action subject to later judicial review of its validity. It may insist on the immediate collection of taxes....It may take possession of property presumptively abandoned by its owner, prior to determination of its action abandonment....For the protection of public health it may order the summary destruction of property without prior notice or hearing....It may summarily requisition property immediately needed for the prosecution of the war....As a measure of public protection the property of alien enemies may be seized and property believed to be owned by enemies taken without prior determination of its true ownership....Similarly public necessity in time of war may justify allowing tenants to remain in possession against the will of the landlord....Even the personal liberty of the citizen may be temporarily restrained as a measure of public safety....Measured by these standards we find no denial of due process under the circumstances in which this Act was adopted and must be applied, in its denial of any judicial stay pending determination of a regulation's validity.

As we have seen Congress, through its power to define the jurisdiction of inferior federal courts and to create such courts for the exercise of the judicial power, could, subject to other constitutional limitations, create the Emergency Court of Appeals, give to it exclusive equity jurisdiction to determine the validity of price regulations prescribed by the Administrator, and foreclose any further or other consideration of the validity of a regulation as a defense to a prosecution for its violation.

Unlike most penal statutes and regulations whose validity can be determined only by running the risk of violation,... the present statute provides a mode of testing the validity of a regulation by an independent administrative proceeding. There is no constitutional requirement that that test be made in one tribunal rather than in another, so long as there is an opportunity to be heard and for judicial review which satisfies the demands of due process, as in the case here....And we are pointed to no principle of law or provision of the Constitution which precludes Congress from making criminal the violation of an administrative regulation, by one who has failed to avail himself of an adequate separate procedure for the adjudication of its validity, or which precludes the practice, in many ways desirable, of splitting the trial for violations of an administrative regulation by committing the determination of the issue of its validity to the agency which created it, and the issue of violation to a court which is given jurisdiction to punish violations. Such a requirement presents no novel constitutional issue.

No procedural principle is more familiar to this Court than that a constitutional right may be forfeited in criminal as well as civil cases by the failure to make timely assertion of the right before a tribunal having jurisdiction to determine it....Courts may for that reason refuse to consider a constitutional objection even though a like objection has previously been sustained in a case in which it was properly taken....While this Court in its discretion sometimes departs from this rule in cases from lower federal courts, it invariably adheres to it in cases from state courts,... and it could hardly be maintained that it is beyond legislative power to make the rule inflexible in all cases....

In the exercise of the equity jurisdiction of the Emergency Court of Appeals to test the validity of a price regulation, a jury trial is not mandatory under the Seventh Amendment....Nor has there been any denial in the present criminal proceeding of the right, guaranteed by the Sixth Amendment, to a trial by a jury of the state and district where the crime was committed. Subject to the requirements of due process, which are here satisfied, Congress could make criminal the violation of a price regulation. The indictment charged a violation of the regulation in the district of trial, and the question whether petitioners had committed the crime thus charged in the indictment and defined by Congress, namely, whether they had violated the statute by willful disobedience of a price regulation promulgated by the Administrator, was properly submitted to the jury....

Affirmed.

Note: The truth was that the powers wielded by the War Production Board (WPB) in the theoretical capacity of advisor to the President, and by OPA in its own right theoretically (but actually subject to presidential control through the Director of Economic Stabilization), exceeded any previous pattern of delegated legislation touching private rights directly. [E. Corwin, The President: Office and Powers 242 (4th ed. 1957).] In fact, in refusing to interfere with the summary method of penalizing the Steuart Company, the Court (in *Steuart Bros.*) acquiesced in an exercise of presidential war power that would seem to have infinite and explosive possibilities. [C. Rossiter, The Supreme Court and the Commander in Chief 99 (Longaker ed. 1976).] And in approving in *Yakus* a novel and summary technique for enforcing administrative orders, the Court virtually abdicated its responsibility for defending the whole pattern of due process against wartime encroachments by such agencies as OPA. [*Ibid.*] Nevertheless, Congress can share its legislative power with the executive branch by delegating aspects of that power to executive agencies. Such legislative delegations will be upheld, as in *Yakus,* unless Congress abdicates one of its powers to the executive agency or fails to give legislative definition of the scope of the agency's power.

Prior to the *Yakus* decision, the Court had already upheld a special statutory scheme set up during World War II to control inflation. Under the Emergency Price Control Act of 1942 an Emergency Court of Appeals was created and vested with exclusive jurisdiction to determine the validity of any regulation, order, or price schedule issued under that Act; the litigants had to follow a specified procedure. [R. Hirschfield, The Constitution and the Court 152 (1962).] Judgments of that court could be reviewed by the Supreme Court. *Lockerty v. Phillips,* 319 U.S. 182 (1943). In *Yakus,* however, the Court upheld the constitutionality of the provisions of the Emergency Price Control Act, which was construed to deprive litigants of the opportunity to attack the validity of a price control regulation in a criminal prosecution violating the Act.

And in another price control case—*Bowles v. Willingham,* 321 U.S. 503 (1944)—rent control was likewise found constitutional. Finally, after the war was over, the Court accepted the notion of congressional delegation of wartime economic authority to the President. In *Lichter v. United States,* 334 U.S. 742 (1948), a decision upholding contract renegotiation as a valid means by which the government could recapture excess profits made on war contracts, the Court declared that a constitutional power "implies a power of delegation of authority under it sufficient to effect its purposes" and that "broad discretion as to the methods to be employed may be essential to an effective use of its war power by Congress." 334 U.S. 778-79. The political branches had no difficulty with the judiciary, therefore, in applying the Constitution to a wartime economy. Whatever controls were necessary could be imposed "constitutionally." [Hirschfield, 155.] The chief beneficiary, of course, was the President.

Chicago & Southern Air Lines v. Waterman S.S. Corp., 333 U.S. 103; 92 L. Ed. 568 (1948)

The underlying principle of the "political question" doctrine—at least with respect to presidential war powers—is that the Court will not decide issues which by their nature, or by a determination that they are delegated to other branches under the separation of powers, are not fitting for judicial resolution. In regard to presidential war powers it is said that traditional judicial standards and reasoning which may be used in other areas of constitutional interpretation cannot be utilized where delicate questions of military judgment and foreign policy are involved. Moreover, traditional remedies (such as injunctions that trigger volatile or unpredictable consequences in a war situation) are instruments a prudent judiciary should never use. Such issues, it is said, are political, with distinctly political consequences, and are beyond judicial competence.

By proceedings not challenged as to regularity, the Board, with express approval of the President, issued an order which denied Waterman Steamship Corporation a certificate of convenience and necessity for an air route and granted one to Chicago and Southern Air Lines, a rival applicant. Routes sought by both carrier interests involved overseas air transportation. Waterman filed a petition for review under section 1006 of the Act with the Circuit Court of Appeals for the Fifth Circuit. Chicago and Southern intervened. Both the latter and the Board moved to dismiss, the grounds pertinent here being that because the order required and had approval of the President, under section 801 of the Act, it was not reviewable. The Court of Appeals disclaimed any power to question or review either the President's approval or his disapproval, but it regarded any Board order as incomplete until court review. Accordingly, it refused to dismiss the petition and asserted jurisdiction. The Supreme Court granted certiorari.

Basic Question: Does the Civil Aeronatics Act (52 Stat. 987), in authorizing judicial review of orders of the Civil Aeronautics Board (CAB), include those that are subject to approval by the President?

Opinion of the Court by Justice Jackson:

This Court long has held that statutes which employ broad terms to confer power of judicial review are not always to be read literally. Where Congress has authorized review of "any order" or used other equally inclusive terms, courts have declined the opportunity to magnify their jurisdiction, by self-denying constructions which do not subject to judicial control orders which, from their nature, from the context of the Act, or from the relation of judicial power to the subject-matter, are inappropriate for review....

The Waterman Steamship Corporation urges that review of the problems involved in establishing foreign air routes are of no more international delicacy or strategic importance than those involved in routes for water carriage. It says, "It is submitted that there is no basic difference between the conduct of the foreign commerce of the United States by air or by sea." From this premise it reasons that we should interpret this statute to follow the pattern of judicial review adopted in relation to orders affecting foreign commerce by rail,... or communications by wire,... and it likens the subject-matter of aeronautics legislation to that of Title VI of the Merchant Marine Act of 1936,... and the function of the Aeronautics Board in respect to overseas and foreign air transportation to that of the Maritime Commission to such commerce when water-borne....

In the regulation of commercial aeronautics, the statute confers on the Board many powers conventional in other carrier regulation under the Congressional commerce power. They are exercised through usual procedures and apply settled standards with only customary administrative finality. Congress evidently thought of the administrative function in terms used by the Court of another of its agencies in exercising interstate commerce power: "Such a body cannot in any proper sense be characterized as an arm or an eye of the executive. Its duties are performed without executive leave and, in the contemplation of the statute, must be free from executive control" *Humphrey's Executor v. United States*, 295 U.S. 602, 628 (1935). Those orders which do not require Presidential approval are subject to judicial review to assure application of the standards Congress has laid down.

But when a foreign carrier seeks to engage in public carriage over the territory or waters of this country, or any carrier seeks the sponsorship of this Government to engage in overseas or foreign air transportation, Congress has completely inverted the usual administrative process. Instead of acting independently of executive control, the agency is then subordinated to it. Instead of its order serving as a final disposition of the application, its force is exhausted when it serves as a recommendation to the President. Instead of being handed down to the parties as the conclusion of the administrative process, it must be submitted to the President, before publication even can take place. Nor is the President's control of the ultimate decision a mere right of veto. It is not alone issuance of such authorizations that are subject to his approval, but denial, transfer, amendment, cancellation or suspension, as well. And likewise subject to his approval are the terms, conditions and limitations of the order....Thus, Presidential control is not limited to a negative but is a positive and detailed control over the Board's decisions, unparalleled in the history of American administrative bodies.

Congress may of course delegate very large grants of its power over foreign commerce to the President....The President also possesses in his own right certain powers conferred by the Constitution on him as Commander-in-Chief and as the Nation's organ in foreign affairs. For present purposes, the order draws vitality from either or both sources. Legislative and Executive powers are pooled obviously to the end that commercial strategic and diplomatic interests of the country may be coordinated and advanced without collision or deadlock between agencies....

It may be conceded that a literal reading of sec. 1006 subjects this order to re-examination by the courts. It also appears that the language was deliberately employed by Congress, although nothing indicates that Congress foresaw or intended the consequences ascribed to it by the decision of the Court below. The letter of the text might with equal consistency be construed to require any one of three things: first, judicial review of a decision by the President; second, judicial review of a Board order before it acquires finality through Presidential action, the court's decision on review being a binding limitation on the President's action; third, a judicial review before action by the President, the latter being at liberty wholly to disregard the court's judgment. We think none of these results is required by usual canons of construction.

In this case, submission of the Board's decision was made to the President, who disapproved certain portions of it and advised the Board of the changes which he required. The Board complied and submitted a revised order and opinion which the President approved. Only then were they made public, and that which was made public and which is before us is only the final order and opinion containing the President's amendments and bearing his approval. Only at that stage was review sought, and only then could it be pursued, for then only was the decision consummated, announced and available to the parties.

While the changes made at direction of the President may be identified, the reasons therefore are not disclosed beyond the statement that "because of certain factors relating to our broad national welfare and other matters for which the Chief Executive has special responsibility, he has reached conclusions which require" changes in the Board's opinion.

The court below considered, and we think quite rightly, that it could not review such provisions of the order as resulted from Presidential direction. The President, both as Commander-in-Chief and as the Nation's organ for foreign affairs, has available intelligence services whose reports neither are nor ought to be published to the world. It would be intolerable that courts, without the relevant information, should review and perhaps nullify actions of the Executive taken on information properly held secret. Nor can courts sit in camera in order to be taken into executive confidences. But even if courts could require full disclosure, the very nature of executive decisions as to foreign policy is political, not judicial. Such decisions are wholly confided by our Constitution to the political departments of the government, Executive and Legislative. They are delicate, complex, and involve large elements of prophecy. They are and should be undertaken only by those directly responsible to the people whose welfare they advance or imperil. They are decisions of a kind for which the Judiciary has neither aptitude, facilities nor responsibility and have long been held to belong in the domain of political power not subject to judicial intrusion or inquiry....We therefore agree that whatever of this order emanates from the President is not susceptible of review by the Judicial Department....

To revise or review an administrative decision, which has only the force of a recommendation to the President, would be to render an advisory opinion in its most obnoxious form—advice that the President has not asked, tendered at the demand of a private litigant, on a subject concededly within the President's exclusive, ultimate control. This Court early and wisely determined that it would not give advisory opinions even when asked by the Chief Executive. It has also been the firm and unvarying practice of Constitutional Courts to render no judgments not binding and conclusive on the parties and none that are subject to later review or alteration by administrative action....

We conclude that orders of the Board as to certificate for overseas or foreign air transportation are not mature and are therefore not susceptible to judicial review at anytime before they are finalized by Presidential approval. After such approval has been given, the final orders embody Presidential discretion as to political matters beyond the competence of the courts to adjudicate. This makes it unnecessary to examine the other questions raised. The petition of the Waterman Steamship Corp. should be dismissed.

Judgment reversed.

Note: The Court in *Waterman* reaffirmed much of the reasoning (and conclusions) of *Curtiss-Wright* as to the unique nature of the President's foreign affairs powers. Thus by constitutional exegesis, practical experience, and congressional and judicial acquiescence, the executive has generally pre-dominated the foreign affairs sphere. And in making the distinction between foreign policy and domestic policy as specifically as it does (in the same way it distinguished between war and peace), is the Supreme Court actually telling us that Hamilton's arguments regarding an expansive international power belonging exclusively to the President—and including his plenary use of discretion—are correct? Indeed, in *Waterman* the Court concluded that whatever portion of the CAB order that emanated from the President was not subject to judicial review. The CAB orders, before presidential approval, are premature and not subject to review. After such presidential approval, they "embody Presidential discretion as to political matters beyond the competence of the courts to adjudicate." [333 U.S. at 114.] This is power, and it borders on the absolute!

5

Roosevelt and Total Emergency, II

Ex Parte Quirin, **317 U.S. 1; 87 L.Ed. 3 (1942)**

The petitioners were all born in Germany. All lived in the United States and returned to Germany between 1933 and 1941. Petitioners attended sabotage school. After completing this training, Quirin and two others boarded a submarine and proceeded to Amagansett Beach, New York. They landed on or about June 13, 1942, carrying a supply of explosives and wearing German infantry uniforms. They buried their uniforms and proceeded to New York City. The four remaining petitioners proceeded by submarine to Ponte Verda Beach, Florida. These men were wearing caps of German marine infantry and carrying explosives. They buried uniform parts and proceeded to Jacksonville, Florida, and thence to various points in the United States. All were taken into custody by agents of the FBI. All had received instructions to destroy war industries and war facilities in the United States. The President, by order of July 2, 1942, appointed a Military Commission and directed it to try petitioners for offenses against the law of war and Articles of War, and prescribed regulations on trial and review of record of the trial and any decision handed down by the Commission. In their appeal to the Supreme Court, the seven Nazi saboteurs claimed that they should have been tried in civilian courts, under civilian law, because they were arrested by civilian authorities while in civilian clothes. The Supreme Court rejected their argument and the sentences were carried out.

Basic Questions: Was trial by a military commission without jury trial legal? Does the President have the constitutional authority to order trial by military commission?

Opinion of the Court by Chief Justice Stone:
The question for decision is whether the detention of petitioners by respond-

ent for trial by Military Commission, appointed by Order of the President of July 2, 1942, on charges preferred against them purporting to set out their violations of the law of war and of the Articles of War, is in conformity to the laws and Constitution of the United States....

The President, as President and Commander in Chief of the Army and Navy,... appointed [on July 2, 1942] a Military Commission and directed it to try petitioners for offenses against the law of war and the Articles of War, and prescribed regulations for the procedure on the trial and for review of the record of the trial and of any judgment declared that "all persons who are subjects, citizens or residents of any nation at war with the United States or who give obedience to or act under the direction of any such nation, and who during time of war enter or attempt to enter the United States ... through coastal or boundary defenses, and are charged with committing or attempting or preparing to commit sabotage, espionage, hostile or warlike acts, or violations of the law of war, shall be subject to the law of war and to the jurisdiction of military tribunals."

The Proclamation also stated in terms that all such persons were denied access to the courts....

The Commission met on July 8, 1942, and proceeded with the trial, which continued in progress while the causes were pending in this Court. On July 27th, before petitioners' applications to the District Court, all the evidence for the prosecution and the defense had been taken by the Commission and the case had been closed except for arguments of counsel. It is conceded that ever since petitioners' arrests the state and federal courts in Florida, New York, and the District of Columbia, and in the states in which each of the petitioners was arrested or detained, have been open and functioning normally....

Petitioners main contention is that the President is without any statutory or constitutional authority to order the petitioners to be tried by military tribunal for offenses with which they are charged; that in consequence they are entitled to be tried in the civil courts with the safeguards, including trial by jury, which the Fifth and Sixth Amendments guarantee to all persons charged in such courts with criminal offenses. In any case it is urged that the President's Order, in pre-scribing the procedure of the Commission and the method for review of its findings and sentence, and the proceedings of the Commission under the Order, conflict with Articles of War adopted by Congress—particularly Articles 38, 43, 46, 50.5 and 70—and are illegal and void.

The Government challenges each of these propositions. But regardless of their merits, it also insists that petitioners must be denied access to the courts, both because they are enemy aliens or have entered our territory as enemy belligerents, and because the President's Proclamation undertakes in terms to deny such access to the class of persons defined by the Proclamation, which aptly describes the character and conduct of petitioners. It is urged that if they are enemy aliens or if the Proclamation has force no court may afford the petitioners a hearing. But there is certainly nothing in the Proclamation to preclude access to the courts for determining its applicability to the particular case. And neither the Proclamation nor the fact that they are enemy aliens foreclosed consideration by the courts of petitioners' contentions that the Constitution and laws of the United States constitutionally enacted forbid their trial by military commission....

We are not here concerned with any question of the guilt or innocence of petitioners. Constitutional safeguards for the protection of all who are charged with offenses are not to be disregarded in order to inflict merited punishment on some who are guilty....But such detention and trial of petitioners—ordered by the President in the declared exercise of his powers as Commander in Chief of the army in time of war and of grave public danger—are not to be set aside by the courts without the clear conviction that they are in conflict with the Constitution or laws of Congress constitutionally enacted....

The Constitution thus invests the President as Commander in Chief with the power to wage war which Congress has declared, and to carry into effect all laws passed by Congress for the conduct of war and for the government and regulation of the Armed Forces, and all laws defining and punishing offenses against the law of nations, including those which pertain to the conduct of war.

By the Articles of War, 10 U.S.C. Secs. 1471-1593,... Congress has provided rules for the government of the Army. It has provided for the trial and punishment, by courts martial, of violations of the Articles by members of the armed forces and by specific classes of persons associated or serving with the Army....But the Articles also recognize the "military commission" appointed by military command as an appropriate tribunal for the trial and punishment of offenses against the law of war not ordinarily tried by court martial or military commission, of those charged with relieving, harboring or corresponding with the enemy and those charged with spying. And Article 15 declares that "the provisions of these articles conferring jurisdiction upon courts-martial shall not be construed as depriving military commissions ... or other military tribunals of concurrent jurisdiction in respect of offenders or offenses that by statute or by the law of war may be triable by such military commissions ... or other military tribunals." Article 2 includes among those persons subject to military law the personnel of our own military establishment. But this, as Article 12 provides, does not exclude from that class "any other persons who by the law of war is subject to trial by military tribunals" and who under Article 12 may be tried by court martial or under Article 15 by military commission....

From the very beginning of its history this Court has recognized and applied the law of war as including that part of the law of nations which prescribes, for the conduct of war, the status, rights and duties of enemy nations as well as of enemy individuals. By the Articles of War, and especially Article 15, Congress has explicitly provided, so far as it may constitutionally do so, that military tribunals shall have jurisdiction to try offenders or offenses against the law of war in appropriate cases. Congress, in addition to making rules for the government of our Armed Forces, has thus exercised its authority to define and punish offenses against the law of nations by sanctioning, within constitutional limitations, the jurisdiction of military commissions to try persons and offenses which, according to the rules and precepts of the law of nations, are more particularly the law of war, are cognizable by such tribunals. And the President, as Commander in Chief, by his Proclamation in time of war has invoked that law. By his Order creating the present Commission he has undertaken to exercise the authority conferred upon him by Congress, and also such authority as the Constitution itself gives the Commander in Chief, to direct the performance of those functions which may constitutionally be performed by the military arm of the nation in time of war....

By universal agreement and practice the law of war draws a distinction between the armed forces and the peaceful populations of belligerent nations and also between those who are lawful and unlawful combatants. Lawful combatants are subject to capture and detention as prisoners of war by opposing military forces. Unlawful combatants are likewise subject to capture and detention, but in addition they are subject to trial and punishment by military tribunals for acts which render their belligerency unlawful. The spy who secretly and without uniform passes the military lines of a belligerent in time of war, seeking to gather military information and communicate it to the enemy, or an enemy combatant who without uniform comes secretly through the lines for the purpose of waging war by destruction of life or property, are familiar examples of belligerents who are generally deemed not be entitled to the status of prisoners of war, but to be offenders against the law of war subject to trial and punishment by military tribunals....

Citizenship in the United States of an enemy belligerent does not relieve him from the consequences of a belligerency which is unlawful because in violation of the law of war. Citizens who associate themselves with the military arm of the enemy government, and with its aid, guidance and direction enter this country bent on hostile acts are enemy belligerents within the meaning of the Hague Convention and the laws of war....It is as an enemy belligerent that [petitioner Haupt is charged with entering the United States], and unlawful belligerency is the gravamen of the offense of which he is accused....

Petitioners, and especially petitioner Haupt, stresses the pronouncement of this Court in the Milligan case,... that the law of war "can never be applied to citizens in states which have upheld the authority of the government, and where the courts are open and their process unobstructed." Elsewhere in its opinion,... the Court was at pains to point out that Milligan, a citizen twenty years resident in Indiana, who had never been a resident of any of the states in rebellion, was not an enemy belligerent either entitled to the status of a prisoner of war or subject to the penalties imposed upon unlawful belligerents. We construe the Court's statement as to the inapplicability of the law of war to Milligan's case as having particular reference to the facts before it. From them the Court concluded that Milligan, not being a part of or associated with the armed forces of the enemy, was a nonbelligerent, not subject to the law of war save as—in circumstances found not there to be presented and not involved here—martial law might be constitutionally established.

The Court's opinion is inapplicable to the case presented by the present record. We have no occasion now to define with meticulous care the ultimate boundaries of the jurisdiction of military tribunals to try persons according to the law of war. It is enough that petitioners here, upon the conceded facts, were plainly within those boundaries, and were held in good faith for trial by military commission, charged with being enemies who, with the purpose of destroying war materials and utilities, entered or after entry remained in our territory without uniform—an offense against the law of war. We hold only that those particular acts constitute an offense against the law of war which the Constitution authorizes to be tried by military commission....

Accordingly, we conclude that Charge I, on which petitioners were detained for trial by the Military Commission alleged an offense which the President is authorized to order tried by military commission; that his Order convening the Commission was a lawful order and that the Commission was lawfully constituted; that the petitioners were held in lawful custody and did not show cause for their discharge. It follows that the orders of the District Court should be affirmed, and that leave to file petitions for habeas corpus in this Court should be denied.

Note: Quirin may be looked at in two contradictory ways. First, the Court was willing to look at the legality of a presidential sponsored military trial, allowed "all" questions of the prisoners to be raised, and prevented the military from proceeding until satisfied with the action of the military tribunal. Second, the Court's participation was little more than ceremonial, as it will not stand in the way of a valid exercise of presidential war powers. The truth, perhaps, lies somewhere between the two extremes.

In accepting the government's position that the military commission had been lawfully constituted and that the saboteurs were clearly subject to its jurisdiction, the Court gave answers of a sort to six points: (1) the President's proclamation did not preclude access to the courts for determining its applicability to this particular case; (2) it was not necessary for the Court to discuss the President's power as commander-in-chief to create this commission, for Congress (in the Fifteenth Article of War) had in effect authorized trial of offenses against the law of war before such commissions; (3) the offenses charged against the law of war has always recognized that unlawful combatants are subject to trial and punishment by military tribunals, for acts which render their belligerency unlawful; (4) the procedural guarantees of the Fifth and Sixth Amendments were never intended to apply to military trials (again the notion of two separate and distinct systems of law); (5) *Ex parte Milligan*, 71 U.S. 2 (1866), did not apply to this situation, and indeed must be confined closely to the facts under which it arose; and (6) the President could validly fix the procedures to be followed by the commission. [C. Rossiter, The Supreme Court and the Commander in Chief 114-15 (R. Longaker ed. 1976).]

Milligan, a prime example of judicial courage when it was easy to be courageous, was assumed to be the law until 1942, when it was overruled sub silentio (without notice being taken) by *Quirin*. [A. Miller, Presidential Power 175 (1977).] In upholding the special military tribunal convened by the President, even though—as in *Milligan*—the civil courts were operating and the United States itself was not a theater of war, the judiciary became perilously close to becoming part of the "executive juggernaut." [*Ibid.*]

Hirabayashi v. United States, 320 U.S. 81; 87 L.Ed. 1774 (1943)

On February 19, 1942, President Roosevelt issued Executive Order 9066, directing all persons excluded from "military areas" be provided with food, shelter, transportation, and other accommodations until other arrangements are made. Such arrangements were made by Executive Order 9102 of March 18, 1942, establishing the War Relocation Authority. On March 21, by voice vote in both houses, Congress in effect ratified the President's orders by establishing penalties for their violation (66 Stat. 173).

Under the directives, Secretary of War Henry Stimson authorized the Western Defense Commander, General DeWitt, first to impose curfews and other restrictions, then to evacuate from their homes in California, Oregon, Washington, and parts of Arizona, and finally to transport to relocation centers in the interior, more than 112,000 persons of Japanese ancestry, of whom over 70,000 were American citizens. The reason given for these drastic actions was "military necessity," that is, the alleged danger of espionage, sabotage, and other "fifth column" operations in the event of an invasion of the West Coast by Japan. Significantly, the exclusion order was not promulgated until May 1942, and all Japanese were not removed from the designated areas until October. But at no time during this period, or later, was any procedure adopted to determine the loyalty or disloyalty of either citizen of alien Japanese; the sole and sufficient criterion for subjection to the restrictions was racial descent.

The appellant, Gordon Keyoshi Hirabayashi, was an American citizen of Japanese ancestry, born and raised in the United States. He had never visited Japan and was personally not suspected of disloyalty to the United States. At the time of his arrest he was a senior at the University of Washington. He was convicted by a federal district court of two crimes: failing to register with other Japanese Americans for evacuation to a military detention camp, and failing to obey a military curfew for persons of his race in the State of Washington. Hirabayashi argued that his reason for violating both orders had been his belief that he would be waiving his rights as an American citizen. The jury returned a verdict of guilty on both counts and Hirabayashi was sentenced to imprisonment for a term of three months on each, the sentences to run concurrently. [In this case the Supreme Court dealt only with the curfew issue, postponing until *Korematsu v. United States,* 323 U.S. 214 (1944), the issue of the constitutionality of the detention program itself].

Basic Questions: Was the particular restriction violated adopted by the military commander in the exercise of an unconstitutional delegation by Congress of its legislative authority? Did the restriction unconstitutionally discriminate between citizens of Japanese ancestry and those of other ancestries in violation of the Fifth Amendment?

Opinion of the Court by Chief Justice Stone:
...The proposed legislation provided criminal sanctions for violation of orders, in terms broad enough to include the curfew order now before us, and the

legislative history demonstrates that Congress was advised that curfew orders were among those intended, and was advised also that regulation of citizen and alien Japanese ... was contemplated.

The conclusion is inescapable that Congress, by the Act of March 21, 1942, ratified and confirmed Executive Order No. 9066....And so far as it lawfully could, Congress authorized and implemented such curfew orders as the commanding officer should promulgate pursuant to the Executive Order of the President. The question then is not one of Congressional power to delegate to the President the promulgation of the Executive Order, but whether, acting in cooperation, Congress and the Executive have constitutional authority to impose the curfew restriction here complained of. We must consider also whether, acting together, Congress and the Executive could leave it to the designated military commander to appraise the relevant conditions and on the basis of that appraisal to say whether, under the circumstances, the time and place were appropriate for the promulgation of the curfew order and whether the order itself was an appropriate means of carrying out the Executive Order for the "protection against espionage and against sabotage" to national defense materials, premises and utilities. For reasons presently to be stated, we conclude that it was within the constitutional power of Congress and the executive arm of the Government to prescribe this curfew order for the period under consideration and that its promulgation by the military commander involved no unlawful delegation of legislative power.

Executive Order No. 9066, promulgated in time of war for the declared purpose of prosecuting the war by protecting national defense resources from sabotage and espionage, and the Act of March 21, 1942, ratifying and confirming the Executive Order, were each an exercise of the power to wage war conferred on the Congress and the President....We have no occasion to consider whether the President, acting alone, could lawfully have made the curfew order in question, or have authorized others to make it. For the President's action has the support of the Act of Congress, and we are immediately concerned with the question whether it is within the constitutional power of the national government, through the joint action of Congress and the Executive, to impose this restriction as an emergency war measure....

The challenged orders were defense measures for the avowed purpose of safeguarding the military area in question, at a time of threatened air raids and invasion by the Japanese forces, from the danger of sabotage and espionage. As the curfew was made applicable to citizens residing in the area only if they were of Japanese ancestry, our inquiry must be whether in the light of all the facts and circumstances there was any substantial basis for the conclusion, in which Congress and the military commander united, that the curfew as applied was a protective measure necessary to meet the threat of sabotage and espionage which would substantially affect the war effort and which might reasonably be expected to aid a threatened enemy invasion. The alternative which appellant insists must be accepted is for the military authorities to impose the curfew on all citizens within the military area, or on none. In a case of threatened danger requiring prompt action, it is a choice between inflicting obviously needless hardship on the many, or sitting passive and unresisting in the presence of the threat. We think that constitutional government, in time of war, is not so powerless and does not compel so hard a choice if those charged with the responsibility of our national defense have reasonable ground for believing that the threat is real....

In the critical days of March 1942, the danger to our war production by sabotage and espionage in this area seems obvious. The German invasion of the Western European countries had given ample warning to the world of the menace of the "fifth column." Espionage by persons in sympathy with the Japanese Government had been found to have been particularly effective in the surprise attack on Pearl Harbor. At a time of threatened Japanese attack upon this country, the nature of our inhabitants' attachments to the Japanese enemy was consequently a matter of grave concern. Of the 126,000 persons of Japanese descent in the United States, citizens and non-citizens, approximately 112,000 resided in California, Oregon and Washington at the time of the adoption of the military regulations. Of these approximately two-thirds are citizens because born in the United States. Not only did the great majority of such persons reside within the Pacific coast states but they were concentrated in or near three of the large cities, Seattle, Portland and Los Angeles, all in Military Area No. 1.

There is support for the view that social, economic and political conditions which have prevailed since the close of the last century, when the Japanese began to come to this country in substantial numbers, have intensified their solidarity and have in large measure prevented their assimilation as an integral part of the white population. In addition, large numbers of children of Japanese parentage are sent to Japanese language schools outside the regular hours of public schools in the locality. Some of these schools are generally believed to be sources of Japanese nationalistic propaganda, cultivating allegiance to Japan. Considerable numbers, estimated to be approximately 10,000, of [the] American-born children of Japanese parentage have been sent to Japan for all or a part of their education....Children born in the United States of Japanese alien parents, and especially those children born before December 1, 1924, are under many circumstances deemed, by Japanese law, to be citizens of Japan....The large number of resident alien Japanese, approximately one-third of all Japanese inhabitants of the country, are of mature years and occupy positions of influence in Japanese communities. The association of influential Japanese residents with Japanese Consulates has been deemed a ready means for the dissemination of propaganda and for the maintenance of the influence of the Japanese Government with the Japanese population in this country....

Viewing these data in all their aspects, Congress and the Executive could reasonably have concluded that these conditions have encouraged the continued attachment of members of this group to Japan and Japanese institutions. These are only some of the many considerations which those charged with the responsibility for the national defense could take into account in deter-mining the nature and extent of the danger of espionage and sabotage, in the event of invasion or air raid attack. The extent of that danger could be definitely known only after the event and after it was too late to meet it. Whatever views we may entertain regarding the loyalty to this country of the citizens of Japanese ancestry, we cannot reject as unfounded the judgment of the military authorities and of Congress that there were disloyal members of that population, whose number and strength could not be precisely and quickly ascertained. We cannot say that the war-making branches of the Government did not have ground for believing that in a critical hour such persons could not readily be isolated and separately dealt with, and constituted a menace to the national defense and safety, which demanded that prompt and adequate measures be taken to guard against it.

Appellant does not deny that, given the danger, a curfew was an appropriate measure against sabotage. It is an obvious protection against the perpetration of sabotage most readily committed during the hours of darkness. If it was an appropriate exercise of the war power its validity is not impaired because it has restricted the citizen's liberty. Like every military control of the population of a dangerous zone in war time, it necessarily involves some infringement of individual liberty, just as does the police establishment of fire lines during a fire, or the confinement of people to their houses during an air raid alarm—neither of which could be thought to be an infringement of constitutional right. Like them, the validity of the restraints of the curfew order depends on all the conditions which obtain at the time the curfew is imposed and which support the order imposing it....

Distinctions between citizens solely because of their ancestry are by their very nature odious to a free people whose institutions are founded upon the doctrine of equality. For that reason, legislative classification or discrimination based on race alone has often been held to be denial of equal protection....We may assume that these considerations would be controlling here were it not for the fact that the danger of espionage and sabotage, in time of war and of threatened invasion, calls upon the military authorities to scrutinize every relevant fact bearing on the loyalty of populations in the danger areas. Because racial discriminations are in most circumstances irrelevant and therefore prohibited, it by no means follows that, in dealing with the perils of war, Congress and the Executive are wholly precluded from taking into account those facts and circumstances which are relevant to measures for our national defense and for the successful prosecution of the war, and which may in fact place citizens of one ancestry in a different category from others....The adoption by Government, in the crisis of war and of threatened invasion, of measures for the public safety, based upon the recognition of facts and circumstances which indicate that a group of one national extraction may menace that safety more than others, is not wholly beyond the limits of the Constitution and is not to be condemned merely because in other and in most circumstances racial distinctions are irrelevant....

Our investigation here does not go beyond the inquiry whether, in the light of all the relevant circumstances preceding and attending their promulgation, the challenged orders and statute afforded a reasonable basis for the action taken in imposing the curfew. We cannot close our eyes to the fact, demonstrated by experience, that in time of war residents having ethnic affiliations with an invading enemy may be a greater source of danger than those of a different ancestry. Nor can we deny that Congress, and the military authorities acting with its authorization, have constitutional power to appraise the danger in the light of facts of public notoriety. We need not now attempt to define the ultimate boundaries of the war power. We decide only the issue as we have defined it— we decide only that the curfew order as applied, and at the time it was applied, was within the boundaries of the war power. In this case it is enough that circumstances within the knowledge of those charged with the responsibility for maintaining the national defense afforded a rational basis for the decision which they made. Whether we would have made it is irrelevant.

What we have said also disposed of the contention that the curfew order involved an unlawful delegation by Congress of its legislative power....The purpose of Executive Order No. 9066, and the standard which the President approved for the orders authorized to be promulgated by the military commander ... was the protection of our war resources against espionage and sabo- tage....Both the Executive Order and the Proclamations were before Congress when the Act of March 21, 1942, was under consideration. To the extent that the Executive Order authorized orders to be promulgated by the military commander to accomplish the declared purpose of the Order, and to the extent that the findings in the Proclamations established that such was their purpose, both have been approved by Congress....

The Constitution as a continuously operating charter of government does not demand the impossible or the impractical. The essentials of the legislative function are preserved when Congress authorizes a statutory command to become operative, upon ascertainment of a basic conclusion of fact by a designated representative of the Government....The present statute, which authorized curfew orders to be made pursuant to Executive Order No. 9066 for the protection of war resources from espionage and sabotage, satisfies those requirements. Under the Executive Order the basic facts, determined by the military commander in the light of knowledge then available, were whether that danger existed and whether a curfew order was an appropriate means of minimizing the danger. Since his findings to that effect were, as we have said, not without adequate support, the legislative function was performed and the sanction of the statute attached to violations of the curfew order. It is unnecessary to consider whether or to what extent such findings would support orders differing from the curfew order.

The conviction under the second count is without constitutional infirmity. Hence we have no occasion to review the conviction on the first count since, as already stated, the sentences on the two counts are to run concurrently and conviction on the second is sufficient to sustain the sentence. For this reason also it is unnecessary to consider the Government's argument that compliance with the order to report to the Civilian Control Station did not necessarily entail confinement in a relocation center.

Affirmed.

Note: In times of declared war, the President acts as a constitutional dictator. There is a tacit understanding that nothing—literally nothing—will be permitted to block the winning of the war. What is necessary, as determined by the President [*Prize Cases,* 67 U.S. 635 (1863)], is done. Legal niceties are given little attention. National survival is the ultimate value. Congress does not interfere with the manner in which the President as commander-in-chief conducts the war; it is a ready ally in almost everything he personally and institutionally wishes to do. Congress, moreover, has in the past drawn on its own war powers to give the President carte blanche—that is, the Lend Lease Act of 1941 (55 Stat. 31) as a qualified declaration of war—to take actions considered by him vital to the defense of the United States.

The Court, on the other hand, lies back, seeking to avoid having to rule on questions of the conduct of the commander-in-chief powers—and when the justices are forced to rule, they usually uphold presidential action. In fact, the Supreme Court has never invalidated any presidential act as commander-in-chief during a wartime emergency.

Hirabayashi is perhaps the most clear-cut case on record of the Court's tendency to insist that unusual military actions be grounded, whenever possible, on the combined powers of the President and Congress, which (when merged) are called simply "the war powers of the United States." The Court was thus faced with two possibilities in adjudicating the legal questions raised: it could review appellant's conviction on both counts, in which case it would have to examine the legality of the order commanding him to report to the control station, and thus might be forced into considering the constitutionality of the entire program of evacuation. [C. Rossiter, The Supreme Court and the Commander in Chief 45 (R. Longaker ed. 1976)]. Or it could confine itself to one count, and, if it found him guilty, could then ignore the other count, since the two sentences ran concurrently. [*Ibid.*] The Court selected the second possibility, fixing its attention rigidly on the much narrower issue of curfew violation. [*Ibid.*] Small wonder the Court had no trouble sustaining the government.

The concurring opinions of Justices Douglas, Murphy, and Rutledge (omitted) warned that there were limits to this sort of thing. One must wonder, nevertheless, why this particular Supreme Court—with its majority of members already on record as defenders of individual rights—should so easily acquiesce in this unprecedented invasion of personal liberty, even in time of war?

Korematsu v. United States, 323 U.S. 214; 89 L.Ed. 194 (1944)

Several portions of Chief Justice Stone's opinion in *Hirabayashi* indicated that the Court was solely troubled by the government's Japanese-American policy. But it had nevertheless dodged the major issue of the case, and it had attempted to avoid future problems by basing the validity of an executive action on the combined "war powers of the United States." Congress had indeed provided penalties for violation of military orders, but the evacuation program (and the curfew as well) were presidentially instituted on the ground of military exigency; they were, in fact, emergency actions based on the President's power as commander-in-chief in time of war. Thus, by its attempt to sidestep the issue of constitutional propriety in *Hirabayashi*, the Court revealed that it was unprepared, even in matters dealing with fundamental personal rights, to contradict the President's determination of "crisis necessity."

The crucial issue left unresolved in 1943 was finally considered eighteen months later. The case involved an American citizen, Fred Toyosaburo Korematsu, who had never been outside the United States. He grew up in Oakland, California, and was a shipyard welder until the Japanese attacked Pearl Harbor, where-upon the Boilermakers' Union expelled him. He refused to obey a military order directing him to report at an evacuation station for removal from his home in California. He challenged the validity of the order, and thus of the entire evacuation program, but was convicted. The conviction was affirmed, and the Supreme Court granted certiorari to review the case. By the time its decision was handed down, the danger of a West Coast invasion was long past and the end of the war with Japan was only nine months off, but a majority of the Court still refused to question the executive's judgment or strike down the emergency regime's extraordinary actions.

Basic Question: Was this a proper exercise of the war powers?

Opinion of the Court by Justice Black:

The 1942 Act was attacked in the *Hirabayashi* case as an unconstitutional delegation of power; it was contended that the curfew order and other orders on which it rested were beyond the war powers of the Congress, the military authorities and the President, as Commander in Chief of the Army; and finally that to apply the curfew order against none but citizens of Japanese ancestry amounted to a constitutionally prohibited discrimination solely on account of race. To these questions, we gave the serious consideration which their importance justified. We upheld the curfew order as an exercise of the power of the government to take steps necessary to prevent espionage and sabotage in an area threatened by Japanese attack.

In the light of the principles we announced in the *Hirabayashi* case, we are unable to conclude that it was beyond the war powers of Congress and the Executive to exclude those of Japanese ancestry from the West Coast war area at the time they did. True, exclusion from the area in which one's home is located is a far greater deprivation than constant confinement to the home from 8 P.M. to 6 A.M. Nothing short of apprehension by the proper military authorities of the gravest imminent danger to the public safety can constitutionally justify either.

But exclusion from a threatened area, no less than curfew, has a definite and close relationship to the prevention of espionage and sabotage. The military authorities, charged with the primary responsibility of defending our shores, concluded that curfew provided inadequate protection and ordered exclusion. They did so ... in accordance with Congressional authority to the military to say who should, and who should not, remain in the threatened areas....

Here, as in the *Hirabayashi* case,... we cannot reject as unfounded the judgment of the military authorities and of Congress that there were disloyal members of that population, whose number and strength could not be precisely and quickly ascertained. We cannot say that the war-making branches of the Government did not have ground for believing that in a critical hour such persons could not readily be isolated and separately dealt with, and constituted a menace to the national defense and safety, which demanded that prompt and adequate measures be taken to guard against it.

Like curfew, exclusion of those of Japanese origin was deemed necessary because of the presence of an unascertained number of disloyal members of the group, most of whom we have no doubt were loyal to this country. It was because we could not reject the finding of the military authorities that it was impossible to bring about an immediate segregation of the disloyal from the loyal that we sustained the validity of the curfew order as applying to the whole group. In the instant case, temporary exclusion of the entire group was rested by the military on the same ground. The judgment that exclusion of the whole group was for the same reason a military imperative answers the contention that the exclusion was in the nature of group punishment based on antagonism to those of Japanese origin. That there were members of the group who retained loyalties to Japan has been confirmed by investigations made subsequent to the exclusion. Approximately five thousand American citizens of Japanese ancestry refused to swear unqualified allegiance to the United States and to renounce allegiance to the Japanese Emperor, and several thousand evacuees requested repatriation to Japan.

We uphold the exclusion order as of the time it was made and when the petitioner violated it....In doing so, we are not unmindful of the hardships imposed by it upon a large group of American citizens....But hardships are part of war, and war is an aggregation of hardships. All citizens alike, both in and out of uniform, feel the impact of war in greater or lesser measure. Citizenship has its privileges, and in time of war the burden is always heavier. Compulsory exclusion of large groups of citizens from their homes, except under circumstances of direst emergency and peril, is inconsistent with our basic governmental institutions. But when under conditions of modern warfare our shores are threatened by hostile forces, the power to protect must be commensurate with the threatened danger....

Since the petitioner has not been convicted of failing to report or to remain in an assembly or relocation center, we cannot in this case determine the validity of those separate provisions of the order. It is sufficient here for us to pass upon the order which petitioner violated. To do more would be to go beyond the issues raised, and to decide momentous questions not contained within the framework of the pleadings or the evidence in this case. It will be time enough to decide the serious constitutional issues which petitioner seeks to raise when an assembly or relocation order is applied or is certain to be applied to him, and we have its terms before us.

Some of the members of the Court are of the view that evacuation and detention in an Assembly Center are inseparable. After May 3, 1942, the date of Exclusion Order No. 34, Korematsu was under compulsion to leave the area not as he would choose but via an Assembly Center. The Assembly Center was conceived as a part of the machinery for group evacuation. The power to exclude includes the power to do it by force if necessary. And any forcible measure must necessarily entail some degree of detention or restraint whatever method of removal is selected. But whichever view is taken, it results in holding that the order under which petitioner was convicted was valid.

It is said that we are dealing here with the case of imprisonment of a citizen in a concentration camp solely because of his ancestry, without evidence or inquiry concerning his loyalty and good disposition towards the United States. Our task would be simple, our duty clear, were this a case involving the imprisonment of a loyal citizen in a concentration camp because of racial prejudice. Regardless of the true nature of the assembly and relocation centers—and we deem it unjustifiable to call them concentration camps with all the ugly connotations that term implies—we are dealing specifically with nothing but an exclusion order. To cast this case into outlines of racial prejudice, without reference to the real military dangers which were presented, merely confuses the issue. Korematsu was not excluded from the Military area because of hostility to him or his race. He was excluded because we are at war with the Japanese Empire, because the properly constituted military authorities feared an invasion of our West Coast and felt constrained to take proper security measures, because they decided that the military urgency of the situation demanded that all citizens of Japanese ancestry be segregated from the West Coast temporarily, and finally, because Congress, reposing its confidence in this time of war in our military leaders—as inevitably it must—determined that they should have the power to do just this. There was evidence of disloyalty on the part of some, the military authorities considered that the need for action was great, and time was short. We cannot—by availing ourselves of the calm perspective of hindsight—now say that at that time these action were unjustified.

Affirmed.

Dissenting opinion by Justice Murphy:

This exclusion of "all persons of Japanese ancestry, both alien and non-alien," from the Pacific Coast area on a plea of military necessity, in the absence of martial law, ought not to be approved. Such exclusion goes over "the very brink of constitutional power" and falls into the ugly abyss of racism....

The judicial test of whether the Government, on a plea of military necessity, can validly deprive an individual of any of his constitutional rights is whether the deprivation is reasonably related to a public danger that is so "immediate, imminent, and impending" as not to admit of delay and not to permit the intervention of ordinary constitutional processes to alleviate the danger....Civilian Exclusion Order No. 34, banishing from a prescribed area of the Pacific Coast "all persons of Japanese ancestry, both alien and non-alien," clearly does not meet that test. Being an obvious racial discrimination, the order deprives all those within its scope of the equal protection of the laws as guaranteed by the Fifth Amendment. It further deprives these individuals of their constitutional rights to live and work where they will, to establish a home where they choose and to move about freely. In excommunicating them without benefit of hearings, this order also deprives them of all their constitutional rights to procedural due process. Yet no reasonable relation to an "immediate, imminent, impending" public danger is evident to support this racial restriction which is one of the most sweeping and complete deprivations of constitutional rights in the history of this nation in the absence of martial law....

No adequate reason is given for the failure to treat these Japanese Americans on an individual basis by holding investigations and hearings to separate the loyal from the disloyal, as was done in the case of persons of German and Italian ancestry....It is asserted merely that the loyalties of this group "were unknown and time was of the essence." Yet nearly four months elapsed after Pearl Harbor before the first exclusion order was issued; nearly eight months went by until the last order was issued; and the last of these "subversive" persons was not actually removed until almost eleven months had elapsed. Leisure and deliberation seem to have been more of the essence than speed. And the fact that conditions were not such as to warrant a declaration of martial law adds strength to the belief that the factors of time and military necessity were not as urgent as they have been represented to be....

Dissenting opinion by Justice Jackson:

...[I]t is said that if the military commander had reasonable military grounds for promulgating the orders, they are constitutional and become law, and the Court is required to enforce them. There are several reasons why I cannot subscribe to this doctrine.

It would be impracticable and dangerous idealism to expect or insist that each specific military command in an area of probable operations will conform to conventional test of constitutionality. When an area is so beset that it must be put under military control at all, the paramount consideration is that its measures be successful, rather than legal. The armed services must protect a society, not merely its Constitution. The very essence of the military job is to marshal physical force, to remove every obstacle to its effectiveness, to give it every strategic advantage. Defense measures will not, and often should not, be held within the limits that bind civil authority in peace. No court can require such a commander in such circumstances to act as a reasonable man; he may be unreasonably cautious and exacting. Perhaps he should be. But a commander in temporarily focusing the life of a community on defense is carrying out a military program; he is not making law in the sense the courts know the term. He issues orders, and they may have a certain authority as military commands, although they may be very bad as constitutional law.

But if we cannot confine military expedients by the Constitution, neither would I distort the Constitution to approve all that the military may deem expedient. That is what the Court appears to be doing, whether consciously or not. I cannot say, from any evidence before me, that the orders of General DeWitt were not reasonably expedient military precautions, nor can I say that they were. But even if they were permissible military procedures, I deny that it follows that they are constitutional. If, as the Court holds, it does follow, then we may as well say that any military order will be constitutional and have done with it....

Much is said of the danger to liberty from the army program for deporting and detaining these citizens of Japanese extraction. But a judicial construction of the due process clause that will sustain this order is a far more subtle blow to liberty than the promulgation of the order itself. A military order, however unconstitutional, is not apt to last longer than the military emergency....But once a judicial opinion rationalizes such an order to show that it conforms to the Constitution, or rather rationalizes the Constitution to show that the Constitution sanctions such an order, the Court for all time has validated the principle of racial discrimination in criminal procedure and of transplanting American citizens. The principle then lies about like a loaded weapon ready for the hand of any authority that can bring forward a plausible claim of an urgent need. Every repetition imbeds that principle more deeply in our law and thinking and expands it to new purposes. All who observe the work of courts are familiar with what Judge Cardozo described as "the tendency of a principle to expand itself to the limit of its logic." A military commander may overstep the bounds of constitutionality, and it is an incident. But if we review and approve, that passing incident becomes the doctrine of the Constitution. There is has a generative power of its own, and all that it creates will be in its own image [emphasis added]. Nothing better illustrates this danger than does the Court's opinion in this case....

I should hold that a civil court cannot be made to enforce an order which violates constitutional limitations even if it is a reasonable exercise of military authority. The courts can exercise only the judicial power, can apply only law, and must abide by the Constitution, or they cease to be civil courts and become instruments of military policy....

Note: On the same day the *Korematsu* decision was handed down, the Supreme Court (with its conscience obviously troubled) also held that a Japanese-American girl of proven loyalty was entitled to a writ of habeas corpus releasing her unconditionally from the custody of the War Relocation Authority (WRA). [*Ex parte Endo*, 323 U.S. 283 (1944).] The young lady was already free by the time her case was decided (the relocation centers were then being disestablished) but she now had the satisfaction of knowing that her detention had been improper all along. The Court did not refer to her prior release, however, nor did it mention that her case had been in the judicial mill for two and one-half years. As for the issue of evacuation of a loyal citizen, it was avoided; and by inference the Court conceded the WRA's power to detain further those evacuees whose loyalty had not yet been proved.

The Court's opinion in *Korematsu* was based on three very simple (and erroneous) propositions: (1) given the fact that there was some rumor of evidence of disloyalty on the part of a very few, the military authorities considered that the need for action was great, and time was short; (2) the evacuation was not founded in racial prejudice—authorities had made their decision on the purely military basis of security; and (3) since the Court had already decided that it was constrained to accept the military's judgment of the extent of the danger, it was likewise constrained to accept its judgment on the extent of "the power to protect." In effect, the Court employed the President's commander-in-chief power as a basis for congressional power also. It thus should be added to the affirmative grants of power in Article I. [C. Rossiter, The Supreme Court and the Commander in Chief 49 (R. Longaker ed. 1976).] That, it should be emphasized, is the doctrine of necessity run riot, with the Supreme Court abjectly acquiescing in government by fiat without regard to the Constitution's due process clause. [A. Miller, Presidential Power 178 (1977).] The fact that there was not one proved instance of sabotage or anti-war behavior did not deter the majority of justices from reading into the Constitution a theory of *raison d'etat* (constitutional reason of state). [*Ibid.*]

More important, *Korematsu* finishes the job (begun earlier in *Quirin*) of destroying the reasoning—and general principles—underlying *Milligan*. There was no suspension of the writ of habeas corpus, no declaration of martial law, no trial by military commission. But there was something that cut even deeper into the liberties of the American people: the wholesale invasion, based on a racial criterion, of the freedom of person of seventy-thousand citizens, an invasion of American liberty made all the more reprehensible by the fact that there was indeed no occasion for martial law. [C. Rossiter, 53-54].

What the Japanese-American cases demonstrated (perhaps more clearly than any other group of cases) was that in time of war the law of necessity was superior to the law of the Constitution. The Court, lacking even a declaration of martial law by which to rationalize the frantic action of the President, and hardly saved by Congress's tardy participation in the matter, found it difficult to uphold what appeared to be a blatant denial of due process. But uphold the exclusion program it did, thereby institutionalizing the crisis principle that in time of war the laws are silent. War and peace are not the same thing and cannot coexist in the same place at the same time.

In 1983, Gordon Hirabayashi and Fred Korematsu filed suits in separate federal courts to have their wartime convictions overturned on the ground that the military's claims of an emergency were based on intentional fabrications and falsehoods and constituted a fraud upon the courts. In 1984, in *Korematsu v. United States,* 584 F.Supp. 1406 (S.D.Cal. 1984), the District Court vacated Korematsu's conviction. Two years later, a federal judge vacated Hirabayashi's conviction for failing to register for evacuation to an internment camp, but let stand the conviction for curfew violation. [*Hirabayashi v. United States,* 627 F.Supp. 1445 (N.D.Cal. 1986).] In 1988, Congress implemented (102 Stat. 903) the recommendations of the Commission on Wartime Relocation and Internment of Civilians by acknowledging "the fundamental injustice of the evacuation, relocation and internment," and apologizing on behalf of the people of the United States. Reparations were approved, and each living survivor of the internment was to be compensated in an amount approximating $20,000. Since, in addition to the lose of their liberty, the internees lost their homes and most of their other property as well, the effort at economic restitution was widely regarded as less than adequate.

Duncan v. Kahanamoku, 327 U.S. 304; 90 L.Ed. 688 (1946)

That the President's powers as commander-in-chief go beyond the use of violence in foreign affairs and the use of military forces to enforce judicial decrees may be seen in the doctrine of "qualified" martial law. The doctrine got its inception during the nineteenth century when state governors used the national guard to enforce judicial decrees issued in labor disputes, mainly to put down strikes. There is, however, a presidential dimension to the doctrine. The President has considerable power in the area of qualified martial law, the dispatching of federal troops or the National Guard to a state where the President deems an insurrection exists. Use of complete martial law contemplates the supersession of civilian courts by military courts. Martial law is proper only in the absence of a functioning civil government, and it may be instituted where civilian courts are in fact closed and it is impossible to administer criminal justice according to law, or where war prevails and it becomes necessary to furnish a substitute for civil authority. Under no circumstances, however, are military trials of nonmilitary persons ever lawful, when civilian courts are in operation. The decision to invoke the doctrine of qualified martial law rests entirely and exclusively with the President as to whether an insurrection exists, and he is to determine whether or not to call out the armed forces. Moreover, while in the case of complete martial law, the actions of the President are judicially reviewable, the declaration of a state to be in insurrection and the subsequent use of troops is not subject to judicial review. This power is vested in the President by Article IV, section 4 of the Constitution and the provisions of the U.S. Code. Also, a state of insurrection continues until the President decides to the contrary. [*United States v. 129 Packages,* 27 F.Cas. 284 (D.C.Mo. 1862) (No. 15,941).]

On December 7, 1941, for reasons that need no explanation, Governor Poindexter, acting upon a clear grant of authority in section 67 of the Organic Act of the Territory of Hawaii (31 Stat. 141), suspended the writ of habeas corpus, declared martial law throughout the islands, and turned over to the Commanding General, Hawaiian Department, the exercise of all his normal powers "during the present emergency and until the danger of invasion is removed." In conformance with the requirements of the statutory grant, a message was rushed off to President Roosevelt asking for approval of this action, and confirmation was immediately forthcoming. Through this action the President took full legal and constitutional responsibility for the initiation of military government.

With the writ of habeas corpus suspended, the civil courts of the territory, although fully prepared to perform their normal tasks, were powerless to give relief to the hundreds of civilians who were punished for the usual run of crimes and misdemeanors by military courts and summary procedures. The state of martial law was not finally terminated until October 24, 1944, when a presidential proclamation cut short a regime that the military would just as soon have prolonged until the end of the war. It was thus in 1944 that two civilians— White, who had been convicted by a military tribunal in August 1942, on a charge of embezzling stock, and Duncan, who had been similarly convicted in March 1944, on a charge of assaulting two Marine sentries in the Pearl Harbor Navy Yard—were able to petition the territorial district court for writs of habeas corpus. In each instance the district court held that the trials had been without authority and that the prisoners were entitled to their freedom. These holding were appealed in tandem to the circuit court and there reversed. The Supreme Court granted certiorari in early 1945, heard arguments in December, and finally handed down its decision February 25, 1946.

Basic Question: Is the military government of Hawaii valid under Section 67 of the Hawaiian Organic Act?

Opinion of the Court by Justice Black:

Did the Organic Act during the period of martial law give the armed forces power to supplant all civilian laws and to substitute military for judicial trials under the conditions that existed in Hawaii at the time these petitioners were tried?...We note first that at the time the alleged offenses were committed the dangers apprehended by the military were not sufficiently imminent to cause them to require civilians to evacuate the area or even to evacuate any of the buildings necessary to carry on the business of the courts. In fact, the buildings had long been open and actually in use for certain kinds of trials. Our question does not involve the well-established power of the military to exercise jurisdiction over members of the armed forces, those directly connected with such forces, or enemy belligerents, prisoners of war, or others charged with violating the laws of war. We are not concerned with the recognized power of the military to try civilians in tribunals established as a part of a temporary military government over occupied enemy territory or territory regained from an enemy where civilian government cannot and does not function. For Hawaii since annexation has been held by and loyal to the United States. Nor need we here consider the power of the military simply to arrest and detain civilians interfering with a necessary military function at a time of turbulence and danger from insurrection or war. And finally, there was no specialized effect of the military, here, to enforce orders which related only to military functions, such as,... curfew rules or blackouts. For these petitioners were tried before tribunals set up under a military program which took over all government and superseded all civil law and courts. If the Organic Act, properly interpreted, did not give the armed forces this awesome power, both petitioners are entitled to their freedom....

Since the Act's language does not provide a satisfactory answer, we look to the legislative history for possible ... aid in interpreting the term "martial law" as used in the statute. The government contends that the legislative history shows that Congress intended to give the armed forces extraordinarily broad powers to try civilians before military tribunals. Its argument is as follows: That portion of the language of Sec. 67 which prescribes the prerequisites to declaring martial law is identical with a part of the language of the original Constitution of Hawaii. Before Congress enacted the Organic Act the Supreme Court of Hawaii had construed that language as giving the Hawaiian President power to authorize military tribunals to try civilians charged with crime whenever the public safety required it....When Congress passed the Organic Act it simply enacted the applicable language of the Hawaiian Constitution and with it the interpretation of that language by the Hawaiian Supreme Court.

In disposing of this argument we wish to point out at the outset that even had Congress intended the decision in [*In re Kalanianaole*, 12 Haw. 29] to become part of the Organic Act, that case did not go so far as to authorize military trials of the petitioners for these reasons. There the defendants were insurrectionists taking part in the very uprising which the military were to suppress, while here the petitioners had no connection with any organized resistance to the armed forces or the established government. If, on the other hand, we should take the *Kalanianaole* case to authorize the complete supplanting of courts by military tribunals, we are certain that Congress did not wish to make that case part of the Organic Act. For that case did not merely uphold military trials of civilians but also held that courts were to interfere only when there was an obvious abuse of discretion which resulted in cruel and inhuman practices or the establishment of military rule for the personal gain of the President and the armed forces. But courts were not to review whether the President's action, no matter how unjustifiable, was necessary for the public safety....[M]ilitary trials of civilians charged with crime, especially when not made subject to judicial review, are so obviously contrary to our political traditions and our institutions of jury trials in courts of law, that the tenuous circumstances offered by the government can hardly suffice to persuade us that Congress was willing to enact a Hawaiian Supreme Court decision permitting such a radical departure from our steadfast beliefs.

Partly in order to meet this objection the government further contends that Congress in enacting the *Kalanianaole* case, not only authorized military trials of civilians in Hawaii, but also could and intended to provide that "martial law" in Hawaii should not be limited by the United States Constitution or by established Constitutional practice. But when the Organic Act is read as a whole and in the light of its legislative history it becomes clear that Congress did not intend the Constitution to have a limited application to Hawaii. Along with Sec. 67 Congress enacted Sec. 5 of the Organic Act which provides "that the Constitution ... shall have the same force and effect within the said Territory as elsewhere in the United States" (31 Stat. 141)....

It follows that civilians in Hawaii are entitled to the Constitutional guarantee of a fair trial to the same extent as those who live in any other part of our country. We are aware that conditions peculiar to Hawaii might imperatively demand extraordinarily and effective speedy measures in the event of actual or threatened invasion. But this also holds true for other parts of the United States. Extraordinary measures in Hawaii, however necessary, are not supportable on the mistaken premise that Hawaiian inhabitants are less entitled to Constitutional protection than others. For here Congress did not in the Organic Act exercise whatever power it might have had to limit the application of the Constitution....The people of Hawaii are therefore entitled to Constitutional protection to the same extent as the inhabitants of the 48 States. And Congress did not enact the Hawaiian Supreme Court's decision ... and, thus, authorize the military trials of petitioners. Whatever power the Organic Act gave the Hawaiian military authorities, such power must therefore be construed in the same way as a grant of power to troops stationed in any one of the states....

Courts and their procedural safeguards are indispensable to our system of government. They were set up by our founders to protect the liberties they valued....Our system of government clearly is the antithesis of total military rule and the founders of this country are not likely to have contemplated complete military dominance within the limits of a Territory made part of this country and not recently not taken from an enemy. They were opposed to governments that placed in the hands of one man the power to make, interpret and enforce the laws. Their philosophy has been the people's throughout our history. For that reason we have maintained legislatures chosen by citizens or their representatives and courts and juries to try those who violate legislative enactments. We have always been especially concerned about the potential evils of summary criminal trials and have guarded against them by provisions embodied in the Constitution itself....Legislatures and courts are not merely cherished American institutions; they are indispensable to our government.

Military tribunals have no such standing....Congress prior to the time of the enactment of the Organic Act had only once authorized the supplanting of the courts by military tribunals. Legislation to that effect was enacted immediately after the South's unsuccessful attempt to secede from the Union. Insofar as that legislation applied to the Southern States after the war was at an end it was challenged by a series of Presidential vetoes as vigorous as any in the country's history. And in order to prevent this Court from passing on the constitutionality of this legislation Congress found it necessary to curtail our appellate jurisdiction [*In re McCardle*, 6 Wall. 318]. Indeed, prior to the Organic Act, the only time this Court had ever discussed the supplanting of courts by military tribunals in a situation other than that involving the establishment of a military government over recently occupied enemy territory, it had emphatically declared that "civil liberty and this kind of martial law cannot endure together; and, in the conflict, one or the other must perish." *Ex parte Milligan*, 4 Wall. 2, 124....

We believe that when Congress passed the Hawaiian Organic Act and authorized the establishment of "martial law" it had in mind and did not wish to exceed the boundaries between military and civilian power, in which our people have always believed, which responsible military and executive officers had heeded, and which had become part of our political philosophy and institutions prior to the time Congress passed the Organic Act. The phrase "martial law" as employed in that Act, therefore, while intended to authorize the military to act vigorously for the maintenance of an orderly civil government and for the defense of the island against actual or threatened rebellion or invasion, was not intended to authorize the supplanting of courts by military tribunals....We hold that both petitioners are now entitled to be released from custody.

Reversed.

Dissenting opinion by Justice Burton (joined by Justice Frankfurter):

With the rest of this Court I subscribe unreservedly to the Bill of Rights. I recognize the importance of the civil courts in protecting individual rights guaranteed by the Constitution. I prefer civil to military control of civilian life and I agree that in war our Constitution contemplates the preservation of the individual rights of all of our people in accordance with a plan of constitutional procedure fitted to the needs of a self-governing republic at war....

On December 7 and in the period immediately following, every inch of the Territory of Hawaii was like a frontier stockade under savage attack with notice that such attack would not be restrained by the laws of civilized nations. Measures of defense had to be taken on the basis that anything could happen. The relation of the Constitution of the United States to such a situation is important. Of course, the Constitution is not put aside. It was written by a generation fresh from war. The people established a more perfect union, in part, so that they might the better defend themselves from military attack. In doing so they centralized far more military power and responsibility in the Chief Executive than previously had been done. The Constitution was built for rough as well as smooth roads. In time of war the nation simply changes gears and takes the harder going under the same power.

The conduct of war under the Constitution is largely an executive function. Within the field of military action in time of war, the executive is allowed wide discretion. While even in the conduct of war, there are many lines of jurisdiction to draw between the proper spheres of legislative, executive and judicial action, it seems clear that at least on an active battle field, the executive discretion to determine policy is there intended by the Constitution to be supreme. The question then arises: What is a battle field and how long does it remain one after the first barrage?...

For this Court to intrude its judgment into spheres of constitutional discretion that are reserved either to the Congress or to the Chief Executive, is to invite disregard of that judgment by the Congress or by the executive agencies under a claim of constitutional right to do so....

In view of the responsibility placed upon the executive branch of the Government and especially upon its armed forces in time of invasion and threatened invasion, it is essential that that branch of the Government have freedom of action equal to its needs. At the center of invasion, military control is the proper control to be applied, subject to provisions of the Constitution, treaties and laws of the United States applicable to the battlefield. On December 7, 1941, I believe that the facts of the invasion and threatened further invasion amply establish such a condition and justified at the time the military control established on that basis throughout the islands....

Now that the war has been won and the safety of the islands has been again assured, there is opportunity, in the calm light of peace, for the readjustment of sentences imposed upon civilians and military personnel during the emergency of war and which have not yet expired. It is important, however, that in reviewing the constitutionality of the conduct of our agencies of government in time of war, invasion and threatened invasion, we do not now make precedents which in other emergencies may handicap the executive branch of the Government in the performance of duties allotted to it by the Constitution and by the exercise of which it successfully defended the nation against the greatest attack ever made upon it.

One way to test the soundness of a decision today that the trial of petitioner White on August 25, 1942, before a provost court on a charge of embezzlement and the trial of petitioner Duncan on March 2, 1944, before a similar court on a charge of maliciously assaulting marine sentries were unconstitutional procedures, is to ask ourselves whether or not on those dates, with the war against Japan in full swing, this Court would have, or should have, granted a writ of habeas corpus, an injunction or a writ of prohibition to release the petitioners or otherwise to oust the provost courts of their claimed jurisdiction. Such a test emphasizes the issue. I believe that this Court would not have been justified in granting the relief suggested at such times. Also I believe that this Court might well have found itself embarrassed had it ordered such relief and then had attempted to enforce its order in the theater of military operations, at a time when the area was under martial law and the writ of habeas corpus was still suspended, all in accordance with the orders of the President of the United States and the Governor of Hawaii issued under their interpretation of the discretion and responsibility vested in them by the Constitution of the United

States and by the Organic Act of Hawaii enacted by Congress....

Note: As it had after the Civil War (and under strikingly similar circumstances), the Court spoke the language of limitation only when the emergency was over. Six months after the hostilities had ceased, a year after President Roosevelt's death, and more than four years after Pearl Harbor, it reviewed and found unconstitutional the President's imposition of martial law in Hawaii. As in *Milligan,* judicial bravery became manifest when the rumble of guns had been silenced. Indeed, while the Court relied heavily on *Milligan,* it treated *Quirin* as though it did not overrule the earlier Civil War precedent *sub silentio;* and it still attempted to avoid the constitutional issue by referring to section 67 of the Hawaiian Organic Act instead of the commander-in-chief clause and presidential power. One would be ill advised to rely on *Duncan* as a significant substantive limitation on presidential emergency power.

The majority justices, in deciding that these military trials could not be brought within the meaning of section 67, had to go behind the testimony of the military authorities concerning the necessities of the moment, read the facts of life in Hawaii in 1942 and 1944 for themselves, and substitute their own judgment for that of the authorities—something they refused to do in *Hirabayashi* and *Korematsu.* In those cases they had accepted at face value all the government argued, along with all the misinformation, half-truths, and insinuations that for years had been directed against Japanese Americans by people with racial and economic prejudices. [C. Rossiter, <u>The Supreme Court and the Commander in Chief</u> 59 (R. Longaker ed. 1976)]. In *Duncan,* however, they accepted nothing. Chief Justice Stone would have come closest to the truth when he said (in his concurrence), "Executive action is not proof of its own necessity," but only if he had added the words, *"now that the war is over."*

The dissenting Justices—Burton and Frankfurter—were quite realistic about the constitutional ability of the Nation, led by the President, to wage war. And, unlike the majority (basically the same majority that handed down *Quirin, Hirabayashi,* and *Korematsu*), were not lured into saying things about limits on the war powers that were simply not true. Ultimately, the dissenters brought out two points that needed to be reemphasized as often as possible. First, Hamilton was correct in <u>The Federalist</u>, No. 23, when he argued that the war power can have no limits placed upon it—and certainly not limits imposed by the courts. Second, the majority conveniently forgot what it earlier said about the war power and the President's exercise of it in the Japanese-American cases; as implied by Burton and Frankfurter, the majority should have remembered Chief Justice Taney's warning in *Luther v. Borden,* 7 How. 1 (1949), that a court that will not strike down a constitutional violation during an emergency has no right (logically speaking) to strike it down after the emergency is over. Perhaps, after all, the proper answer when confronted with such an issue is the one suggested by Jackson in his *Korematsu* dissent.

One additional point: the same year the *Hawaiian Martial Law Cases* were decided, the Court rendered its opinion in *In re Yamashita,* 327 U.S. 1 (1946). Here, a majority of the Court asserted the right to scrutinize the authority and proceedings of a military commission, and once again found them either satisfactory or unreviewable. It was upon this latter element of Chief Justice Stone's opinion—the unreviewability of the manifestly irregular methods employed in Yamashita's trial—that Justices Murphy and Rutledge seized upon in two separate, elaborate dissents.

The lesson of this case—and generally speaking of the vast majority of wartime cases considered here—is that the Supreme Court cannot be expected to set itself up as a sort of supermilitary commission to oversee the worldwide activities of the punitive tribunals that the President has authorized, often in conjunction with our allies, to pursue the laws of war to their harsh but imperative conclusions. [C. Rossiter, 118-19.] If we did commit a moral and practical blunder at Nuremberg and Tokyo and Manila, the person to correct it (if correction was even possible) is the person history will hold accountable— the President of the United States. What he and his commanders have done in the occupied countries they have done *politically,* in the purest sense of the word, and the trials of these alleged war criminals were part of that pattern. [*Id.* at 119.] The trials of the war criminals are one type of "judicial" proceeding in which the standards are set and maintained by the President, not the Court. [*Ibid.*] His sins the justices may lament, but not in public. This would seem to be the general rule for the Supreme Court's review and control of these extraordinary military commissions. [For a more complete analysis on this point, *see, e.g.,* Fairman, Some New Problems of the Constitution Following the Flag, 1 Stan.L.Rev. 587 (1949); Perlman, Habeas Corpus and Extraterritoriality, 36 A.B.A.J. 187 (1950); A. Reel, The Case of General Yamashita (1949)].

Woods v. Cloyd W. Miller Co., 333 U.S. 138; 92 L.Ed. 596 (1948)

If a President may recognize the commencement of a state of war, and thereby deprive citizens and aliens of certain legal rights, is it not logical to conclude that he may also continue to deprive them of those rights by declaring that the state of war continues even after hostilities have come to an end? In *Freeborn v. The Protector,* 79 U.S. (12 Wall.) 700 (1872), the Court decided that the Civil War ended when the President said it ended, but in that instance his proclamation coincided with the end of hostilities. In cases arising out of World War I and World War II, the Count consistently treated this question as "political" and beyond its jurisdiction, but in every case the President's "war measures" in the postwar interim between the end of hostilities and the signing of peace treaties were carried out pursuant to a legislative authorization and were not clearly contrary to the legislative will.

The District Court for the Northern District of Ohio declared unconstitutional Title II of the Housing and Rent Act of 1947 (61 Stat. 193), which continued in force rent control provisions of previous legislation. The Act became effective on July 1, 1947 (more than twenty-two months after the last shot of the war had been fired), and the following day the appellee demanded of its tenants 40 percent and 60 percent increases for rental accommodations in the Cleveland Defense Rental Area. This was an admitted violation of the act. The district court declared the act an unconstitutional violation of congressional war power.

Basic Question: Does the right of Congress to establish rent controls by virtue of its war powers carry beyond the cessation of hostilities?

Opinion of the Court by Justice Douglas:

The District Court ... was of the view that the authority of Congress to regulate rents by virtue of the war power ... ended with the Presidential Proclamation terminating hostilities on December 31, 1946, since that proclamation inaugurated "peace-in-fact" though it did not mark termination of the war. It also concluded that even if the war power continues, Congress did not act under it because it did not say so, and only if Congress says so, or enacts provisions so implying, can it be held that Congress intended to exercise such power. That Congress did not so intend, said the District Court, follows from the provision that the Housing Expediter can end controls in any area without regard to the official termination of the war, and from the fact that the preceding federal rent control laws (which were concededly exercises of the war power) were neither amended nor extended. The District Court expressed the further view that rent control is not within the war power because "the emergency created by housing shortages came into existence long before the war." It held that the Act "lacks in uniformity of application and distinctly constitutes a delegation of legislative power not within the grant of Congress" because of the authorization to the Housing Expediter to lift controls in any area before the Act's expiration. It also held that the Act in effect provides "low rentals for certain groups without taking the property or compensating the owner in any way."...

We conclude, in the first place, that the war power sustains this legislation. The Court said in *Hamilton v. Kentucky Distilleries* ... that the war power includes the power "to remedy the evils which have arisen from its rise and progress" and continues for the duration of that emergency. Whatever may be the consequences when war is officially terminated, the war power does not necessarily end with the cessation of hostilities....In *Hamilton* ... and *Ruppert v. Caffey* ... prohibition laws which were enacted after the Armistice in World War I were sustained as exercises of the war power because they conceived manpower and increased efficiency of production in the critical days during the period of demobilization, and helped to husband the supply of grains and cereals depleted by the war effort. Those cases followed the reasoning of *Stewart v. Kahn* ... which held that Congress had the power to toll the statute of limitations of the States during the period when the process of their courts were not available to litigants due to the conditions obtaining in the Civil War.

The constitutional validity of the present legislation follows a fortiori from those cases. The legislative history of the present Act makes abundantly clear that there has not yet been eliminated the deficit in housing which in considerable measure was caused by the heavy demobilization of veterans and by the cessation or reduction in residential construction during the period of hostilities due to the allocation of building materials to military projects. Since the war effort contributed heavily to that deficit, Congress has the power even after the cessation of hostilities to act to control the forces that a short supply of the needed article created....

We recognize the force of the argument that the effects of war under modern conditions may be felt in the economy for years and years, and that if the war power can be used in days of peace to treat all the wounds which war inflicts on our society, it may not only swallow up all other powers of Congress but largely obliterate the Ninth and Tenth Amendments as well. There are no such implications in today's decision....

The question of the constitutionality of action taken by Congress does not depend on recitals of the power which it undertakes to exercise. Here it is plain from the legislative history that Congress was invoking its war power to cope with a current condition of which the war was a direct and immediate cause. Its judgment on that score is entitled to the respect granted like legislation enacted pursuant to the police power....

Objection is made that the Act by its exemption of certain classes of housing accommodations violates the Fifth Amendment. A similar argument was rejected under the Fourteenth Amendment when New York made like exemptions under the rent-control statute which was here for review in *Marcus Brown Holding Co. v. Feldman*....Certainly Congress is not under greater limitations. It need not control all rents or none. It can select those areas or those classes of property where the need seems the greatest....This alone is adequate answer to the objection, equally applicable to the original Act sustained in *Bowles v. Willingham* ... that the present Act lacks uniformity in application.

The fact that the property regulated suffers a decrease in value is not more fatal to the exercise of the war power ... than it is where the police power is invoked to the same end.

Affirmed.

Concurring opinion by Justice Jackson:

I agree with the result of this case, but the arguments that have been addressed to us lead me to utter more explicit misgivings about war powers than the Court has done. The Government asserts no constitutional basis for this legislation other than this vague, undefined and undefinable "war powers."

No one will question that this power is the most dangerous one to free government in the whole catalogue of powers. It usually is invoked in haste and excitement when calm legislative consideration of constitutional limitation is difficult. It is executed in a time of patriotic fervor that makes moderation unpopular. And, worse, it is interpreted by the judges under the influence of the same passions and pressures. Always, as in this case, the Government urges hasty decision to forestall some emergency or serve some purpose and pleads that paralysis will result if its claims to power are denied or their confirmation delayed [emphasis added].

Particularly when the war power is invoked to do things to the liberties of people, or to their property or economy that only indirectly affect conduct of the war and do not relate to the management of the war itself, the constitutional basis should be scrutinized with care.

I think we can hardly deny that the war power is as valid a ground for federal rent control now as it has been at any time. We still are technically in a state of war. I would not be willing to hold that war powers may be indefinitely prolonged merely by keeping legally alive a state of war that had in fact ended. I cannot accept the argument that war powers last as long as the effects and consequences of war for if so they are permanent—as permanent as the war debts. But I find no reason to conclude that we could find fairly that the present state of war is merely technical. We have armies abroad exercising our war power and have made no peace terms with our allies not to mention our principle enemies. I think the conclusion that the war power has been applicable during the lifetime of this legislation is unavoidable.

Note: In addition to all else ascribed to the war power it is a source of domestic legislative authority. The Court has ruled—for example, *Home Building & Loan Assoc. v. Blaisdell,* 290 U.S. 398, 426 (1934) and *United States v. Macintosh,* 283 U.S. 605, 622 (1931)—that the power to declare war implies the power to wage war and supports what is necessary and proper to wage war successfully. During World War II Congress totally mobilized the manpower and the resources of the country and regulated down to the smallest detail the lives of the people.

The war powers, moreover, do not begin with the declaration of war and do not end with the coming of peace. The power to declare and wage war implies power to prepare for war and to act to deter and prevent war. In fact, the power also allows the legislature/executive to deal with the aftermath and the consequences of war—by providing for the renegotiation of wartime contracts and the control of prices and rentals years after the fighting ended. *Woods* stands for the proposition that there is always "a war after the war," and the same economy that was regulated during the fighting can be regulated in the same way after peace has been declared. As *Woods* demonstrates, even in spite of Jackson's warning that there are lines that cannot be crossed, the Supreme Court has never declared any limit to the war powers during war or peace or even intimated where such limits might lie.

One year earlier, the Court had already rejected the contentions of private interests by holding that the war emergency had not come to an end. In *Fleming v. Mohawk Wrecking & Lumber Co.,* 331 U.S. 111 (1947), the Court denied that

President Truman's proclamation of a "cessation of hostilities" on December 31, 1947, had ended the state of war. Citing the earlier wartime cases of *Hamilton v. Kentucky Distilleries,* 251 U.S. 146 (1919) and *Stewart v. Kahn,* 78 U.S. (11 Wall.) 493 (1870), Justice Douglas said: "The cessation of hostilities does not necessarily end the war power....Whatever may be the reach of that power, it is plainly adequate to deal with problems of law enforcement which arise during the period of hostilities but do not cease with them." [331 U.S. at 116.] At issue was an executive order of December 2, 1946, consolidating the OPA and three other agencies into the Office of Temporary Controls. The order was issued under the authority of the First War Power Act of 1941 (55 Stat. 838), which granted the President the broad power of administrative reorganization "only in matters relating to the conduct of the present war" and "during the continuance of the present war and for six months after the termination of the war."

Once again we come full circle back to the warning articulated by Chief Justice Taney in *Luther v. Borden,* 48 U.S. (7 How.) 1 (1849). By the end of World War II the warning had become, if you cannot question the President's authority to decide when an emergency is over—or, at the opposite end, decide when an emergency begins—how can you ever question what he does during the emergency?

Ludecke v. Watkins, 335 U.S. 160; 92 L.Ed. 1881 (1948)

Petitioner, a German alien enemy, was arrested on December 8, 1941, and, after proceedings before an Alien Enemy Hearing Board on January 16, 1942, was interned by order the Attorney General, dated February 9, 1942. Under authority of the Alien Enemy Act of 1798, the President, on July 14, 1945, directed the removal from the United States of all alien enemies" who shall be deemed by the Attorney General to be dangerous to the public peace and safety of the United States" [Proclamation 2655, 10 Fed.Reg. 8947]. Accordingly, the Attorney General, on January 18, 1946, ordered petitioner's removal. Denial of a writ of habeas corpus for release from detention under this order was affirmed by the court below.

Basic Question: May the President order deportation of an enemy alien, under the terms of the Alien Enemy Act of 1798, three years after the fighting has ceased?

Opinion of the Court by Justice Frankfurter:

As Congress explicitly recognized in the recent Administrative Procedure Act, some statutes "preclude judicial review."...Barring questions of interpretation and constitutionality, the Alien Enemy Act of 1798 is such a statute. Its terms, purpose, and construction leave no doubt....The very nature of the President's power to order the removal of an enemy aliens rejects the notion that courts may pass judgment upon the exercise of his discretion....

The power with which Congress vested the President had to be executed by him through others. He provided for the removal of such enemy aliens as were "deemed by the Attorney General" to be dangerous. But such a finding, at the President's behest, was likewise not to be subjected to the scrutiny of the courts. A war power of the President not subject to judicial review is not transmuted into a judicially reviewable action because the President chooses to have that power exercised within narrower limits than Congress authorized....

...War does not cease with a cease-fire order, and power to be exercised by the President such as that conferred by the Act of 1798 is a process which begins when war is declared but is not exhausted when the shooting stops. ..."The state of war" may be terminated by treaty or legislation or Presidential proclamation. Whatever the mode, its termination is a political act. Whether and when it would be open to this Court to find that a war though merely formally kept alive had in fact ended, is a question too fraught with gravity even to be adequately formulated when not compelled. Only a few months ago the Court rejected the contention that the state of war in relation to which the President has exercised the authority now challenged was terminated. *Woods v. Cloyd W. Miller Co.,* 333 U.S. 138. Nothing that has happened since calls for a qualification of that view....

The political branch of the Government has not brought the war with Germany to an end. On the contrary, it has proclaimed that "a state of war still exists."...The Court would be assuming the functions of the political agencies of the Government to yield to the suggestion that the unconditional surrender of Germany and the disintegration of the Nazi Reich have left Germany without a government capable of negotiating a treaty of peace. It is not for us to question a belief by the President that enemy aliens who were justifiably deemed fit subjects for internment during active hostilities do not lose their potency for mischief during the period of confusion and conflict which is characteristic of a state of war even when the guns are silent but the peace of Peace has not come. These are matters of political judgment for which judges have neither technical competence nor official responsibility....

This brings us to the final question. Is the statute valid as we have construed it? The same considerations of reason, authority, and history, that led us to reject reading the statutory language "declared war" to mean "actual hostilities," support the validity of the statute. The war power is the war power. If the war, as we have held, has not in fact ended, so as to justify local rent control, a fortiori, it validly supports the power given to the President by the Act of 1798 in relation to alien enemies. Nor does it require protracted argument to find no defect in the Act because resort to the courts may be had only to challenge the construction and validity of the statute and to question the existence of the "declared war," as has been done in this case. The Act is almost as old as the Constitution, and it would savor of doctrinaire audacity now to find the statute offensive to some emanation of the Bill of Rights. The fact that hearing are utilized by the Executive to secure an informed basis for the exercise of summary power does not argue the right of courts to retry such hearings, nor bespeak denial of due process to withhold such power from the courts.

Such great war powers may be abused, no doubt, but that is a bad reason for having judges supervise their exercise, whatever the legal formulas within which such supervision would nominally be confined. In relation to the distribution of constitutional powers among the three branches of the Government, the optimistic Eighteenth Century language of Mr. Justice Iredell, speaking of this very Act, is still pertinent:

All systems of government suppose they are to be administered by men of common sense and common honesty. In our country, as all ultimately depends on the voice of the people, they have it in their power, and it is to be presumed they generally will choose men of this description; but if they will not, the case, to be sure, is without remedy. If they choose fools, they will have foolish laws. If they choose knaves, they will have knavish ones. But this can never be the case until they are generally fools or knaves themselves, which, thank God, is not likely ever to become the character of the American people. *Case of Fries*, 9 F. Cas. at 836 (No. 5126).

Accordingly, we hold that full responsibility for the just exercise of this great power may validly be left where the Congress has constitutionally placed it—on the President of the United States. The Founders in their wisdom made him not only the Commander-in-Chief but also the guiding organ in the conduct of our foreign affairs. He who was entrusted with such vast powers in relation to the outside world was also entrusted by Congress, almost throughout the whole life of the nation, with the disposition of alien enemies during a state of war.

Judgment affirmed and stay order entered February 2, 1948, vacated.

Note: Here, some three years after the fighting had ended, the Court was forced to consider the applicability of the Alien Enemy Act of 1798 (1 Stat. 577, as amended by 40 Stat. 531), which gave the President broad authority to restrain and remove alien enemies "wherever there is a declared war between the United

States and any foreign nation or government." In siding with the government's argument the majority in *Ludecke* clarified several points: (1) war does not cease with a cease-fire order—it is the President who determines when hostilities actually end, (2) war powers are "political," (3) the exercise of the President's discretion is not to be subjected to judicial review, and (4) courts cannot end wars. In effect, then, the war powers are treated differently from all other positive and discretionary powers found in the Constitution; and the Civil War, World War I, and World War II periods seem to suggest that we have one Constitution in peace and another in war.

The dissenters in *Ludecke* (Black, Douglas, Murphy, and Rutledge) once again argued that the war is over (really) and that the peacetime Constitution should apply. Yet even here the basic distinction is acknowledged—war and peace are not the same thing, and each must be governed by different rules— and, moreover, three of the four dissenters took active part in sustaining the constitutional dictatorship during World War II.

6

Cold War Cases

Youngstown Sheet & Tube Co. v. Sawyer, 343 U.S. 579; 96 L.Ed. 1153 (1952)

For the United States the cold war began in earnest with the decision to assume leadership of the free world against the threat of Communist expansion. This decision, impelled by a realization that postwar economic and political instability in the non-Communist nations might open the door to Soviet domination, was manifested first in President Harry S. Truman's proposal of the Greek-Turkish aid program in 1947 and then in two major programs for Western European economic and military defense—the Marshall Plan and the NATO Alliance. These initial moves were followed quickly by the development of a "containment policy" and the creation of a system of alliances encircling the globe. Tension between the free and Communist worlds was highest at those points where they confronted each other across a common border. The Thirty-eighth parallel in Korea was such a point, and it was there that the antagonism exploded in armed conflict on June 25, 1950.

President Truman responded to this challenge on his own initiative (he acted in the Lincolnian tradition) by ordering American forces to defend the invaded country. The President characterized this move as a "police action" designed to uphold the rule of international law, and it was quickly given international sanction through a UN resolution. But in fact he had committed the United States, and its allies, to war. Viewing the American Presidency as the focal position of the free world alliance, and American military power as the principle instrument for preserving Western security and global peace, he had acted as both American and Western chief executive and commander-in-chief to meet the national and international emergency. [R. Hirschfield, The Constitution and the Court 168-69 (1962).] America's new position of global responsibility had expanded the President's authority into new and uncharted areas of action.

The President had not declared the existence of a "national emergency" after the Communist attack, nor had he requested Congress to ratify his initial actions.

He did address the legislators on July 10, however, at which time (in addition to a request for funds) he asked for the delegation of limited powers to allocate and determine priorities for scarce materials, to stabilize wages and prices, and to requisition property essential to the war effort. He also asked Congress to consider tax increases and other measures to prevent inflation, and he hinted at the possible need for price control and rationing. However, reflecting both a recognition of hostility to his domestic policies in the Republican-dominated legislature and a desire to limit the emergency's impact on American society, the President did not seek the delegation of vast war power. [*Id.* at 169.] Nor did Congress insist on greater participation in the crisis regime. The conflict had begun as a "presidential war" and so it would remain.

In December 1950, Communist China entered the conflict, and the crisis became even more serious than before. Although President Truman decided to maintain the policy of limited war in Korea, despite this change in circumstances, the Chinese intervention led him to proclaim the formal existence of a national emergency on December 16, 1950. The proclamation was designed to accomplish two purposes: it automatically activated over sixty statutes applicable to emergency periods as well as laying the base for resort to other forms of presidential authority, and it emphasized for both Congress and the Nation the dangers of the new situation. The President's action was attacked by his opponents in Congress as an unnecessary and "dictatorial" move to expand executive power, but the popular reaction was not unfavorable, and Congress did not attempt to repeal any of the measures which had been reactivated or to impose limitations on the exercise of presidential power. [*Id.* at 170].

The *Steel Seizure Case* arose out of a long and bitter labor-management dispute resulting in the issuance of a strike notice by the United Steelworkers in December 1951. Attempts by federal mediation agencies failed to achieve a settlement, and President Truman refused to invoke the "cooling-off period" provisions of the Taft-Hartley Act (61 Stat. 136), which he regarded as an antilabor measure and which had been repassed by Congress over his veto in 1947. The union postponed its first strike call at the President's request, but when the settlement efforts failed, it set a nationwide walkout for April 9, 1952.

To avert this strike, President Truman, on April 8, issued Executive Order 10340, directing Secretary of Commerce Sawyer to seize and operate the country's steel plants. Citing the existence of a national emergency, and asserting that a work stoppage in the steel industry would jeopardize and imperil the national defense, the President based the seizure order on his inherent power under "the Constitution and laws of the United States, and as President of the United States and Commander-in-Chief of the armed forces."

The next day Truman informed Congress of his action and, in effect, requested its approval and support. But neither then nor two weeks later when he again asked for congressional participation in the affair did the legislature enter the controversy. Meanwhile, the steel companies had sought a temporary restraining order from the District of Columbia district court. Their request was denied on the ground that no evidence of irreparable injury had been presented and that "to issue a restraining order ... and in effect to nullify an order of the

President of the United States, promulgated by him to meet a nationwide emergency problem is something that the court should not do, unless there is some very vital reason for the court stepping in." [*Youngstown,* 103 F.Supp. 978, 981 (D.D.C. 1952).] But on a second try in the same court, a different judge, noting that the issue which had been raised "requires a discussion of the fundamental principles of constitutional government," denounced the President's action as unconstitutional and granted a preliminary injunction. [103 F.Supp. 569, 573 (D.D.C. 1952).] This injunction was stayed by the Court of Appeals because five of its members considered the issue to be of such importance that the Supreme Court should make a determination, 197 F.2d 582 (D.C. Cir. 1952), and on May 3 the high court granted certiorari. One month later—and only nine weeks after the seizure order had been issued—a "majority" opinion, five concurrences, and a three-man dissent were announced.

Basic Question: Is the seizure order within the constitutional power of the President?

Opinion of the Court by Justice Black:

We are asked to decide whether the President was acting within his constitutional power when he issued an order directing the secretary of Commerce to take possession of and operate most of the Nation's steel mills. The mill owners argue that the President's order amounts to law-making, a legislative function which the Constitution has expressly confided to the Congress and not to the President. The Government's position is that the order was made on findings of the President that his action was necessary to avert a national catastrophe which would inevitably result from a stoppage of steel production, and that in meeting this grave emergency the President was acting within the aggregate of his constitutional powers as the Nation's Chief Executive and the Commander in Chief of the Armed Forces of the United States....

The President's power, if any, to issue the order must stem either from an act of Congress or from the Constitution itself. There is no statute that expressly authorizes the President to take possession of property as he did here. Nor is there any act of Congress to which our attention has been directed from which such a power can fairly be implied....

Moreover, the use of the seizure technique to solve labor disputes in order to prevent work stoppages was not only unauthorized by any congressional enactment; prior to this controversy, Congress had refused to adopt that method of settling labor disputes. When the Taft-Hartley Act was under consideration in 1947, Congress rejected an amendment which would have authorized such governmental seizures in cases of emergency....Instead, the plan sought to bring about settlements by use of the customary devices of mediation, conciliation, [and] investigation by boards of inquiry....In some instances temporary injunctions were authorized to provide cooling-off periods. All this failing, unions were left free to strike after a secret vote by employees as to whether they wished to accept their employers' final settlement offer.

It is clear that if the President had authority to issue the order he did, it must be found in some provisions of the Constitution. And it is not claimed that express constitutional language grants this power to the President. The contention is that presidential power should be implied from the aggregate of his powers under the Constitution. Particular reliance is placed on provisions in Article II which say that "the executive Power shall be vested in a President ..."; that "he shall take Care that the Laws be faithfully executed"; and that he "shall be Commander in Chief of the Army and Navy of the United States."

The order cannot properly be sustained as an exercise of the President's military power as Commander in Chief of the Armed Forces. The Government attempts to do so by citing a number of cases upholding broad powers in military commanders engaged in day-to-day fighting in a theater of war. Such cases need not concern us here. Even though "theater of war" be an expanding concept, we cannot with faithfulness to our constitutional system hold that the Commander in Chief of the armed Forces has the ultimate power as such to take possession of private property in order to keep labor disputes from stopping production. This is a job for the Nation's lawmakers, not for its military authorities.

Nor can the seizure order be sustained because of the several constitutional provisions that grant executive power to the President. In the framework of our Constitution, the President's power to see that the laws are faithfully executed refutes the idea that he is to be a lawmaker. The Constitution limits his functions in the lawmaking process to the recommending of laws he thinks wise and the vetoing the laws he thinks bad. And the Constitution is neither silent nor equivocal about who shall make laws which the President is to execute....

The President's order does not direct that a congressional policy be executed in a manner prescribed by Congress—it directs that a presidential policy be executed in a manner prescribed by the President. The preamble of the order itself, like that of many statutes, sets out reasons why the President believes certain policies should be adopted, proclaims these policies as rules of conduct to be followed, and again, like a statute, authorizes a government official to promulgate additional rules and regulations consistent with the policy proclaimed and needed to carry that policy into execution. The power of Congress to adopt such public policies as those proclaimed by the order is beyond question. It can authorize the taking of private property for public use. It can make laws regulating the relationships between employers and employees, prescribing rules designed to settle labor disputes, and fixing wages and working conditions in certain fields of our economy. The Constitution did not subject this law-making power of Congress to presidential or military supervision or control.

It is said that other Presidents without congressional authority have taken possession of private business enterprises in order to settle labor disputes. But even if this be true, Congress has not thereby lost its exclusive constitutional authority to make laws necessary and proper to carry out the powers vested by the Constitution "in the Government of the United States, or in any Department or Officer thereof."

The Founders of this Nation entrusted the law making power to the Congress alone in both good and bad times. It would do no good to recall the historical events, the fears of power and the hopes for freedom that lay behind their choice. Such a review would but confirm our holding that this seizure order cannot stand.

The judgment of the District Court is affirmed.

Concurring opinion by Justice Jackson:
...We may well begin by a somewhat over-simplified grouping of practical

situations in which a President may doubt, or others may challenge, his powers, and by distinguishing roughly the legal consequences of this fact of relativity.

1.   When the President acts pursuant to an express or implied authorization of Congress, his authority is at its maximum, for it includes all that he possesses in his own right plus all that Congress can delegate. In these circumstances, and in these only, may he be said (for what it may be worth), to personify the federal sovereignty.   If his act is held unconstitutional under these circumstances, it usually means that the Federal Government as an undivided whole lacks power. A seizure executed by the President pursuant to an Act of Congress would be supported by the strongest of presumptions and the widest latitude of judicial interpretation, and the burden of persuasion would rest heavily upon any who might attack it.

2.   When the President acts in absence of either a congressional grant or denial of authority, he can only rely upon his own independent powers, but there is a zone of twilight in which he and Congress may have concurrent authority, or in which its distribution is uncertain.   Therefore, congressional inertia, indifference or quiescence may sometimes, at least as a practical matter, enable, if not invite, measures on independent presidential responsibility.   In this area, any actual test of power is likely to depend on the imperatives of events and contemporary imponderables rather than on abstract theories of law.

3.   When the President takes measures incompatible with the expressed or implied will of the Congress, his power is at its lowest ebb, for then he can rely only upon his own constitutional powers minus any constitutional powers of Congress over the matter.   Courts can sustain exclusive Presidential control in such a case only by disabling the Congress from acting upon the subject. Presidential claim to a power at once so conclusive and preclusive must be scrutinized with caution, for what is at stake is the equilibrium established by our constitutional system.

Into which of these classifications does this executive seizure of the steel industry fit? It is eliminated from the first by admission, for it is conceded that no congressional authorization exists for this seizure....Can it then be defended under flexible tests available to the second category? It seems clearly eliminated from that class because Congress has not left seizure of private property an open field but has covered it by three statutory policies inconsistent with this seizure....This leaves the current seizure to be justified only by the severe tests under the third grouping, where it can be supported only by any remainder of executive power after subtractions of such powers as Congress may have over the subject.   In short, we can sustain the President only by holding that seizure of such strike-bound industries is within his domain and beyond control by Congress.   Thus, this Court's first review of such seizures occurs under circumstances which leave Presidential power most vulnerable to attack and in the least favorable of possible constitutional postures....

Dissenting opinion by Chief Justice Vinson (concurred in by Justices Reed and Minton):
          ...Because we cannot agree that affirmance is proper on any ground, and because of the transcending importance of the questions presented not only

in this critical litigation but also to the powers the President and of future Presidents to act in time of crisis, we are compelled to register this dissent.

In passing upon the question of Presidential powers in this case, we must first consider the context in which those powers were exercised.

Those who suggest that this is a case involving extraordinary powers should be mindful that these are extra-ordinary times....The President has the duty to execute the foregoing legislative programs [designed to support the Korean action]. Their successful execution depends upon continued production of steel and stabilized prices for steel. Accordingly, when ... a strike shutting down the entire basic steel industry was threatened, the President acted to avert a complete shut-down of steel production....

Accordingly, if the President has any power under the Constitution to meet a critical situation in the absence of express statutory authorization, there is no basis whatever for criticizing the exercise of such power in this case....Admitting that the Government could seize the mills, plaintiffs claim that the implied power of eminent domain can be exercised only under an Act of Congress; under no circumstances, they say, can that power be exercised by the President unless he can point to an express provision in enabling legislation....Under this view, the President is left powerless at the very moment when the need for action may be most pressing and when no one, other than he, is immediately capable of action. Under this view, he is left powerless because a power not expressly given to Congress is nevertheless found to rest exclusively with Congress....

A review of executive action demonstrates that our Presidents have on many occasions exhibited the leadership contemplated by the Framers when they made the President Commander in Chief, and imposed upon him the trust to "take care that the Laws be faithfully executed." With or without explicit statutory authorization, Presidents have at such times dealt with national emergencies by acting promptly and resolutely to enforce legislative programs, at least to save those programs until Congress could act. Congress and the courts have responded to such executive initiative with consistent approval....

This is but a cursory summary of executive leadership. But it amply demonstrates that Presidents have taken prompt action to enforce the laws and protect the country whether or not Congress happened to provide in advance for the particular method of execution. At the minimum, the executive actions reviewed herein sustain the action of the President in this case. And many of the cited examples of Presidential practices go far beyond the extent of power necessary to sustain the President's order to seize the steel mills. The fact that temporary executive seizures of industrial plants to meet an emergency have not been directly tested in this Court furnishes not the slightest suggestion that such actions have been illegal. Rather, the fact that Congress and the courts have consistently recognized and given their support to such executive action indicates that such a power of seizure has been accepted throughout our history....

Much of the argument in this case has been directed at straw men. We do not now have before us the case of a President acting solely on the basis of his own notions of the public welfare. Nor is there any question of unlimited executive power in this case. The President himself closed the door to any such claim when he sent his Message to Congress stating his purpose to abide by any action of Congress, whether approving or disapproving his seizure action. Here, the President immediately made sure that Congress was fully informed of the temporary action he had taken only to preserve the legislative programs from destruction until Congress could act....

The diversity of views expressed in the six opinions of the majority, the lack of reference to authoritative precedent, the repeated reliance upon prior dissenting opinions, the complete disregard of the uncontroverted facts showing the gravity of the emergency and the temporary nature of the taking all serve to demonstrate how far afield one must go to affirm the order of the District Court.

The broad executive power granted by Article II to an officer on duty 365 days a year cannot, it is said, be invoked to avert disaster. Instead, the President must confine himself to sending a message to Congress recommending action. Under this messenger-boy [or magistrate] concept of the Office, the President cannot even act to preserve legislative programs from destruction so that Congress will have something left to act upon. There is no judicial finding that the executive action was unwarranted because there was in fact no basis for the President's finding of the existence of an emergency for, under this view, the gravity of the emergency and the immediacy of the threatened disaster are considered irrelevant as a matter of law....

...Presidents have been in the past, and any man worthy of the Office should be in the future, free to take at least interim action necessary to execute legislative programs essential to survival of the Nation. A sturdy judiciary should not be swayed by the unpleasantness of unpopularity of necessary executive action, but must independently determine for itself whether the President was acting, as required by the Constitution, to "take Care that the Laws be faithfully executed."...

Note: Marking only the second time since the post-Civil War era that a presidential resort to emergency power had been struck down, and the first time the Supreme Court has taken such action while a declared emergency was in existence, the *Youngstown* decision should be regarded as a "significant" commentary on American crisis government. [R. Hirschfield, 184.] But its importance as a viable limitation on presidential power should not be overstated; and the "opinions" of the Court avoided the main issue and the case may be rightfully referred to—in Corwin's words, as a "judicial brick without straw." [Corwin, The Steel Seizure Case: A Judicial Brick without Straw, 53 Colum. L. Rev. 53 (1953).]

The decision itself reflected neither a deep division on the Court, nor a significant departure from its previous position on emergency rule. There can be no doubt that the seizure would have been upheld if Congress and the President has agreed on its necessity; and there was every likelihood that even as an independent action it would have been upheld if legislation directly related to the situation had not existed. [R. Hirschfield, 184-85.] For four of the majority justices the crux of the matter (and their principle point of disagreement with the minority) was that Congress had taken a definite stand against the use of the seizure technique in labor-management disputes—and had thereby precluded the exercise of discretionary power by the President. But with the minority's basic contention that the President during critical periods possessed a residium of authority in addition to (or as a consequence of) his specific constitutional powers, and that in the absence of explicitly restrictive legislation he was free to exercise such authority as he deemed necessary for the national defense—on these crucial points, at least four of the majority indicated agreement. [*Id.* at 185.]

Thus both the vote and the holding in *Youngstown* were deceptive. There was a wide (though unstated) area of agreement on the fundamental issue, and in terms of limiting executive authority in time of crisis, the decision's applicability to future situations was doubtful. The holding—and the reasoning sustaining it—was illogical and self-refuting. Since Congress could have ordered the seizure of the steel mills, the President lacked the power to seize them without congressional authorization. That was separation of powers theory; but the majority pushed it further than it was capable of going. According to Corwin,

If the principle of the Separation of Powers prevents the President from doing anything that Congress may do, then by the same token it bars the Supreme Court from doing anything that Congress may do. Yet everybody conceded that Congress could have ended the seizure of the steel mills at any time—precisely what the Supreme Court undertook to do in this case! [E. Corwin, The President: Office and Powers 155 (4th ed. 1957)].

Moreover, certain circumstances peculiar to the case limited its effect on presidential power: the absence of firm popular support for the President's action and the hostility to him in Congress. By the time the case was argued truce talks were beginning to make progress; the emergency in Korea had passed its most critical stage. Had the circumstances been different or had the danger seemed more immediate, it was unlikely that the justices would have written even the cautious opinions that they did. [R. Hirschfield, 185.]

What was most significant about *Youngstown* was that by 1952—after so long a period of recurrent national emergencies—the Supreme Court had once again seized an opportunity to speak the language of constitutional limitation. For it was by then evident that the United States had entered an era in which crisis would be the "normal" condition of the Nation's life, and that a major casualty of this era might be the Constitution itself. The impact of the cold war on the Constitution had already been felt in the increasing activity of congressional investigating committees, in the executive's establishment of a loyalty-security program, in the emergence of McCarthyism, and in the Court's own decision in *Dennis v. United States,* 341 U.S. 494 (1951), broadening the restrictive power of government over freedom of political belief and expression. If the Court had acquiesced in the President's resort to extraordinary power in *Youngstown,* as it had acquiesced in the face of emergency since 1933, it would have extended into an indefinite period of protracted emergency the wartime concept of unlimited governmental power, and thereby dealt another—and perhaps even fatal—blow to the basic law. [*Id.* at 186.] Remember, wartime government on a permanent basis would mean the end of constitutional rule and the freedom which it guarantees.

One last point: in his dissenting opinion, the Chief Justice—where he reviewed the occasions on which Presidents from Washington to Roosevelt exercised emergency power without congressional authorization—quoted from a statement made by John W. Davis as Solicitor General of the United States in *United States v. Midwest Oil Co.,* 236 U.S. 459 (1915), and in 1952 chief counsel for the steel companies:

The function of making laws is peculiar to Congress, and the Executive cannot exercise that function to any degree. But this is not to say that all of the subjects concerning which laws might be made are perforce removed from the possibility of Executive influence. The Executive may act upon things and upon men in many relations which have not, though they might have, been actually regulated by Congress. In other words, just as there are field which are peculiar to Congress and ... to the Executive, so there are fields which are common to both, in the sense that the Executive may move within them until they shall have been occupied by legislative action....This situation results from the fact that the President is the active agent, not of Congress, but of the Nation....He is the agent of the people of the United States, deriving all his power from them and responsible directly to them. In no sense is he the agent of Congress....Therefore it follows that in ways short of making laws or disobeying them, the Executive may be under a grave constitutional duty to act for the national protection in situations not covered by the acts of Congress, and in which, even, it may not be said that his action is the direct expression of any particular one of the independent powers which are granted to him specifically by the Constitution. Instances wherein the President has felt and fulfilled such a duty have not been rare in our history, though, being for the public benefit and approved by all, his acts have seldom been challenged in the courts. [343 U.S. at 690-91.]

The lesson of the case, practically speaking, was that just as nature abhors a vacuum, so does the age of emergency. Let Congress see to it that no such vacuum occurs.

United States ex rel. Toth v. Quarles, 350 U.S. 11; 100 L.Ed. 8 (1955)

The great increase in the number of civilian and military officials of the United States on duty in all parts of the world makes relevant a consideration of the problem of the Constitution following the flag. Does the Bill of Rights define the obligations of an American official toward American military personnel or civilians abroad? If the entire Constitution is not controlling under these circumstances, is a standard of due process in force? Has an American official a lower obligatory standard of conduct toward foreign nationals? Does it make a difference whether the United States official acts on leased American property abroad or in territory occupied by American forces? What if the occupation is conducted jointly with other nations? If the Constitution defines the duties of American officials overseas, what agency of the Government enforces it? The judiciary? Or the executive alone?

After serving with the United States Air Force in Korea, Robert W. Toth was honorably discharged. He returned to his home in Pittsburgh. Five months later he was arrested by military authorities on charges of murder and conspiracy to commit murder while an airman in Korea. The charges were violations of Articles 118 and 81 of the Uniform Code of Military Justice (64 Stat. 140, 134). At the time of his arrest he had no relationship of any kind with the military. He was taken to Korea to stand trial before a court-martial under authority of a 1950 Act of Congress (64 Stat. 109). The Court of Appeals for the District of Columbia sustained the Act, rejecting the contention that civilian ex-servicemen like Toth could not constitutionally be subjected to trial by court-martial. The Supreme Court granted certiorari.

Basic Question: Can a discharged serviceman be subjected to court-martial for offenses committed in the service?

Opinion of the Court by Justice Black:

The 1950 Act cannot be sustained on the constitutional power of Congress "To raise and support Armies," "To declare War," or to punish "Offenses against the Law of Nations."...And this assertion of military authority over civilians cannot rest on the President's power as commander-in-chief, or on any theory of martial law....The Government's contention is that the Act is a valid exercise of the power granted Congress in Article I of the Constitution "To make Rules for the Government and Regulation of the land and naval Forces," as supplemented by the Necessary and Proper Clause.

The Court has held that the Article I clause ... authorizes Congress to subject persons actually in the armed service to trial by court-martial for military and naval offenses. Later it was held that court-martial jurisdiction could be exerted over a dishonorably discharged soldier then a military prisoner serving a sentence imposed by a prior court-martial. It has never been intimated by this Court, however, that Article I military jurisdiction could be extended to civilian ex-soldiers who had severed all relationship with the military and its institutions. To allow this extension of military authority would require an extremely broad construction of the language used in the constitutional provision relied on. For given it natural meaning, the power granted Congress ... would seem to restrict court-martial jurisdiction to persons who are actually members or part of the armed forces. There is a compelling reason for construing the clause this way: any expansion of court-martial jurisdiction like that in the 1950 Act necessarily encroaches on the jurisdiction of federal courts set up under Article III of the Constitution where persons on trial are surrounded with more constitutional safeguards than in military tribunals.

Article III provides for the establishment of a court system as one of the separate but coordinate branches of the National Government. It is the primary, indeed the sole business of these courts to try cases and controversies between individuals and between individuals and the Government. This includes trial of criminal cases....

We find nothing in the history or constitutional treatment of military tribunals which entitles them to rank along with Article III courts as adjudicators of the guilt or innocence of people charged with offenses for which they can be deprived of their life, liberty or property. Unlike courts, it is the primary business of armies and navies to fight or be ready to fight wars should the occasion arise. But trial of soldiers to maintain discipline is merely incidental to an army's primary fighting function....And conceding to military personnel that high degree of honesty and sense of justice which nearly all of them undoubtedly have, it still remains true that military tribunals have not been and probably never can be constituted in such a way that they can have the same kind of qualifications that the Constitution has deemed essential to fair trials of civilians in federal courts....

Moreover, there is a great difference between trial by jury and trial by selected members of the military forces....

The 1950 Act here considered deprives of jury trial and sweeps under military jurisdiction over 3,000,000 persons who have become veterans since the Act became effective....[This figure points] up what would be the enormous scope of a holding that Congress could subject every ex-serviceman and woman in the land to trial by court-martial for any alleged offense committed while he or she had been a member of the armed forces. Every veteran discharged since passage of the 1950 Act is subject to military trial for any offense punishable by as much as five years' imprisonment unless the offense is now punishable in a civilian court....

None of the ... reasons suggested by the Government are sufficient to justify a broad construction of the constitutional grant of power to Congress to regulate the armed forces. That provision itself does not empower Congress to deprive people of trials under Bill of Rights safeguards, and we are not willing to hold that power to circumvent those safeguards should be inferred through the Necessary and Proper Clause. It is impossible to think that the discipline of the Army is going to be disrupted, its morale impaired, or its orderly process disturbed, by giving ex-servicemen the benefit of a civilian court trial when they are actually civilians....

There are dangers lurking in military trials which were sought to be avoided by the Bill of Rights and Article III of our Constitution. Free countries of the world have tried to restrict military tribunals to the narrowest jurisdiction deemed absolutely essential to maintaining discipline among troops in active service. Even as late as the Seventeenth Century standing armies and court-martial were not established institutions in England. Court-martial jurisdiction sprang from the belief that within the military ranks there is need for a prompt, ready-at-hand means of compelling obedience and order. But Army discipline will not be improved by court-martialing rather than trying by jury some civilian ex-soldier who has been wholly separated from the service for months, years or perhaps decades. Consequently considerations of discipline provide no excuse for new expansion of court-martial jurisdiction at the expense of the normal and constitutionally preferable system of trial by jury.

Determining the scope of the constitutional power of Congress to authorize trial by court-martial presents another instance calling for limitations to "the least possible power adequate to the end proposed." We hold that Congress cannot subject civilians like Toth to trial by court-martial. They, like other civilians, are entitled to have the benefit of safeguards afforded those tried in the regular courts authorized by Article III of the Constitution.

Reversed.

Note: One simple answer to the problem—often suggested but never approved—would be for Congress to provide for holding terms of United States district courts overseas, for the trial of dependents of the armed forces, and of civilian employees, thus affording the protections of Article III and the Fifth and Sixth Amendments. [*See* Sutherland, The Constitution, the Civilian, and Military Justice, 36 St. John's L.Rev. 215 (1961).]

Toth may be added to a long line of decisions, dating back to *Ex parte Milligan,* 71 U.S. (4 Wall.) 2 (1866), that denies the military establishment (*i.e.,* the President) legal authority to try civilians before courts-martial or military tribunals. Absent the overriding justification of war, rebellion, or national emergency, the Constitution (peacetime version) does apply.

Reid v. Covert, 354 U.S. 1; 1 L.Ed.2d 1148 (1957)

Clarice Covert killed her husband, a sergeant in the U.S. Air Force, at an airbase in England. Mrs. Covert, who was not a member of the armed services, was residing on the base with her husband at the time. She was tried by a court-martial for murder under Article 118 of the Uniform Code of Military Justice (UCMJ). The trial was on charges preferred by Air Force personnel and the court-martial was composed of Air Force officers.

Counsel for Mrs. Covert contended that she was insane at the time she killed her husband, but the military tribunal found her guilty of murder and sentenced her to life imprisonment. The judgment was affirmed by the Air Force Board of Review, but was reversed by the Court of Military Appeals because of prejudicial errors concerning the defense of insanity. While Mrs. Covert was being held in this country pending a proposed retrial by court-martial in the District of Columbia, her counsel petitioned the District Court for a writ of habeas corpus to set her free on the grounds that the constitution forbade her trial by military authorities. Construing *United States ex rel. Toth v. Quarles* as holding that "a civilian is entitled to a civilian trial," the District Court held that Mrs. Covert could not be tried by court-martial and ordered her release from custody. The Government appealed directly to the Supreme Court.

During the previous term a majority of the Supreme Court, with three Justices dissenting and one reserving opinion, held that the military trial of Mrs. Covert was constitutional. [*Reid v. Covert,* 351 U.S. 470 (1956).] The majority held that the provisions of Article III and the Fifth and Sixth Amendments, which require that crimes be tried by a jury after indictment by a grand jury, did not protect an American citizen when tried by the American Government in foreign lands for offenses committed there and that Congress could provide for the trial of such offenses in any manner it saw fit so long as the procedures established were reasonable and consonant with due process.

Basic Question: Can Congress, under Article 118 of the Uniform Code of Military Justice (UCMJ), legally order the court-martial trial of a civilian military dependent?

Opinion of the Court by Justice Black:

These cases raise basic constitutional issues of the utmost concern. They call into question the role of the military under our system of government. They involve the power of Congress to expose civilians to trial by military tribunals, under military regulations and procedures, for offenses against the United States thereby depriving them of trial in civilian courts, under civilian laws and procedures and with all the safeguards of the Bill of Rights. These cases are particularly significant because for the first time since the adoption of the Constitution wives of soldiers have been denied trial by jury in a court of law and forced to trial before courts-martial....

At the beginning we reject the idea that when the United States acts against citizens abroad it can do so free of the Bill of Rights. The United States is entirely a creature of the Constitution. Its power and authority have no other source. It can only act in accordance with all the limitations imposed by the Constitution. When the Government reaches out to punish a citizen who is abroad, the shield which the Bill of Rights and other parts of the Constitution provide to protect his life and liberty should not be stripped away just because he happens to be in another land. This is not a novel concept. To the contrary, it is as old as government....The rights and liberties which citizens of our country enjoy are not protected by custom and tradition alone, they have been jealously preserved from the encroachments of Government by express provisions of our written Constitution....

The keystone of supporting authorities mustered by the Court's opinion last June to justify its holding that Art. III, sec. 2, and the Fifth and Sixth Amendments did not apply abroad was *In re Ross*, 140 U.S. 453. The *Ross* case is one of those cases that cannot be understood except in its peculiar setting; even then, it seems highly unlikely that a similar result would be reached today....The *Ross* approach that the Constitution has no applicability abroad has long since been directly repudiated by numerous cases. That approach is obviously erroneous if the United States Government, which has no power except that granted by the Constitution, can and does try citizens for crimes committed abroad. Thus the *Ross* case rested, at least in substantial part, on a fundamental misconception and the most that can be said in support of the result reached there is that the consular court jurisdiction had a long history antedating the adoption of the Constitution. The Congress has recently buried the consular system of trying Americans. We are not willing to jeopardize the lives and liberties of Americans by disinterring it. At best, the *Ross* case should be left as a relic from a different era.

The Court's opinion last Term also relied on the *Insular Cases* [95 U.S. 138] to support its conclusion that Article III and the Fifth and Sixth Amendments were not applicable to the trial of ... Mrs. Covert. We believe that reliance was misplaced. The Insular Cases, which arose at the turn of the century, involved territories which had only recently been conquered or acquired by the United States. These territories, governed and regulated by Congress under Art. IV, sec. 3, had entirely different cultures and customs from those of this country. This Court, although closely divided, ruled that certain constitutional safeguards were not applicable to those territories since they had not been "expressly or implicitly incorporated" into the Union by Congress. While conceding that "fundamental" constitutional rights applied everywhere, the majority found that it would disrupt long-established practices and would be inexpedient to require a jury trial after an indictment by a grand jury in the insular possessions.

The *Insular Cases* can be distinguished from the present cases in that they involve the power of Congress to provide rules and regulations to govern temporarily territories with wholly dissimilar traditions and institutions whereas here the basis for governmental power is American citizenship. None of these cases had anything to do with military trials and they cannot properly be used as vehicles to support an extension of military jurisdiction to civilians. Moreover, it is our judgment that neither the cases nor their reasoning should be given any further expansion. The concept that the Bill of Rights and other constitutional protections against arbitrary government are inoperative when they become inconvenient or when expediency dictates otherwise in a very dangerous doctrine and if allowed to flourish would destroy the benefit of a written Constitution and undermine the basis of our government....

There is nothing new or unique about what we say here. This Court has regularly and uniformly recognized the supremacy of the Constitution over a treaty....This Court has also repeatedly taken the position that an Act of Congress, which must comply with the Constitution, is on a full parity with a treaty, and that when a statute which is subsequent in time is inconsistent with a treaty, the statute to the extent of conflict renders the treaty null. It would be completely anomalous to say that a treaty need not comply with the Constitution when such an agreement can be overridden by a statute that must conform to that instrument.

There is nothing in ... *Missouri v. Holland*, 252 U.S. 416, which is contrary to the position taken here. There the Court carefully noted that the treaty involved was not inconsistent with any specific provision of the Constitution. The Court was concerned with the Tenth Amendment which reserves to the States or the people all power not delegated to the National Government. To the extent that the United States can validly make treaties, the people and the States have delegated their power to the National Government and the Tenth Amendment is no barrier.

In summary, we conclude that the Constitution in its entirety applied to the [trial of Mrs. Covert]. Since [her] court-martial did not meet the requirements of Article III, sec. 2, or the Fifth and Sixth Amendments we are compelled to determine if there is anything within the Constitution which authorizes the military trial of dependents accompanying the armed forces overseas....

The *Milligan, Duncan* and *Toth* cases recognized and manifested the deeply rooted and ancient opposition in this country to the extension of military control over civilians. In each instance an effort to expand the jurisdiction of military courts to civilians was repulsed....

It is urged that the expansion of military jurisdiction over civilians claimed here is only slight, and that the practical necessity for it is very great. The attitude appears to be that a slight encroachment on the Bill of Rights and other safeguards in the Constitution need cause little concern. But to hold that these wives could be tried by the military would be a tempting precedent. Slight encroachments create new boundaries from which legions of power can seek new territory to capture....Moreover we cannot consider this encroachment a slight one. Throughout history many transgressions by the military have been called "slight" and have been justified as "reasonable" in light of the "uniqueness" of the times. We cannot close our eyes to the fact that today the peoples of many nations are ruled by the military....

Ours is a government of divided authority on the assumption that in division there is not only strength but freedom from tyranny. And under our Constitution courts of law alone are given power to try civilians for their offenses against the United States....

In No. 701, *Reid v. Covert*, the judgment of the District Court directing that Mrs. Covert be released from custody is affirmed.

Note: The reversing of the earlier holding in *Reid v. Covert,* 351 U.S. 470 (1956), came about in part as a result of the retirement of two justices (Reed and Minton), two justices who changed their minds (Frankfurter and Harlen), and the appointment of Justice Brennan. [C. Rossiter, The Supreme Court and the Commander in Chief 156 (R. Longaker ed. 1976).] *Reid* stands out among a line of important cases imposing judicial control over military trials and, more broadly, civilian control over the military. To *Milligan, Duncan, Toth,* and *Reid,* can also be added *McElroy v. United States ex rel. Guagliardo,* 361 U.S. 281 (1960) and *Grisham v. Hagan,* 361 U.S. 278 (1960) [American civilian employees of the armed forces cannot be tried by military courts for capital or noncapital offenses], *Latney v. Ignatius,* 416 F.2d 821 (D.C. Cir. 1969) and *United States v. Averette,* U.S.M.C.A. 363 (1970) [efforts to apply a "time of war" exception in the legislation for the trial of civilians during the Vietnam war were rejected], and *O'Callahan v. Parker,* 395 U.S. 258 (1969) [for a crime to be within military jurisdiction it must be service connected]. *Cf. Parker v. Levy,* 417 U.S. 733 (1974) and *Wilson v. Girard,* 354 U.S. 524 (1957).

Reid also stands for the proposition that treaties and executive agreements cannot be used to limit the application of the Bill of Rights. Indeed, while not undermining the rationale of *Belmont* and *Pink*—which concluded that a President has independent power to make executive agreements—the majority in *Reid* established that there were limitations emanating from the Bill of Rights; and it staked a claim for the judiciary in determining those limitations. As for Congress, fifteen years passed after the *Reid* decision before concern about executive discretion produced a constructive reaction. In 1972 Congress passed a mild measure requiring that all executive agreements be reported to Congress within sixty days (Pub.L. No. 92-403).

Dames & Moore v. Regan, 453 U.S. 654; 69 L.Ed.2d 918 (1981)

Following the seizure of the American Embassy in Tehran on November 4, 1979, which resulted in the capture and holding hostage of our diplomatic personnel by the Iranians, President Jimmy Carter ordered a freeze on the removal and transfer of all assets held by the Iranian government or its instrumentalities within American jurisdiction. On the day the Carter Administration left office, the hostages were released by Iran pursuant to an agreement under which the United States was obliged "to terminate all legal proceedings in United States courts involving claims of United States persons and institutions against Iran and its state enterprises, to nullify all attachments and judgments obtained therein, [and] to prohibit all future litigation based on these claims." In addition, the United States was to transfer all Iranian assets held in this country by the following July. A billion dollars of these assets were to be transferred to a security account in the Bank of England to be used to satisfy awards rendered against Iran by an Iran-United States Claims Tribunal. The day before his term of office ended, President Carter implemented the terms of the agreement through several Executive Orders which revoked all licenses permitting the exercise of power over Iranian assets, nullified all non-Iranian interests in the assets, and required banks holding Iranian funds to transfer them to the Federal Reserve Bank of New York to be held or transferred at the direction of the Secretary of the Treasury. Five weeks later, these orders were reaffirmed by the incoming Reagan Administration.

Petitioner, which had obtained a prejudgment attachment of assets of certain Iranian banks, brought an action against the Secretary of Treasury seeking to prevent enforcement of the various executive orders and regulations implementing the hostage release agreement with Iran. The District Court for the Central District of California dismissed the complaint for failure to state a claim upon which relief could be granted. Appeal was taken to the Court of Appeals for the Ninth Circuit, but before judgment was reached the Supreme Court granted certiorari on an expedited basis.

Basic Question: Is the agreement concluded with Iran to terminate the hostage crisis in which claims between the two countries will be transferred from American courts to an Iran-United States Claims Tribunal constitutionally infirm?

Opinion of the Court by Justice Rehnquist:

The parties and the lower courts, confronted with the instant questions, have all agreed that much relevant analysis is contained in *Youngstown Sheet & Tube Co. v. Sawyer,* 343 U.S. 579 (1952). Justice Black's opinion for the Court in that case, involving the validity of President Truman's effort to seize the country's steel mills in the wake of a nation-wide strike, recognized that "[t]he President's power, if any, to issue the order must stem either from an act of Congress or from the Constitution itself."...Justice Jackson's concurring opinion elaborated in a general way the consequences of different types of interaction between the two democratic branches in assessing Presidential authority to act in any given case. When the President acts pursuant to an express or implied authorization from

Congress, he exercises not only his powers but also those delegated by Congress. In such a case the executive action "would be supported by the strongest of presumptions and the widest latitude of judicial interpretation, and the burden of persuasion would rest heavily upon any who might attack it."...When the President acts in the absence of congressional authorization he may enter "a zone of twilight in which he and Congress may have concurrent authority, or in which its distribution is uncertain."...In such a case the analysis becomes more complicated, and the validity of the President's action, at least so far as separation-of-powers principles are concerned, hinges on a consideration of all the circumstances which might shed light on the views of the Legislative Branch toward such action, including "congressional inertia, indifference or quiescence."...Finally, when the President acts in contravention of the will of Congress, "his power is at its lowest ebb," and the Court can sustain his actions "only by disabling the Congress from acting upon the subject."...

Although we have in the past found and do today find Justice Jackson's classification of executive actions into three general categories analytically useful,... [he] himself recognized that his three categories represented "a somewhat over-simplified grouping," ... and it is doubtless the case that executive action in any particular instance falls, not nearly in one of three pigeonholes, but rather at some point along a spectrum running from explicit congressional authorization to explicit congressional prohibition. This is particularly true as respects cases such as the one before us, involving responses to international crises the nature of which Congress can hardly have been expected to anticipate in any detail.

In nullifying post-November 4, 1979, attachments and directing those persons holding blocked Iranian funds and securities to transfer them to the Federal Reserve Bank of New York for ultimate transfer to Iran, President Carter cited five sources of express or inherent power. The Government, however, has principally relied on Sec. 203 of the IEEPA [International Emergency Economic Power Act], 91 Stat. 1626, as authorization for these actions. Section 1702(a)(1) provides in part [that the President may]: (b) investigate, regulate, direct and compel, nullify, void, prevent or prohibit, any acquisition, holding, withholding, use, transfer, withdrawal, transportation, importation or exportation of, or dealing in, or exercising any right, power, or privilege with respect to, or transactions involving, any property in which any foreign country or a national thereof has any interest; by any person, or with respect to any property, subject to the jurisdiction of the United States.

The Government contends that the acts of "nullifying" the attachments and ordering the "transfer" of the frozen assets are specifically authorized by the plain language of the above statute. The two Courts of Appeals that have considered the issue agreed with this contention....

Petitioner contends that we should ignore the plain language of this statute because an examination of its legislative history as well as the history of Sec. 5(b) of the Trading With the Enemy Act [TWEA], 40 Stat. 411,... from which the pertinent language of Sec. 1702 is directly drawn, reveals that the statute was not intended to give the President such extensive power over the assets of a foreign state during times of national emergency. According to the petitioner, once the President instituted the November 14, 1979 blocking order, Sec. 1702 authorized him "only to continue the freeze or to discontinue controls." Brief for Petitioner, at 32.

We do not agree and refuse to read out of Sec. 1702 all meaning to the words "transfer," "compel," or "nullify." Nothing in the legislative history of either

Sec. 1702 or Sec. 5(b) of the TWEA requires such a result. To the contrary, we think both the legislative history and cases interpreting the TWEA fully sustain the broad authority of the Executive when acting under this congressional grant of power....

This Court has previously recognized that the congressional purpose in authorizing blocking orders is "to put control of foreign assets in the hands of the President."...Such orders permit the President to maintain the foreign assets at his disposal for use in negotiating the resolution of a declared national emergency. The frozen assets serve as a "bargaining chip" to be used by the President when dealing with a hostile country. Accordingly, it is difficult to accept petitioner's argument because the practical effect of it is to allow individual claimants throughout the country to minimize or wholly eliminate this "bargaining chip" through attachments, garnishments, or similar encumbrances on property. Neither the purpose the statute was enacted to serve nor its plain language supports such a result.

Because the President's action in nullifying the attachments and ordering the transfer of the assets was taken pursuant to specific congressional authorization, it is "supported by the strongest of presumptions and the widest latitude of judicial interpretation, and the burden of persuasion would rest heavily upon any who might attack it."...Under the circumstances of this case, we cannot say that petitioner has sustained that heavy burden. A contrary ruling would mean that the Federal Government as a whole lacked the power exercised by the President ... and that we are not prepared to say.

Although we have concluded that the IEEPA constitutes specific congressional authorization to the President to nullify the attachments and orders the transfer of Iranian assets, there remains the question of the President's authority to suspend claims pending in American courts....

Although we have declined to conclude that the IEEPA or the Hostage Act directly authorizes the President's suspension of claims for the reasons noted, we cannot ignore the general tenor of Congress' legislation in this area in trying to determine whether the President is acting alone or at least with the acceptance of Congress. As we have noted, Congress cannot anticipate and legislate with regard to every possible action the President may find it necessary to take or every possible situation in which he might act. Such failure of Congress specifically to delegate authority does not, "especially ... in the areas of foreign policy and national security," imply "congressional disapproval" of action taken by the Executive. *Haig v. Agee*, 453 U.S. 280, 291 (1981). On the contrary, the enactment of legislation closely related to the question of the President's authority in a particular case which evinces legislative intent to accord the President broad discretion may be considered to "invite" measures on independent presidential responsibility....At least this is so where there is no contrary indication of legislative intent and when, as here, there is a history of congressional acquiescence in conduct of the sort engaged in by the President....

Crucial to our decision today is the conclusion that Congress has implicitly approved the practice of claim settlement by executive agreement. This is best demonstrated by Congress' enactment of the International Claims Settlement Act of 1949 (64 Stat. 13)....

In addition to congressional acquiescence in the President's power to settle claims, prior cases of this Court have also recognized that the President does have some measure of power to enter into executive agreements without obtaining the advice and consent of the Senate. In *United States v. Pink* ... the

Court upheld the validity of the Litvinov Assignment, which was part of an Executive Agreement whereby the Soviet Union assigned to the United States amounts owed to it by American nationals so that outstanding claims of other American nationals could be paid. The Court explained that the resolution of such claims was integrally connected with normalizing United States' relations with a foreign state....

[W]e do not believe that the President has attempted to divest the federal courts of jurisdiction. Executive Order No. 12294 purports only to "suspend" the claims, not divest the federal courts of "jurisdiction." As we read the Executive Order, those claims not within the jurisdiction of the Claims Tribunal will "revive" and become judicially enforceable in the United States courts. This case, in short, illustrates the difference between modifying federal-court jurisdiction and directing the courts to apply a different rule of law....The President has exercised the power, acquiesced in by Congress, to settle claims and, as such, has simply effected a change in the substantive law governing the lawsuit....

In light of the foregoing ... we conclude that the President was authorized to suspend pending claims pursuant to Executive Order No. 12294. As Justice Frankfurter pointed out in *Youngstown*,... "a systematic, unbroken, executive practice, long pursued to the knowledge of the Congress and never before questioned ... may be treated as a gloss on 'Executive Power' vested in the President by Sec. 1 of Art. II." Past practice does not, by itself, create power, but "long- continued practice, known to and acquiesced in by Congress would raise a presumption that the [action] has been [taken] in pursuance of its consent." *United States v. Midwest Oil Co.*, 236 U.S. 458, 474 (1915). Such practice is present here and such a presumption is also appropriate. In light of the fact that Congress may be considered to have consented to the President's action in suspending claims, we cannot say that action exceeded the President's powers....

Just as importantly, Congress has not disapproved of the action taken here. Though Congress has held hearings on the Iranian Agreement itself, Congress has not enacted legislation, or even passed a resolution, indicating its displeasure with the Agreement. Quite the contrary, the relevant Senate Committee has stated that the establishment of the Tribunal is "of vital importance to the United States."...We are thus clearly not confronted with a situation in which Congress has in some way resisted the exercise of Presidential authority.

Finally, we re-emphasize the narrowness of our decision. We do not decide that the President possesses plenary power to settle claims, even as against foreign governmental entities....But where, as here, the settlement of claims has been determined to be a necessary incident of the resolution of a major foreign policy dispute between our country and another, and where, as here, we can conclude that Congress acquiesced in the President's action, we are not prepared to say that the President lacks the power to settle such claims....

The judgment of the District Court is accordingly affirmed....

Note: The decision in *Dames & Moore* underscored the same principle articulated almost a half-century earlier in *Curtiss-Wright*—the President was the primary governmental authority over matters of foreign policy; and in times of emergency the President's power expands. Nevertheless, in a very narrowly crafted opinion, the Court upheld the constitutionality of the Executive Orders—and the executive agreements—relying in large part on Jackson's seminal analysis in *Youngstown.* Here, prior congressional authorization existed and the

President stood on much firmer constitutional ground when acting with the assent of Congress.

At the same time Rehnquist's opinion placed great emphasis on the history of congressional acquiescence in the settlement of international claims by the executive. What the Congress allowed the President to do in the field of foreign relations had become a "gloss" (*Midwest Oil*) on the meaning of the law. Moreover, the Court held that the presidential order nullifying attachments on Iranian assets and allowing a transfer of those assets out of the country did not constitute a compensable taking of property because the President had statutory authority to prevent or condition the allowance of such attachments. The *Dames & Moore* opinion, however, ignored a contrary ruling by the Court of Claims in *Seery v. United States,* 127 F.Supp. 601 (Ct.Cl. 1955), *cert. denied,* 359 U.S. 943 (1959).

Perhaps the ruling was little more than a "political" decision after all. Consider the following:

To understand the Supreme Court's decision in *Dames & Moore v. Reagan,* one should perceive at the outset that it is basically a compromise between harsh international reality and abstract constitutional norms. Although crafted in familiar lawyers' language, Justice Rehnquist's opinion for the Court reeks with the odor of compromise forced by necessity. Principle, as usual, gave way to *realpolitik.* The Justices had, in the last analysis, no choice save to sustain the validity of President Carter's hurried deal for the release of the hostages. [Miller, Dames & Moore v. Regan: A Political Decision by a Political Court, 29 U.C.L.A. L.REV. 1104 (1982).]

Crockett v. Reagan, 558 F.Supp. 893 (D.D.C. 1982)

The ability of the executive to deploy the military to foreign nations to fight in informal wars created a growing discontent with what many have regarded as the President's assumption of congressional war power during the Vietnam conflict. To restore what has been argued by some to be the balance intended by the Framers, Congress passed the War Powers Resolution (WPR) (87 Stat. 555) over a presidential veto on November 7, 1973. The Resolution restricts the executive's authority to involve the United States in foreign controversies without congressional approval. Specific provisions of the Resolution, however, insure that the President has authority to send the military into combat without requesting authorization from Congress if the United States or one of her territories is attacked.

The War Powers Resolution raises many interesting and unresolved questions. Is the Resolution binding? If it is, who has standing to sue claiming a violation of the provisions? No specific language in the Resolution resolves the standing issue. Perhaps Justice Brennan's theory that the only requirement for standing is injury in fact, expressed in the different context of other cases— *Association of Data Processing Service v. Camp,* 397 U.S. 150 (1970) and *Barlow v. Collins,* 397 U.S. 159 (1970)—could provide a basis for military personnel sent abroad in violation of the resolution to sue the President. If standing is found to exist, it may well be that judicial review of cases under this law is foreclosed by the doctrine of political questions. The impact on foreign affairs of a judicial decision contrary to the President's military actions already underway may suggest that questions regarding provisions of the War Powers Resolution should be considered nonjusticiable and immune from judicial review as political questions.

Even if the War Powers Resolution were reviewable and subject to litigation, its constitutionality might be subject to a presidential claim that the Resolution improperly seeks to subtract from his inherent powers. However, in that case, the War Powers Resolution should still be relevant, for under Justice Jackson's analysis in *Youngstown,* the President's war powers should be at their lowest ebb: if he should act contrary to the War Powers Resolution, he would then have only his own powers minus any constitutional powers of Congress to reduce his powers.

Twenty-nine members of Congress sued President Ronald Reagan, Secretary of Defense Caspar Weinberger, and Secretary of State Alexander Haig for failing to file a report that would start the clock running on his use of American military advisers in the civil war in El Salvador. The plaintiffs sought a declaratory judgment that the President had violated the resolution and a court order directing the withdrawal of American forces and other aid.

Basic Question: May the President be sued for nonperformance under the War Powers Resolution? Are the issues raised here covered by the "political question" doctrine?

Opinion of the District Court by Judge Green:

...[I]n order to determine the application of the 60-day provision, the court would be required to decide at exactly what point in time U.S. forces had been introduced into hostilities or imminent hostilities, and whether that situation continues to exist. This inquiry would be even more inappropriate for the judiciary.

In *Baker v. Carr*, 369 U.S. 186 (1962), Justice Brennan identified several categories of "political questions." The question here belongs to the category characterized by a lack of judicially discoverable and manageable standards for resolution. The court disagrees with defendants that this is the type of political question which involves potential judicial interference with executive discretion in the foreign affairs field. Plaintiffs do not seek relief that would dictate foreign policy but rather to enforce existing law concerning the procedures for decision-making. Moreover, the issue here is not a political question simply because it involves the apportionment of power between the executive and legislative branches. The duty of courts to decide such questions has been repeatedly reaffirmed by the Supreme Court....

However, the question presented does require judicial inquiry into sensitive military matters. Even if the plaintiffs could introduce admissible evidence concerning the state of hostilities in various geographical areas in El Salvador where U.S. forces are stationed and the exact nature of U.S. participation in the conflict (and the information may well be unavailable except through inadmissible newspaper articles), the court no doubt would be presented conflicting evidence on those issues by defendants. The court lacks the resources and expertise (which are accessible to the Congress) to resolve disputed questions of fact concerning the military situation in El Salvador....

...The subtleties of factfinding in this situation should be left to the political branches. If Congress doubts or disagrees with the Executive's determination that U.S. forces in El Salvador have not been introduced into hostilities or imminent hostilities, it has the resources to investigate the matter and assert its wishes. The court need not decide here what type of congressional statement or action would constitute an official congressional stance that our involvement in El Salvador is subject to the WPR, because Congress has taken absolutely no action that could be interpreted to have that effect. Certainly, were Congress to pass a resolution to the effect that a report was required under the WPR, or to the effect that the forces should be withdrawn, and the President disregarded it, a constitutional impasse appropriate for judicial resolution would be presented....

Defendants do not dispute the interpretation of the basic purpose of the WPR presented here and emphasized by plaintiffs. However, they deny that it is self-executing in a situation where a report has not been submitted. They argue that the decision as to whether a situation warrants a report under the WPR is left to the President's discretion in the first instance. In their view, his failure to submit a report does not justify a court action, and the 60-day period does not begin to run for the time he assertedly should have filed the report. Rather, in instances of disagreement between the President and Congress as to whether a report is required, a "second trigger" is needed to bring the WPR into play. Congress must either take action to express its view that the WPR is applicable to the situation and that a report is required, or, if it desires immediate withdrawal of forces, pass a concurrent resolution directing removal of the forces....

The court finds that the legislative scheme did not contemplate court-ordered withdrawal when no report has been filed, but rather, it leaves open the possibility for a court to order that a report be filed or, alternatively, withdrawal 60-days after a report was filed or required to be filed by a court or Congress....If plaintiffs' position is correct, total congressional inaction (which perhaps could signify general agreement with the President's appraisal that no report is required) could result in mandatory withdrawal of U.S. forces if a court adjudges that they had been introduced into hostilities or imminent hostilities more than 60 days previously. In all of the extensive debate on the mandatory withdrawal provision, this possibility was never entertained....[I]n a situation where no report has been filed, and the priority procedures would not be invoked, the majority of Congress might not be of the opinion that a specific authorization is necessary for continued involvement and take no action, unaware that this course would result in mandatory withdrawal. In that instance court-ordered withdrawal could thwart the will of the majority of Congress. Therefore, when a report has not been filed, it is consistent with the purposes and structure of the WPR to require further congressional action before the automatic termination provision operates....

The arguments discussed above convince the court that the cause must be dismissed. Therefore, it is unnecessary to reach the other asserted bases for dismissal, which include standing, equitable discretion and lack of a private right of action. As already stated, the court does not decide that all disputes under the [WPR] would be inappropriate for judicial resolution....

While a court upon scrutiny of detailed discovery might not agree with the President's assessment of the human rights situation in El Salvador, and could possibly conclude that the provision of security assistance under these circumstances violates section 502B of the Foreign Assistance Act, the equitable discretion doctrine prevents consideration of these issues on behalf of congressional plaintiffs. Their dispute is primarily with their fellow legislators. Action by this court would not serve to mediate between branches of government, but merely aid plaintiffs in circumventing the democratic process available to them.

Therefore, it is this 4th day of October, 1982, hereby ORDERED, that defendants' motion to dismiss be, and it hereby is, granted, and this cause stands dismissed.

Note: The motion to dismiss granted in *Crockett* was upheld in the court of appeals, 720 F.2d 1355 (D.C. Cir. 1983), cert. denied, 467 U.S. 1251 (1984). Nevertheless, several questions arose that were not successfully answered by Judge Green's opinion. Do you agree with Judge Green that a court is not capable of determining whether American forces have been introduced into foreign hostilities? Is Congress more capable than the courts of ascertaining such facts? Who within Congress is "capable" of issuing an authoritative finding of fact: a committee, one house, both houses? Suppose that one or both houses had authorized the suit. Would that authorization amount to a finding by Congress that American forces had, in fact, been introduced into hostilities? [C. Pyle & R. Pious, The President, Congress, and the Constitution 372 (1984).]

Suppose that one or both houses of Congress did ask the court to remedy a presidential violation of the reporting requirement of the War Powers Resolution? What is the appropriate remedy: an order that the President file a report and start the clock, or an order directing the withdrawal of all forces? Does the resolution clearly establish the following two-trigger procedure: the first a congressionally requested court order to start the clock and the second a court order sixty days later requiring withdrawal? What effect does Judge Green's opinion have on the sixty-day timetable? [*Id.* at 372-73.]

On February 4, 1983, according to inadmissible newspaper reports, an unarmed American military advisor to El Salvador was wounded by sniper fire as his helicopter swooped low over a rebel position. The Department of Defense (DOD) insisted that the mission on which the advisor was flying was solely for the purpose of repairing a communications line, and therefore did not involve the introduction of American forces "into hostilities or into situations where imminent hostilities are clearly indicated by the circumstances." No report was filed under the WPR. Nor was any report filed when a marine was killed by a land mine in Beirut and a marine captain confronted an Israeli tank commander with a loaded weapon. Should reports have been filed in these circumstances? Should President Carter have filed reports when he sent a carrier task force into the Persian Gulf during the Iran-Iraq war or when he dispatched four AWAC aircraft to Saudi Arabia to monitor that war by radar? In September, 1983, President Reagan denied the existence of "imminent hostilities" in Lebanon even though marines had been killed by artillery and American warships had shelled artillery positions. As public fear of another Vietnam mounted, many members of Congress began asserting that the sixty-day clock of the WPR had begun running on August 29, when the marines in Beirut had first come under hostile fire. Do you agree? Would it be legitimate for a court, or Congress, to so rule months later in order to justify an order of immediate withdrawal? Or should a court or Congress always start the clock running from the time they decide that it should be running? That is what Congress decided to do in October 1983, when it agreed to authorize American participation in the international peace keeping force in Lebanon for eighteen months—past the November 1984, presidential and congressional elections. [*Id.* at 373.]

The problem, however, remains the same: the President does not play by the required rules of the WPR, and Congress does not have the courage to impose accountability on the President. On September 29, 1982, shortly after introducing marines into Beirut, Lebanon, President Reagan sent the Speaker of the House and the President Pro Tempore of the Senate a two-page letter stating that "there is no intention or expectation that U.S. armed forces will become involved in hostilities." Following the example set by Presidents Ford and Carter, Reagan did not specify which, if any, section of the WPR he was fol-lowing in making this report. On the contrary, he declared that the deployment "is being undertaken pursuant to the President's constitutional authority with respect to the conduct of foreign relations and as Commander in Chief...." Similarly, in informing Congress that he had ordered the invasion of Grenada on October 25, 1983, Reagan refused to report that troops had been introduced "into hostilities," even though they were clearly engaged in combat and had taken casualties. In short, he refused to say anything that might trigger the 60-day clock. If Presidents will not start the war powers clock voluntarily, how is it to be started?

7

Vietnam and Gulf War Cases

Berk v. Laird, **429 F.2d 302 (2d Cir. 1970)**

When President Harry Truman ordered American troops into Korea in June 1950, a new era in the use of presidential power began. The constitutional rationale for the President's action was spelled out by the Department of State soon after issuance of the order to intervene [Authority of the President to Repel the Attack in Korea, 23 Dep't St.Bull. 173 (1950).] While secondary reliance was placed on the United Nation's Charter and the Security Council's resolution requesting support for those resisting North Korean aggression, primary reliance was on plenary presidential power and its exercise independent of other agencies, including Congress. The entry into Korea was an act of independent presidential power.

It is generally agreed that there were *two* constitutional legacies of the Korean War. On the one hand, there was the exercise of greater caution in the use of troops by the Eisenhower administration; on the other hand, there was the legacy that said that President Truman had established a clear precedent for later presidential initiatives. Consequently, when the United States became deeply involved in Vietnam in the mid-1960s, there was no firm grounding in either post-World War II precedent or practice, for the proposition that Congress needed to "authorize" the use of troops abroad if their use was to be constitutional. On the contrary, the presidential position was that while any formal support that Congress might wish to extend in a given instance would be welcomed, the independent power of the executive was sufficient. And this was the way it had always been since the founding of the Republic.

The Tonkin Gulf Resolution (78 Stat. 384), which preceded by several months the massive buildup of troops in Vietnam by President Lyndon Johnson in 1965, in specific terms "authorized" nothing, but supported a great deal. [C. Rossiter, The Supreme Court and the Commander in Chief 137 (R. Longaker ed.

1976).] So did subsequent appropriations for the war. In the resolution, Congress approved "the determination of the President as Commander in Chief, to take all necessary measures to repel any armed attack against the forces of the United States and to prevent further aggression." 78 Stat. 384. The clause added little to constitutional theory, for it was generally recognized that a President could repel an armed attack against the nation or its forces on his own authority. The second clause was even more expansive. The Congress, adopting language prepared by the executive proclaimed: "[T]he United States is ... prepared, as the President determines, to take all necessary steps, including the use of armed force, to assist any member or protocol state of the Southeast Asia Collective Defense Treaty requesting assistance in defense of its freedom." *Id.* The usage banished any presumed limitations on the power of the President to use military force and accomplished an apparent delegation of the putative war powers of Congress without a clear understanding of the scope of their exercise. [C. Rossiter, 138]. Not surprising, the administration took the resolution to be the "functional equivalent" of a declaration of war—similar to the position taken by President Franklin Roosevelt with the Lend Lease Act of 1941.

The central paradox of the Johnson Administration's response to the Tonkin resolution was that, while the administration requested the resolution and employed it openly as the justification for the use of armed forces in Asia, the administration also declared that the resolution was not necessary [Meeker, The Legality of the United States Participation in the Defense of Viet Nam, 54 Dep't St.Bull. 474 (1966)]: The President is empowered to meet force with force anywhere or even anticipate it. His decision need be based only on his own judgment and authority—in other words, the President's own "inherent" authority.

As congressional disillusionment developed and intensified, the opposition went through several mutations—sense resolutions, threats to cut off funds, and, especially, repeal of the Tonkin resolution. Similarly, the purported reasons for the use of force shifted as the war would down and led to variations in the constitutional rationale. First, the President (by this time Richard Nixon) abandoned reliance on the South East Asia Treaty Organization (SEATO) Treaty which, at best, had always been a dubious basis for American involvement. Then, when the Tonkin Gulf Resolution was repealed, the administration relied on argumentation based on historical precedent—some 200 instances in which troops had been used abroad by Presidents—and the alleged ratification of the war by continuing appropriations and other legislation, including the renewal of the Selective Service Act (81 Stat. 100). And, even without these verifications of its support, there was the President's independent power as commander-in-chief over forces committed in the field.

This independent power was, as it has always been, sub-stantive authority to dispatch and command the armed forces, but now it was viewed by the administration more broadly as the power of the President to use force as a negotiating instrument to assure the independence of Vietnam and to protect American troops during the process of withdrawal from the war. [C. Rossiter, 141.] Approval was said to be implicit in military appropriations by Congress.

In other words, congressional participation was the functional equivalent to a "declaration" of war. And, by a turn of inverse interpretation, any sense resolutions by the House or Senate, or both, which attempted to place limits on the executive were said to be not binding. Thus, when Congress "advised" the President in the Mansfield Amendment to the Military Procurement Act (85 Stat. 423) to limit his actions solely to bring about the negotiation of a cease-fire and withdrawal of all American forces, the President stated that the limiting amendment was "without force or effect." [*Id.*]

Given the above background, the following development merits closer attention: a sustained pattern of avoidance by the Supreme Court of any determination on the constitutionality of the war in Vietnam, which stance obscured growing restlessness in the courts below. [*Id.* at 145.] At no time did the Supreme Court reach the merits of the war's constitutionality, nor did the Court specify reasons for rejecting appeals from the decisions of the lower federal courts. The persistent efforts by opponents of the war to litigate the constitutional issues and the increasing unpopularity of the war led to a greater inclination, as time passed, to hear argument about the war's constitutionality. Although many of the federal courts finally wrapped themselves in the protective mantle of the political questions doctrine (as seen in the cases that follow), especially during the depths of American involvement, several were willing to treat the war as a justiciable issue. The sum total of all of the Vietnam cases, approximately seventy in number, left no coherent legacy. But in significant instances the political question doctrine crumbled noticeably, and standards began to emerge. It was a significant indication that the judicial deference which was assumed as a judicial fact of life in the immediate post World War II years could no longer be taken for granted in the 1970s.

Berk, an enlisted member of the Army, challenged the constitutional basis for the presence of the United States armed forces in Vietnam and sought an injunction against sending him to Vietnam or Cambodia. Berk contended that the U.S. Government had exceeded its constitutional authority by commanding him to participate in military activity not properly authorized by Congress. His complaint alleged that these orders violated rights protected by the Fifth, Ninth, Tenth and Fourteenth Amendments to the Constitution, as well as section 5 of the New York Civil Rights Law (McKinney's Consol.Laws, ch. 6). The court denied a preliminary injunction on the grounds that the balance of equities inclined toward the Government because if Berk succeeded in obtaining a preliminary injunction, there would be a flood of similar applications which would have to be granted thereby causing "a drastic interference with the war effort" by a decision on a preliminary motion.

Basic Questions: Is the issue of a "undeclared war" justiciable? Was the participation by Congress the "functional equivalent" of a declaration of war?

Opinion of the Court of Appeals by Circuit Judge Anderson:

As the appellant correctly points out, the issue on this appeal is not whether the courts are empowered to "second-guess" the President in his decision to commit the armed forces to action, but whether they have the power to make a particular kind of constitutional decision involving the division of powers between legislative and executive branches....The appellees' position is essentially that the President's authority as Commander in Chief, in the absence of a declared war, is co-extensive with his broad and unitary power in the field of foreign affairs....If this were the case, Berk's claim would not be justiciable because the congressional power to "declare" war would be reduced to an antique formality, leaving no executive "duty" to follow constitutional steps which can be judicially identified....However, the power to commit American military forces under various sets of circumstances is shared by Congress and the executive. History makes clear that the congressional power "to declare War" conferred by Article I, Section 8, of the Constitution was intended as an explicit restriction upon the power of the Executive to initiate war on his own prerogative which was enjoyed by the British sovereign. Although Article II specifies that the President "shall be Commander in Chief of the Army and Navy of the United States" and also vests the "executive power" in him and requires that he "take Care that the Laws be faithfully executed," these provisions must be reconciled with the congressional war power....Since orders to fight must be issued in accordance with proper authorization from both branches under some circumstances, executive officers are under a threshold constitutional "duty [that] can be judicially identified and its breach judicially determined."...

Even if it possesses this general attribute of justiciability, however, a claim still may not be decided if it involves a political question....The challenge framed at this point by the appellant—"Which branch has the power to decide if an order has been issued in violation of the Constitution"—may not be answered by stating that courts alone inevitably pass upon allegations of constitutional violations, as Berk seems to suppose. If the issue involved in this case is "political," Congress and the executive will "decide" whether there has been a usurpation of authority by the latter, through political means.

The political question doctrine itself requires that a court decline to adjudicate an issue involving "a lack of judicially discoverable and manageable standards for resolving it."...If the executive branch engaged the nation in prolonged foreign military activities without any significant congressional authorization, a court might be able to determine that this extreme step violated a discoverable standard calling for some mutual participation by Congress in accordance with Article I, Section 8. But in this case, in which Congress definitely has acted, in part expressly through the Gulf of Tonkin Resolution and implicitly through appropriations and other acts in support of the project over a period of years, it is more difficult to Berk to suggest a set of manageable standards and escape the likelihood that his particular claim about this war at this time is a political question. It may be that he will be able to provide a method for resolving the question of when specified joint legislative-executive action is sufficient to authorize various levels of military activity, but no such standard has yet been presented to us....Even if a distinction can be drawn between offensive and defensive conflicts and if some rather explicit congressional authorization is required for the former, there still remains the problem of determining whether a broad approving resolution followed by nonrepeal meets the proposed criterion of "explicit" approval....

Finally, even if Berk is able to show that his claim does not raise an unmanageable political question, he will be required to show the district court that congressional debates and actions, from the Gulf of Tonkin Resolution through the events of the subsequent six years, fall short of whatever "explicit approval" standard he propounds. This will invoke a multitude of considerations concerning which neither the district court nor this court has been adequately informed, and we cannot, in good con-science, now say that the appellant has shown probability of success on the merits if this stage is reached, although ... we do not foreclose the appellant from seeking to establish his claims.

In summary, the appellant raises a claim which meets the general standard of justiciability set out in *Powell v. McCormick* ... and *Baker v. Carr* ..., but must still be shown to escape the political question doctrine. Even though he has perhaps raised substantial questions going to the merits, neither the likelihood of success nor the balance of equities inclines so strongly in his favor that a preliminary injunction is required....

The denial of a preliminary injunction is affirmed and the case is remanded to the district court for further proceedings consistent with this opinion. The current stay of the military orders detaching appellant to South Vietnam shall expire and the mandate shall issue seven days from the date thereof to allow appellant to seek further relief in the Supreme Court. It is also suggested that the proceedings in the district court on the underlying action proceed with expedition.

So ordered.

Note: Upon rehearing, the district court held that—notwithstanding the lack of a explicit declaration of war—Congress had authorized hostilities in Vietnam in a manner sufficiently explicit to satisfy all constitutional requirements, and the question whether Congress *should have* made an explicit declaration of war was a political question with respect to which the court would not interfere. [*Berk v. Laird,* 317 F.Supp. 715 (E.D.N.Y. 1970).] In essence, the lower court argued that ever since *Bas v. Tingy,* 4 U.S. 37 (1800), the distinction had existed between a "perfect war" or total war, initiated by a formal declaration of war, and an "imperfect war" or partial war, which involved military action *authorized* by Congress without a formal declaration of war. Indeed, through twenty-four statutes (including appropriation bills and selective service laws) Congress passed to facilitate the war, proof existed of joint action or mutual participation that had become so systematic, persuasive and comprehensive that it amounted in every practical sense to ratification. What Congress refused to do expressly, it did indirectly and *sub silentio.*

Berk was decided while the war was in full sway. Nevertheless, the court shifted significantly from the absolute bar of the political question doctrine by asserting that there was a functional equivalent of an authorization by continued congressional action supporting the President's position. Consequently, the political question doctrine did *not* foreclose judicial inquiry into whether there had been the mutual participation required to prolonged hostilities. But the form and the "propriety" of the participation, that is, whether or not an explicit authorization was required, was a political question for Congress, not the judiciary, to decide.

Similar results, and acceptance of the functional equivalent theory, occurred in *Orlando v. Laird,* 317 F.Supp. 1013 (E.D.N.Y. 1970), *aff'd,* 423 F.2d 1039 (2d Cir. 1971); *Massachusetts v. Laird,* 451 F.2d 26 (1st Cir. 1971); and, earlier, *Mora v. McNamara,* 387 F.2d 862 (D.C. Cir. 1967), *cert. denied,* 389 U.S. 934

(1967). *See especially,* Bickel, <u>Congress, the President, and the Power to Wage War</u>, 48 Chi.-Kent L.Rev. 131 (1971) and Van Alstyne, <u>Congress, the President, and the Power to Declare War</u>, 121 U.Pa.L.Rev. 1 (1972). *Cf.* Monaghan, <u>Presidential War-Making</u>, 50 B.U.L.Rev. 19 (1970) and Harmon, <u>Presidential Power to Use the Armed Forces Abroad without Statutory Authority</u>, 4A U.S.Op.,Off. Legal Couns. 185 (Feb. 12, 1980).

Mitchell v. Laird, 488 F.2d 611 (D.C. Cir. 1973)

The facts of the case, and the basic questions, are contained in the opinion of the court.

Opinion of the Court of Appeals by Senior District Judge Wyzanski:

On April 7, 1971 thirteen members of the United States House of Representatives, as plaintiffs, filed in the District Court a complaint against the President of the United States, the Secretaries of State, Defense, Army, Navy, and Air Force, and the United States of America. Plaintiffs alleged that for seven years the United States, by the named individual defendants and their predecessors, has been engaged in a war in Indo-China without obtaining "either a declaration of war or an explicit, intentional and discrete authorization of war" and thereby "unlawfully impair and defeat plaintiffs' constitutional right, as members of the Congress of the United States, to decide whether the United States should fight a war." Plaintiffs prayed for first, an order that defendants be enjoined from prosecuting the war in Indo-China unless, within 60 days from the date of such order, the Congress shall have explicitly, intentionally and discretely authorized a continuation of the war, and, second, "a declaratory judgment that defendants are carrying on a war in violation of Article I, Section 8, Clause 11 of the United States Constitution."

The District Court dismissed the action as to the President, on the authority of *Mississippi v. Johnson*, 71 U.S. (4 Wall.) 475 (1866), and as to the other defendants, on the authority of *Luftig v. McNamara*, 373 F.2d 664 (D.C. Cir. 1967), *cert. denied*, 387 U.S. 945 (1967)....

The first issue presented in whether the case is now moot. Recently, the President has purported formally to end hostilities in Vietnam and Laos. There has been no similar action with respect to Cambodia, another part of Indo-China. The continuation of hostilities there precludes our holding that this case is moot....

The second issue is whether the dismissal of the action against the United States was correct for a reason not given by the District Court. We are unanimously of the view that as to the government the dismissal was correct because the sovereign has not consented to be sued.

The third issue is whether the dismissal of the action as to the remaining defendants was proper for another reason not given by the District Court: to wit, that plaintiffs have no standing to sue. Nine of the judges who heard this appeal are persuaded that plaintiffs are sound in their explicit reliance upon defendants' alleged duty not to interfere with what the complaint alleges is "plaintiffs" constitutional right, as members of the Congress of the United States, to decide whether the United States should fight a war."

Implicit in plaintiffs' contention is their assumption that the Constitution gives to the Congress the exclusive right to decide whether the United States should fight all types of war. Without at this point exhaustively considering all possibilities, we are unanimously of the opinion that there are some types of war which, without Congressional approval, the President may begin to wage: for example, he may respond immediately without such approval to a belligerent attack, or in a grave emergency he may, without Congressional approval, take the initiative to wage war. Otherwise the country would be paralyzed....In such unusual situations necessity confers the requisite authority upon the President....

However, plaintiffs are not limited by their own concepts of their standing to sue. We perceive that in respects which they have not alleged they may be entitled to complain. If we, for the moment, assume that defendant's actions in continuing the hostilities in Indo-China were or are beyond the authority conferred upon them by the Constitution, a declaration to that effect would bear upon the duties of plaintiffs to consider whether to impeach defendants, and upon plaintiffs' quite distinct and different duties to make appropriations to support the hostilities, or to take other legislative actions related to such hostilities, such as raising an army or enacting other civil or criminal legislation. In our view, these considerations are sufficient to give plaintiffs a standing to make their complaint....

The fourth issue is whether plaintiffs seek adjudication of a "political question" beyond the jurisdiction conferred upon the courts by Article III of the Constitution. Despite *Luftig* ..., which admittedly indicates that it is beyond judicial competence to determine the allocation, between the executive and the legislative branches, of the powers to wage war, we are now persuaded that there may be, in some cases, such competence....

Here the critical question to be initially decided is whether the hostilities in Indo-China constitute in the Constitutional sense a "war," both within and beyond the meaning of that term in Article I, Section 8, Clause 11. That the hostilities have been not merely of magnitude but also of long duration is plainly alleged in paragraph 4 of the complaint....As of the present, one million human beings, including 50,000 Americans have been killed in the war, and at least one hundred billion dollars has been spent by the United States in and for the prosecution of the war....[I]n our opinion,... there has been a war in Indo-China. Nor do we see any difficulty in a court facing up to the question as to whether because of the war's duration and magnitude the President is or was without power to continue the war without Congressional approval.

But the aforesaid question invites inquiry as to whether Congress has given, in a Constitutionally satisfactory form, the approval requisite for a war of considerable duration and magnitude. Originally Congress gave what may be argued to have been its approval by the passage of the Gulf of Tonkin Resolution (78 Stat. 384)....However, that resolution cannot serve as justification for the indefinite continuance of the war since it was repealed by subsequent Congressional action (84 Stat. 2055). Apparently recognizing that point, the Government contends that Congressional approval has been given by appropriation acts, by extension of the Selective Service and Training act, and by other measures.

We are unanimously agreed that it is constitutionally permissible for Congress to use another means than a formal declaration of war to give its approval to a war such as is involved in the protracted and substantial hostilities in Indo-China....Any attempt to require a declaration of war as the only permissible form of assent might involve unforeseeable domestic and international consequences, without any obvious compensating advantages other than a formal declaration of war does have special solemnity and does present to the legislature an unambiguous choice. While those advantages are not negligible, we deem it a political question, or, to phrase it more accurately, a discretionary matter for Congress to decide in which form, if any, it will give its consent to the continuation of a war already begun by a President acting alone. ...That is, we regard the Constitution as contemplating various forms of Congressional assent, and we do not find any authority in the courts to require Congress to employ one rather than another form, if the form chosen by Congress be in itself constitutionally permissible. That conclusion, however, leaves unanswered the further question whether the particular forms which the Government counsel at our bar refer to as having been used by Congress in the Indo-China war are themselves of that character which makes them *in toto*, if not separately, a constitutionally permissible form of assent.

The overwhelming weight of authority,... hold that the appropriation, draft extension, and cognate laws enacted with direct or indirect reference to the Indo-China war,... did constitute a constitutionally permissible form of assent....Judge Tamm is content to adhere to that line of authority.

But Chief Judge Bazelon and I now regard that body of authority as unsound. It is, of course, elementary that in many areas of the law appropriations by Congress have been construed by the courts as involving Congressional assent to, or ratification of, prior or continuing executive action originally undertaken without Congressional legislative approval....[I]t is more relevant to emphasize the special problem which is presented when one seeks to spell out from military appropriation acts, extensions of selective service laws, and cognate legislation the purported Congressional approval or ratification of a war already being waged at the direction of the President alone. This court cannot be unmindful of what every schoolboy knows: that in voting to appropriate money or to draft men a Congressman is not necessarily approving of the continuation of a war no matter how specifically the appropriation or draft act refers to that war. A Congressman wholly opposed to the war's commencement and continuation might vote for the military appropriations and for the draft measures because he was unwilling to abandon without support men already fighting. An honorable, decent, compassionate act of aiding those already in peril is not proof of consent to the actions that place and continued them in that dangerous posture. We should not construe votes cast in pity and piety as though they were votes freely given to express consent. Hence Chief Judge Bazelon and I believe that none of the legislation drawn to the court's attention may serve as a valid assent to the Vietnam war.

Yet it does not follow that plaintiffs are entitled to prevail. When on January 20, 1969 President Nixon took office, and when on the same or even later dates the other individual defendants took their present office, they were faced with a belligerent situation not of their creation. Obviously, the President could not properly execute the duties of his office or his responsibility as Commander-in-Chief by ordering hostilities to cease on the very day he took office. Even if his predecessors had exceeded their constitutional authority, President Nixon's duty did not go beyond trying, in good faith and to the best of his ability, to bring the war to an end as promptly as was consistent with the safety of those fighting and with profound concern for the durable interests of the nation—its defense, its honor, its morality.

Whether President Nixon did so proceed is a question which at this stage in history a court is incompetent to answer. A court cannot procure the relevant evidence: some is in the hands of foreign governments, some is privileged. Even if the necessary facts were to be laid before it, a court would not substitute its judgment for that of the President, who has an unusually wide measure of discretion in this area, and who should not be judicially condemned except in a case of clear abuse amounting to bad faith. Otherwise a court would be ignoring the delicacies of diplomatic negotiation, the inevitable bargaining for the best solution of an international conflict, and the scope which in foreign affairs must be allowed to the President if this country is to play a responsible role in the council of nations.

In short, we are faced with what has traditionally been called a "political question" which is beyond the judicial power conferred by Article III of the United States Constitution. And on that ground the complaint was properly dismissed by the District Court.

Appeal dismissed.

Dissenting opinion of Circuit Judge MacKinnon (joined by Circuit Judges Tamm, Robb and Wilkey): [The dissenting opinion was based solely on the ground that the mutual participation of Congress was the functional equivalent of a declaration of war and, accordingly, a rehearing *en blanc* was necessary.]

Note: In *Mitchell* the appeals court rejected the functional equivalent theory and did not decide the case in favor of the plaintiffs. Instead it determined that the case involved a political question. The holding itself made two specific points, while omitting a third, regarding presidential war powers: (1) the President in certain circumstances had the power to initiate a war, but not to continue it indefinitely without congressional approval, and (2) even if Congress had originally given by the Gulf of Tonkin Resolution a power to continue the Indochina war, the President has no constitutional power to continue the hostilities except to withdraw in safety the forces already committed. What the court did not consider (the third point) was whether the President had exceeded his constitutional power by assuming the role of "dictatorial" commander-in-chief. Invoking the political question doctrine was one thing; it was quite another thing to not face a vital, necessary constitutional issue. By doing nothing on the question of the President's possible violation of his constitutional duties, the disease remained far worse than the possible cure.

Eventually, Congress would recognize that it, not the courts, had the authority to ensure that the separation of powers and checks and balances function as originally intended.

Holtzman v. Schlesinger, 361 F.Supp. 553 (E.D.N.Y. 1973)

After Congress "advised" the President in the Mansfield Amendment to the Military Procurement Act of 1972 (85 Stat. 423) to limit his actions solely to bring about the negotiation of a cease-fire and the withdrawal of all American forces, it would take another eighteen months to extricate those troops and an additional six months to bring the war to a "conclusion." When the troop withdrawal was completed in March 1973, reliance on the commander-in-chief clause for further military action in Indochina seemed to be undermined. Moreover, opposition in Congress to the war had reached an intensity which severely strained the argument that there was continuing implicit authorization in congressional acquiescence. And when, with the departure of all American forces from Vietnam, the President ordered bombing of Cambodia and Laos, his constitutional resources became exceedingly thin. He could not rely on his power as commander-in-chief to repel attacks on American forces, because there were none left to be attacked. [C. Rossiter, The Supreme Court and the Commander in Chief 142 (R. Longaker ed. 1976)].

In May 1973, Congress passed the Eagleton "End the War" Amendment to the Supplemental Appropriations Act of 1973 (87 Stat. 130) ordering an absolute cutoff of funds for combat activities in Cambodia and Laos on August 15. The following month (June 1973), Congress and the President moved toward a direct confrontation when the Senate attached an absolute cutoff of funds to the Debt Ceiling Act and the House did likewise with a Continuing Resolution. A presidential veto, if upheld, would have left the Government without funds to operate in the new fiscal year. The confrontation was avoided when Congress received assurance from the President that he would not veto the legislation; in turn, Congress tacitly agreed that the bombing could continue until August 15, but not beyond that time. Congress had, at long last, spoken unambiguously, and the President acceded. The immediate resolution of the issue in August 1973, was that Congress refused to share further in the responsibility for military action in Cambodia. The presidential theory of unlimited authority over the disposition of American troops—the constitutional theory of the post-World War II era—ran head on into the brute fact of the appropriations power. [*Id.* at 144.]

Plaintiff, a member of the United States House of Representatives, along with several Air Force officers, sought a determination that the President of the United States and the military personnel under his direction and control may not engage in intensive combat operations in Cambodia and elsewhere in Indochina in the absence of congressional authorization required under Article I, section 8, clause 11 of the Constitution. The plaintiff asked for a motion for summary judgment, as well as declaratory relief. [The *Holtzman* case is presented here in both versions—at the District Court level and before the Court of Appeals. All case commentary will appear after the second version].

Basic Questions: Do plaintiffs have standing to sue? Does the judiciary have adequate standards to determine when a "political question" is justiciable? Must the President halt military operations lacking congressional authorization?

Opinion of the District Court by Judge Judd:

The Court of Appeals of this circuit has spoken several times concerning earlier aspects of the Vietnam hostilities. The teaching of *Dacosta v. Laird*, 471 F.2d 1146 (2d Cir. 1970), *Orlando v. Laird*, 443 F.2d 1039 (2d Cir. 1971), and *Berk v. Laird*, 429 F.2d 302 (2d Cir. 1970), is that the question of the balance of constitutional authority to declare war, as between the executive and legislative branches, is not a political question and hence presents a justiciable issue, if plaintiffs can succeed in showing that there are manageable standards to resolve the controversy.

The Court of Appeals in *Berk* ... stated that there might be manageable standards to determine whether "prolonged foreign military activities without any significant congressional authorization" might violate a discoverable standard calling for some mutual participation by Congress in accordance with Article I, Section 8. The count on remand found that Congress in appropriations bills from 1965 through 1969 had shown "its continued support for the Vietnam action" and that Congress' choice of appropriations bills rather than a formal declaration of war to effectuate its intent involved a political question which did not prevent the finding that the fighting in Vietnam was authorized by Congress and that such fighting was not a usurpation of power by either of the Presidents who had been in office after 1964....

Nevertheless, appropriations bills do not necessarily indicate an open-ended approval of all military operations which may be conducted....

In affirming this court's *Berk* [and *Orlando* decisions] ... the Court of Appeals stated the test of whether there were manageable standards for adjudication as being "whether there is any action by the Congress sufficient to authorize or ratify the military activity in question."...It found that there was evidence of "an abundance of continuing mutual participation in the prosecution of the war."...

More recently in *Dacosta v. Laird*, 471 F.2d 1146 (2d Cir. 1973), the Court of Appeals dealt with the question "whether within the context of a lawful war, the President's order to mine the harbors of North Vietnam was properly authorized." It held in that instance that judges could not determine "whether a specific military operation constitutes an 'escalation' of the war or is merely a new tactical approach within a continuing strategic plan."...

The court finds no evidence of intentional bombing of civilians, but the mining of North Vietnam harbors was a part of the war in Vietnam. If bombing of Cambodia is not part of the war in Vietnam, there may be a standard available here which the Court of Appeals did not find in *Dacosta*.

Therefore the manageable standard which this court must apply is the existence of Congressional authority for the present bombing activities over Cambodia, now that American forces have been withdrawn and prisoners of war have been repatriated. In order to be entitled to relief, plaintiffs must show, under this standard, and the test of "continuing mutual participation" set forth in *Orlando*, either that Congress has not participated with the executive in the authorization of the hostilities in Cambodia or that Congress has terminated any such authorization....

Applying principles of the law of agency, as this court did in the *Berk* case ... it is the usual rule that the principal (Congress) may limit the duration of any authorization which it gives to the agent (the Executive)....

In considering the continued bombing of Cambodia, the removal of American forces and prisoners of war from Vietnam represents a basic change in the situation, which must be considered in determining the scope and duration of any Congressional authorization....

The Congressional action before and after the beginning of hostilities in Cambodia does not include authorization to bomb Cambodia in order to achieve a Cambodian cease-fire or even to protect the Vietnamese cease-fire as urged by defendants. The extent of the power granted by Congress depends on the language used by Congress, not on the President's statements to Congress.

An emergency does not create power unless Congress has granted it. *Youngstown Sheet & Tube Co. v. Sawyer*, 343 U.S. 579 (1952). The Constitution provides (Article II, Section 3) that the President shall recommend to the Congress "such Measures as he shall deem necessary and expedient" and that "he shall take Care that the Laws be faithfully executed." Nonaction by Congress does not constitute an implied grant of power....

The question here is not the one posed by the government, whether aerial action in Cambodia is the termination of a continuing war or the initiation of a new and distinct war; but whether Congress has authorized bombing in Cambodia after the withdrawal of American troops from Vietnam and the release of prisoners of war.

Authority to bomb Cambodia was not granted by the provisions adopted by both Houses of Congress on June 29, 1973 and signed by the President on July 1, 1973, forbidding any expenditures over Cambodia after August 15, 1973. This is made clear by the statements of Senator Fulbright and others during the debate in the Senate, where Senator Fulbright stated: "The acceptance of an August 15 cutoff date should in no way be interpreted as recognition by the committee of the President's authority to engage U.S. forces in hostilities until that date. The view of most members of the committee has been and continues to be that the President does not have such authority in the absence of specific congressional approval."...

This is not a situation where the views of a few members of Congress, holding attitudes antithetical to the majority, are being proffered to defeat what Congress had intended to be a grant of authority. There is no indication of a contrary majority sentiment. Majorities in both Houses had previously made plain that they were opposed to any continuation of bombing in Cambodia, and they included an August 15 cutoff date merely in order to avoid the veto which had met their earlier efforts.

The defendants urge that Congress' will as expressed through bills which were not enacted cannot be used as a factor in interpreting the July 1 legislation. But this contention misconstrues the basic issue. The question is not whether Congress has affirmatively acted to disavow participation, but whether Congress has acted to authorize the continuation of hostilities in Cambodia. While Congress can exercise its war-making power through measures other than an express declaration of war, courts should not easily infer the exercise of such a grave responsibility. Legislative history as evidenced through bills that were vetoed is relevant to a judicial inquiry of whether or not Congress intended to participate in the military campaign under challenge.

It cannot be the rule that the President needs a vote of one-third plus one of either House in order to conduct a war, but this would be the consequence of holding that Congress agreed to hold off any action affirmatively cutting off funds for military purposes until August 15, 1973.

This does not reach the question whether such activities had previously been authorized.

The period from now until August 15 is relatively short, the court necessarily having taken several weeks in studying the matter and preparing this memorandum. However, the court cannot say that the Cambodian and American lives which may be lost during the next three weeks are so unimportant that it should defer action in this case still further.

There is no disputed issues of material fact. The issues relate to the interpretation of Congressional acts.

Even if part of the fighting in Cambodia is being conducted by North Vietnamese troops rather than Khmer insurgents, the court has found that there is no Congressional authorization to fight in Cambodia after the withdrawal of American troops and the release of American prisoners of war. Even though the executive and the military may consider Cambodian bombing an effective means of enforcing paragraph 20 of the Paris Agreement of January 27, 1973, it does not appear that Congress has given its authority for such acts.

There is no indication that any of the classified information mentioned by the government will affect the interpretation of the Congressional acts or that the testimony of the officials suggest as witnesses will do so. The reasons which may have led the executive to continue bombing in Cambodia are not decisive, in the absence of continuing authority from Congress to do so....

Holtzman v. Schlesinger, 484 F.2d 1307 (2d Cir. 1973)

Appeal was taken from judgment of the District Court granting declaratory and injunctive relief against the continuation of bombing and other military activities in Cambodia.

Opinion of the Court of Appeals by Circuit Judge Mulligan:

At the outset, as the parties agreed below and on the argument on appeal, we should emphasize that we are not deciding the wisdom, the propriety or the morality of the war in Indo-China and particularly the on-going bombing in Cambodia. This is the responsibility of the Executive and the Legislative branches of the government. The role of the Judiciary is to determine the legality of the challenged action and the threshold question is whether under the "political question" doctrine we should decline even to do that....

The most recent holding of this court now pertinent is *Dacosta v. Laird*, 471 F.2d 1146 (2d Cir. 1973) where an inductee urged that the President's unilateral decision to mine the harbors of North Vietnam and to bomb targets in that country constituted an escalation of the war, which was illegal in the absence of additional Congressional authorization. Judge Kaufman found that this was a political question which was non-justiciable, recognizing that the court was incapable of assessing the facts....

We fail to see how the present challenge involving the bombing in Cambodia is in any significant manner distinguishable from the situation discussed by Judge Kaufman in *Dacosta*....Judge Judd found that the continuing bombing of Cambodia, after the removal of American forces and prisoners of war from Vietnam, represents "a basic change in the situation; which must be considered in determining the duration of prior Congressional authorization." He further found such action a tactical decision not traditionally confided in the Commander-in-Chief. These are precisely the questions of fact involving military and diplomatic expertise not vested in the judiciary, which make the issue political and thus beyond the competence of that court or this court to determine. We are not privy to the information supplied to the Executive by his professional military and diplomatic advisers and even if we were, we are hardly competent to evaluate it. If we were incompetent to judge the significance of the mining and bombing of North Vietnam's harbors and territories, we fail to see our competence to determine that the bombing of Cambodia is a "basic change" in the situation and that it is not a "tactical decision" within the competence of the President....

The court below and our dissenting Brother assume that since American ground forces and prisoners have been removed and accounted for, Congressional authorization has ceased as determined by virtue of the so-called Mansfield Amendment....The fallacy of this position is that we have no way of knowing whether the Cambodia bombing furthers or hinders the goals of the Mansfield Amendment....Moreover, although Sec. 601(a)(1) of the Amendment urges the President to remove all military forces contingent upon release of American prisoners, it also in Sec. 601 (a)(2) urges him to negotiate for an immediate cease fire of all parties in the hostilities in Indo-China. In our view, the return and repatriation of American troops only represents the beginning and not the end of the inquiry as to whether such a basic change has occurred that the Executive at this stage is suddenly bereft of power and authority....The strictures of the political question doctrine cannot be avoided by resort to the law of agency as the court did below, finding the Congress the principle and the President an agent or servant. Judicial *ipse dixits* cannot provide any proper basis particularly for the injunctive relief granted here which is unprecedented in American jurisprudence.

Since the argument that continuing Congressional approval was necessary, was predicated upon a determination that the Cambodian bombing constituted a basic change in the war not within the tactical discretion of the President and since that is a determination we have found to be a political question, we have not found it necessary to dwell at length upon Congressional participation....We cannot resist however commenting that the most recent expression of Congressional approval by appropriation, the Joint Resolution Continuing Appropriations for Fiscal 1974 ... enacted into law July 1, 1973, contains the following provision [Sec. 108]: "Notwithstanding any other provision of law, on or after August 15, 1973, no funds herein or heretofore appropriated may be obligated or expended to finance directly or indirectly combat activities by United States military forces in or over or from off the shores of North Vietnam, South Vietnam, Laos or Cambodia."

Assuming arguendo that the military and diplomatic issues were manageable and that we were obliged to find some participation by Congress, we cannot see how this provision does not support the proposition that the Congress has approved the Cambodian bombing. The statute is facially clear but its applicability is contested by plaintiffs on several grounds which were essentially adopted by the court below. The argument is made that the Congress didn't really mean what it said because it was coerced by the President who had vetoed Congressional Bills which would have immediately cut off Cambodia funds. Not being able to muster sufficient strength to overcome the veto, the argument runs, the Congress was forced willy nilly to enact the appropriation legislation. Resort is made to the floor debate which it is argued bolsters view that individual legislators expressed personal disapproval of the bombing and did not interpret the appropriation as an approval to bomb but simply a recognition that it gave the President the power to bomb. It is further urged that since the Constitution entrusts the power to declare war to a majority of the Congress, the veto exercised makes it possible for the President to thwart the will of Congress by holding one-third plus one of the members of either House. We find none of these arguments persuasive....

We cannot agree that the Congress was "coerced" by the President's veto. There was unquestionably a Congressional impasse resulting from the desire of a majority of Congress to stop bombing immediately and the desire of the President that his discretion be unfettered by an arbitrarily selected date. Instead of an acute constitutional confrontation as Senator Javits noted an "agreement" was reached....

While the Constitution vests the war declaring authority in the Congress, the Founding Fathers also conferred the veto power upon the President. The suggestion that the veto power is impotent with respect to an authority vested solely in Congress by the Constitution is unsupported by any citation of authority and is hardly persuasive. It of course assumes here that the Cambodian bombing constitutes a new war requiring a new declaration and that it is not part of the extrication of a long suffering nation from an Indo-China war lasting for several years. This again in our view is the nucleus of the issue and we have no way of resolving that question particularly here on a motion for summary judgment.

We finally note, although again not necessarily in view of our holding in Part I, our disagreement with our colleague Judge Oakes that any of the parties plaintiff have standing....[W]e held that a serviceman does have standing if he is under orders to fight in the combat to which he objects. Here none of the servicemen plaintiffs are presently under orders to fight in Cambodia. They have been relieved of any such military obligation and indeed one has been separated from the service....Neither do we see any adequate support for the standing of Representative Holtzman. She has not been denied any right to vote on Cambodia by any action of the defendants. She has fully participated in the Congressional debates which have transpired since her election to the Congress. The fact that her vote was ineffective was due to the contrary votes of her colleagues and not the defendants herein. The claim that the establishment of illegality here would be relevant in possible impeachment proceedings against the President would in effect be asking the judiciary for an advisory opinion which is precisely and historically what the "cases and controversy" conditions set forth in Article III, Section 2 of the Constitution forbid....

The judgment is reversed and the case is remanded with instructions to dismiss the complaint....

Dissenting opinion by Circuit Judge Oakes:
I believe there is standing for Congresswoman Holtzman under *Baker v. Carr*, 369 U.S. 186 (1962) and *Coleman v. Miller*, 307 U.S. 423 (1939). I believe there is standing for the airmen-appellees under *Berk v. Laird*, 429 F.2d 302 (2d Cir. 1970) and *Massachusetts v. Laird*, 451 F.2d 26 (1st Cir. 1971) which has not been mooted by their return to the United States....

I believe there is justiciability under *Dacosta v. Laird*, 471 F.2d 1146 (2d Cir. 1973)....There is here "a manageable standard" under ... *Youngstown Sheet & Tube Co. v. Sawyer*, 343 U.S. 579 (1952), since there has been such a "radical change in the character of war operations." The Defense Department is continuing to bomb in Cambodia despite the cease-fire in Vietnam and despite the return of our prisoners of war from North Vietnam. The justiciable question then is whether there is any Constitutional authorization for the employment of United States armed forces over Cambodia, now that the war in Vietnam has come to an end. There is no question under the law of this Circuit ... that the Executive lacks unilateral power to commit American forces to combat absent a "belligerent attack" or "a grave emergency."...

Has Congress ratified or authorized the bombing in Cambodia by appropriations acts or otherwise?...

The combination of concealment of the facts from Congress together with the enactment of a policy of "earliest practicable" withdrawal did not amount in my mind to an appropriations carte blanche to the military to carry on bombing in Cambodia after the cease-fire, withdrawal of our troops from Vietnam, and return of our prisoners of war from North Vietnam....

If we return to fundamentals, as I think we must in a case of any conflict of view between the other two Branches of Government, it will be recalled that the Founding Fathers deliberately eschewed the example of the British Monarchy in which was lodged the authority to declare war and to raise and regulate fleets and armies....Rather, these powers were deliberately given to the Legislative Branch of the new American Republic in Article I, Section 8 of the Constitution....I fail to see, and the Government in its able presentation has failed to point out, where the Congress ever authorized the continuation of bombing in Cambodia after the cease-fire in Vietnam, the withdrawal of our forces there, and the return of our prisoners of war to our shores. Accordingly, I must dissent, and although on a somewhat different analysis would affirm the judgment below.

Note: If national security was—and is—the overriding value during times of declared war, with the consequence that the President as commander-in-chief is a constitutional dictator, what may be said about his commander-in-chief powers when Congress has not declared war? The question (as these Vietnam era cases demonstrate) was not easily answered, and there was no neat and tidy way to summarize the various considerations save in high-level abstractions. Certain principles, however, were discernible. First, there was an absence of authoritative precedent, the courts being only too willing to leave the questions that have arisen up to the political branches of government. Second, the commander-in-chief power, despite the constitutional language, was to some immeasurable but nonetheless definite extent (since it relates to the war power) shared with Congress. [A. Miller, Presidential Power 163 (1977).] Third, the President as commander- in-chief does have responsibilities and powers to protect the lives and property of American citizens abroad, to carry out treaty obligations, to protect the national security, to deal with aggression from other nations (aggression not against the United States proper but in geographical areas deemed important to American interests), and to conduct paramilitary operations (such as covert activities of the Central Intelligence Agency). Here, as elsewhere, the legal situation was foggy because of the absence of precedent—no one has a correlative right to force presidential action via the courts—and because of a combination of vague constitutional terms, statutory enactments, and (indeed) failures of Congress to act with respect to certain situations. [C. Rossiter, The Supreme Court and the Commander in Chief 150-51 (R. Longaker ed. 1976).] Furthermore, much of this activity was conducted in either relative or absolute secrecy, so that neither the American people nor members of Congress were privy to the details of what was done in the name of national security. [*Id.*] The result was that the President as commander-in-chief and with all the executive power was free to operate with vast discretion.

The essence of the debate over the President's commander-in-chief powers outside of declared war was whether he had independent power to use military forces not only to protect the nation from attack but to further the nation's interests—as he alone perceived those interests. [A. Miller, 191.] In *Holtzman I* (at the district court level), the court reasoned that earlier cases had presumed continuing mutual participation by the President and Congress in the use of force. Noting the withdrawal of American troops and the resolution of Congress which specified the date on which appropriations could no longer be used to sustain hostilities in Southeast Asia, the court found that the August 15 compromise could not be viewed as an affirmative authorization by Congress.

Indeed, given the more fluid setting of troop withdrawal, a peace agreement, and continued bombing, past congressional authorizations in no way could be interpreted to cover a changed situation. Mutual participation was lacking! [C. Rossiter, 149]. The court concluded, in citing *Youngstown*, that in whatever way an executive might interpret an emergency, emergency did not create power unless Congress shared in giving authority for its use.

In *Holtzman II* (at the court of appeals level), the decision exposed judicial ambivalence. Here the court concluded that the nature of military tactics used by a President to wind down a war was a political question beyond the capacity of courts to judge; and it was beyond the judicial function to determine whether a military situation has changed to such an extent that a renewed authorization was required from Congress. Moreover, the appeals court embraced the functional equivalent theory by accepting the notion that the August 15 compromise could be interpreted, in its terms, as an act of mutual participation. The court suggested, ultimately, what some other lower courts had affirmed, namely that there were judicially discoverable and manageable standards—in this instance the August 15 cutoff—which courts could examine as to the sufficiency of mutual participation.

The ambivalence, however, came from the way the court of appeals treated the "political question" doctrine. Did it mean that while the Constitution was law, it contained law that the courts may not apply, or did it mean that there were legal requirements in the Constitution that may be violated without giving rise to correlative rights that courts may remedy? [C. Pyle & R. Pious, The President, Congress, and the Constitution 359 (1984).] If it meant the latter, what was to be made of the right to life guaranteed by the Fifth Amendment's due process clause? [*Id.*] If the President was under no enforceable legal obligation to follow "due process" in the use of the military, then did he not have the equivalent of an absolute royal prerogative to send citizens to their death in military operations of his own choosing? [*Id.*] Would it be too candid to say that the political question doctrine (during the Vietnam era and all emergency situations) was simply an unprincipled device whereby judges avoided confrontations with elected officials on major fundamental issues of such political passion that the judges were likely to be ignored, or, if they were not ignored, would require policy reversals too massive in scale, cost, or embarrassment to be ordered by nonelected officials? [*Id.*]

Holtzman was appealed to the Supreme Court. The issue of independent presidential power might have been presented squarely if it had reached the Court after the August 15 date, then a week away, and if the President had continued the bombing. It was altogether likely that given the force of the *Youngstown* decision—if presidential seizures of private property contrary to congressional intent fell under Justice Jackson's category III, surely the continued bombing of Cambodia in the face of specific congressional opposition would similarly fall into category III—the conflict would have created votes sufficient at least for argument to be heard. Instead, with presidential compliance virtually assured (the Court was not then in session), Justice Marshall speaking for his circuit, refused to issue a stay. [*Holtzman v. Schlesinger,* 414 U.S. 1304 (1973).] The only point of potential legal significance in Marshall's opinion was that he referred positively to "a respectable and growing body of lower court opinion holding that Art. I, Sec. 8, Cl. 11, imposes some judicially manageable standards as to congressional authorization for war-making ... [and] as a matter of substantive law, it seems likely that the President may not wage war without some form of congressional approval—except, perhaps, in the case of a pressing emergency or when the [P]resident is in the process of extricating himself from a war Congress once authorized." [414 U.S. at 1311-13.]

The Vietnam cases raised more questions than they ever answered. Their major contribution was the mutual participation theory (the functional equivalent of a declaration of war), which found its legislative expression in the War Powers Resolution (Pub.L. No. 93-148)—an enactment which found its origin, in part, in the very failure of the courts to take a more active role in determining the scope of presidential power to commit troops abroad.

Dellums v. Bush, 752 F.Supp. 1141 (D.D.C. 1990)

The War Powers Resolution was a compromise product re-passed after a presidential veto. It called for the "collective judgment" of both Congress and the President before American troops are sent into combat. It recognized that the President may use military force without prior congressional authorization for sixty days (with the option of extending this period to ninety days), but longer military engagements would require congressional action. Politically that had been the case. Presidents Ford, Carter, Reagan, and Bush had all used military force without seeking congressional authorization, but each operation was of a short-term nature: Ford's rescue of the U.S. merchant ship *Mayaguez,* which had been seized by Cambodians; Carter's attempted rescue of American hostages in Iran; Reagan's invasion of Grenada and air strikes against Libya; and Bush's intervention in Panama. More extensive operations, such as the commitment of troops to Lebanon in 1983 and to the Middle East in 1991, had been authorized by Congress.

Part of the War Powers Resolution never functioned as contemplated. Its framers anticipated that the President would re-port to Congress when he dispatched troops to hostilities or imminent hostilities, and that the report would trigger the sixty to ninety day clock. However, under section 4(a)(1), the clock did not actually begin to tick unless the President reported under this particular provision. Not surprising, Presidents did not report under that provision. Instead, they reported "consistent with the War Powers Resolution." Only President Ford reported under section 4(a)(1) for the *Mayaguez* capture, but by the time he reported to Congress the operation was over. The only other time section 4(a)(1) started the clock was in 1983 when Congress passed a statute authorizing military action in Lebanon (97 Stat. 805).

In August 1990, President Bush sent military forces to Saudi Arabia after Iraq invaded Kuwait. Although members of Congress expressed concern about the President's deployment of troops, there was little discussion about his constitutional authority until November when he more than doubled the size of American forces to create an offensive capability. Administrative officials claimed that President Bush could shift from a *defensive* posture to *offensive* operations without first obtaining authority from Congress.

The plaintiffs were fifty-three members of the House of Representatives and one U.S. Senator who brought suit requesting an injunction directed to the President to prevent him from going to war against Iraq without first securing a declaration of war or other explicit congressional authorization for such action.

Basic Questions: Do these issues raise a political question? Do plaintiffs have standing to bring suit? Does the doctrine of remedial discretion negate this action? Is the controversy ripe for adjudication?

Opinion of the District Court by Judge Green:

The House of Representatives and the Senate have in various ways expressed their support for the President's past and present actions in the Persian Gulf. However, the Congress was not asked for, and it did not take, action pursuant to Article I, Section 8, Clause 11 of the Constitution "to declare war" on Iraq. On November 19, 1990, the congressional plaintiffs brought this action, which proceeds on the premise that the initiation of offensive United States military action is imminent, that such action would be unlawful in the absence of a declaration of war by the Congress, and that a war without concurrence by the Congress would deprive the congressional plaintiffs of the voice to which they are entitled under the Constitution. The Department of Justice, acting on behalf of the President, is opposing the motion for preliminary injunction, and it has also moved to dismiss. Plaintiffs thereafter moved for summary judgment.

The Department raises a number of defenses to the lawsuit—most particularly that the complaint presents a nonjusticiable political question, that plaintiffs lack standing to maintain the action, that their claim violates established canons of equity jurisprudence, and that the issue of the proper allocation of the war making powers between the branches is not ripe for decision. These will now be considered seriatim....

It is the position of the Department of Justice on behalf of the President that the simultaneous existence of all these provisions [Art. II, Sec. 1, Cl. 1 and Sec. 2] renders it impossible to isolate the war-declaring power. The Department further argues that the design of the Constitution is to have the various war-and military-related provisions construed and acting together, and that their harmonization is a political rather than a legal question. In short, the Department relies on the political question doctrine.

The doctrine is premised both upon the separation of powers and the inherent limits of judicial abilities....In relation to the issues involved in this case, the Department of Justice expands on its basic theme, contending that by their very nature the determination whether certain types of military actions require a declaration of war is not justiciable, but depends instead upon delicate judgments by the political branches. On that view, the question whether an offensive action taken by American armed forces constitutes an act of war (to be initiated by a declaration of war) or an "offensive military attack" (presumably undertaken by the President in his capacity as commander-in-chief) is not one of objective fact but involves an exercise of judgment based upon all the vagaries of foreign affairs and national security....Indeed, the Department contends that there are no judicially discoverable and manageable standards to apply, claiming that only the political branches are able to determine whether or not this country is at war. Such a determination, it is said, is based upon "a political judgment" about the significance of those facts. Under this rationale, a court cannot make an independent determination on this issue because it cannot take adequate account of these political considerations.

This claim on behalf of the Executive is far too sweeping to be accepted by the courts. If the Executive had the sole power to determine that any particular offensive military operation, no matter how vast, does not constitute war-making but only an offensive military attack, the congressional power to declare war will be at the mercy of a semantic decision by the Executive. Such an "interpretation" would evade the plain language of the Constitution, and it cannot stand.

That is not to say that, assuming that the issue is factually closed or ambiguous or fraught with intricate technical military and diplomatic baggage, the courts would not defer to the political branches to determine whether or not particular hostilities might qualify as a "war." However, here the forces involved are of such magnitude and significance as to present no serious claim that a war would not ensue if they became engaged in combat, and it is therefore clear that congressional approval is required if Congress desires to become involved....

Given these factual allegations and the legal principles outlined above, the court has no hesitation in concluding that an offensive entry into Iraq by several hundred thousand United States servicemen under the conditions described above could be described as a "war" within the meaning of Article I, Section 8, Clause 11, of the Constitution. To put it another way: the court is not prepared to read out of the Constitution the clause granting to the Congress, and to it alone, the authority "to declare war."

The Department of Justice argues next that the plaintiffs lack "standing" to pursue this action.

The Supreme Court has established a two-part test for determining standing under Article III of the Constitution. The plaintiff must allege: (1) that he personally suffered actual or threatened injury, and (2) that the "injury 'fairly can be traced to the challenged action' and 'is likely to be redressed by a favorable decision.'" *Valley Forge Christian College v. Americans United for Separation of Church and State,* 454 U.S. 464, 472 (1982)....For the purpose of determining standing on a motion to dismiss, the Court must "accept as true all material allegations of the complaint, and must construe the complaint in favor of the complaining party." *Warth v. Seldin,* 422 U.S. 490, 501 (1975). Accordingly, plaintiffs' allegations of an imminent danger of hostilities between the United States forces and Iraq must be accepted as true for this purpose.

Plaintiffs further claim that their interest guaranteed by the War Clause of the Constitution is in immediate danger of being harmed by military actions the President may take against Iraq. That claim states a legally cognizable injury, for as the Court of Appeals for this Circuit stated in a leading case, members of Congress plainly have an interest in protecting their right to vote on matters entrusted to their respective chambers by the Constitution. *Moore v. United States House of Representatives,* 773 F.2d 946 (D.C. Cir. 1984). Indeed, Moore pointed out even more explicitly that where a congressional plaintiff suffers "unconstitutional deprivation of [his] constitutional duties or rights ... if the injuries are specific and discernible," a finding of harm sufficient to support standing is justified. *Id.* at 952....

With close to 400,000 United States troops stationed in Saudi Arabia, with all troop rotation and leave provisions suspended, and with the President having acted vigorously on his own as well as through the Secretary of State to obtain from the United Nations Security Council a resolution authorizing the use of all available means to remove Iraqi forces from Kuwait, including the use of force, it is disingenuous for the Department to characterize plaintiffs' allegations as to the imminence of the threat of offensive military action for standing purposes as "remote and conjectural."...For these reasons, the [c]ourt concludes that the plaintiffs have adequately alleged a threat of injury in fact necessary to support standing....

The plaintiffs in this case do not have a remedy available from their fellow legislators. While action remains open to them which would make the issue involved more concrete, and hence make the matter ripe for review by the court, these actions would not remedy the threatened harm plaintiffs assert. A joint resolution counseling the President to refrain from attacking Iraq without a congressional declaration of war would not be likely to stop the President from initiating such military action if he is persuaded that the Constitution affirmatively gives him the power to act otherwise.

Plaintiffs in the instant case, therefore, cannot gain "substantial relief" by persuasion of their colleagues alone. The "remedies" of cutting off funding to the military or impeaching the President are not available to these plaintiffs either politically or practically. Additionally, these "remedies" would not afford the relief sought by the plaintiffs—which is the guarantee that they will have the opportunity to debate and vote on the wisdom of initiating a military attack against Iraq before the United States military becomes embroiled in belligerency with that nation.

Although, as discussed above, the court rejects several of defendant's objections to the maintenance of this lawsuit, and concluded that, in principle, an injunction may issue at the request of Members of Congress to prevent the conduct of a war which is about to be carried on without congressional authorization, it does not follow that these plaintiffs are entitled to relief at this juncture. For the plaintiffs are met with a significant obstacle to such relief: the doctrine of ripeness.

It has long been held that, as a matter of deference that is due to the other branches of government, the Judiciary will undertake to render decisions that compel action by the President or the Congress only if the dispute before the court is truly ripe, in that all the factors necessary for a decision are present then and there. The need for ripeness as a prerequisite to judicial action has particular weight in a case such as this. The principle that the courts shall be prudent in the exercise of their authority is never more compelling than when they are called upon to adjudicate on such sensitive issues as those trenching upon military and foreign affairs. Judicial restraint must, of course, be even further enhanced when the issue is one—as here—on which the other two branches may be deeply divided. Hence the necessity for determining at the outset whether the controversy is truly "ripe" for decision or whether, on the other hand, the judiciary should abstain from rendering a decision on ripeness grounds....

For these reasons, this court has elected to follow the course described by Justice Powell in his concurrence in *Goldwater v. Carter*, 444 U.S. 996 (1979). In that opinion, Justice Powell provided a test for ripeness in cases involving a confrontation between the legislative and executive branches that is helpful here. ...[He] proposed that "a dispute between Congress and the President is not ready for judicial review unless and until each branch has taken action asserting its constitutional authority." Id. at 997. He further explained that in *Goldwater* there had been no such confrontation because there had as yet been no vote in the Senate as to what to do in the face of the President's action to terminate the treaty with Taiwan, and he went on to say that the "Judicial Branch should not decide issues affecting the allocation of power between the President and Congress until the political branches reach a constitutional impasse. Otherwise we would encourage small groups or even individual Members of Congress to seek judicial resolution of issues before the normal political process has the opportunity to resolve the conflict....It cannot be said that either the Senate or the House has rejected the President's claim. If the Congress chooses not to confront the President, it is not our task to do so." *Id.* at 997-98....

All these difficulties are avoided by a requirement that the plaintiffs in an action of this kind be or represent a majority of the Members of the Congress: a majority of the body that under the Constitution is the only one competent to declare war, and there-fore also the one with the ability to seek an order from the courts to prevent anyone else, *i.e.,* the Executive, from in effect declaring war. In short, unless the Congress as a whole, or be a majority, is heard from, the controversy here cannot be deemed ripe; it is only if the majority of the Congress seeks relief from an infringement on its constitutional war declaration power that it may be entitled to receive it....

Should the congressional ripeness issue ... be resolved in favor of a finding of ripeness as a consequence of actions taken by the Congress as a whole, there will still be time enough to determine whether, in view of the conditions as they are found to exist at that time, the Executive is so clearly committed to early military operations amounting to "war" in the constitutional sense that the court would be justified in concluding that the remainder of the test of ripeness has been met. And of course an injunction will be issued only if, on both of the aspects of the doctrine discussed above, the court could find that the controversy is ripe for judicial decision. That situation does not, or at least not yet, prevail, and plaintiffs' request for a preliminary injunction will therefore not be granted.

Note: In holding that the dispute was not ripe for judicial determination, the district court nevertheless forcefully rejected many of the sweeping claims for unlimited presidential authority advanced by the Justice Department. In fact, the decision in *Dellums* probably contributed somewhat to prompting the Bush Administration to rethink its constitutional theories about presidential power. On January 8, 1991, about a week before a deadline established by the United Nations for Iraq to withdraw from Kuwait if it wanted to avoid war, President Bush sent a letter to congressional leaders recommending legislative action. Although his letter did not explicitly acknowledge the need for congressional authority, it recognized that the United States would be on firmer ground if it proceeded with joint action between Congress and the President. Congress, in turn, passed legislation on January 12, 1991, authorizing the use of military force (105 Stat. 3) "pursuant to United Nations Security Council Resolution 678."

The decision by the President—after the *Dellums* holding and the earlier ruling in *Lowry v. Reagan,* 676 F.Supp. 333 (D.C.C. 1987), which declared that escort operations of Kuwait oil tankers in the Persian Gulf constituted a political question—to seek congressional support for military action in the Persian Gulf reflected a policy that had developed with the executive branch (though not always adhered to) in the post Vietnam War years. To fight a war successfully, particularly an extended war, the President ought to secure the support and cooperation of Congress. Secretary of State Henry Kissinger stated in 1975: "Comity between the executive and legislative branches is the only possible basis for national action. The decade-long struggle in this country over executive dominance in foreign policy is over. The recognition that the Congress is a coequal branch of government is the dominant fact of national politics today. The executive accepts that the Congress must have both the sense and the reality of participation: foreign affairs must be a shared enterprise." [75 Dep't St.Bull. 562 (1975).] And in 1984 Secretary of Defense Caspar Weinberger also concluded that American troops should not be sent into combat without congressional and public support.

There is still a hollow ring to all this, however, as the overwhelming majority of the cases indicate. What is being suggested—real cooperation—is no doubt the wisest policy, and closest to the intention of the Framers; but until a majority of members of Congress finds the courage to say no to the President (who must simultaneously learn to govern under democratic constraints) and not go along no matter what, it is only a suggestion, not a reality. The problem that seems to be forever overlooked is the unwillingness of the American people, along with their legislators and judges, to understand that war and peace are not the same thing and cannot coexist in the same place at the same time. As a result, we have—and use—a Constitution for peace and another one for war.

8

Constitutional Government and Dictatorship

Few would disagree that the growth of presidential power after World War II was more the result of the pressures of the contemporary world than from presidential personal ambition or self-aggrandizement (although the final verdict is not yet in on Richard Nixon). Moreover, in spite of the presidential excesses that dominate this period of our history, most observers would agree that vigorous presidential leadership is not only necessary but can be used for beneficial purposes and with a fundamental respect for the Constitution.[1] Indeed, any effort to impose restraints on presidential initiative, discretion, and power by means of judicial intervention or legislative restrictions can be damaging to the Nation's larger security interests as well as to the constitutional scheme itself.[2] Nevertheless, these excessive exercises of constitutional power did not go unchallenged, and judicial and legislative sensitivity to limitations on presidential emergency powers seemed to have matured into a special concern for the Bill of Rights and the separation of powers and checks and balances.[3] These institutions of government rediscovered what the Framers knew only too well: under no circumstances should we return to the old British system of Crown Prerogatives, which gave the monarch not only the power to declare and make war, but the power to raise fleets and armies and to demand funds to finance them.[4]

The essence of the debate over the President's power as commander-in-chief outside of declared wars is whether he has independent power to use military forces not only to protect the Nation from attack but to further the Nation's interests—as he perceives those interests. When President Harry Truman ordered American troops into Korea in June 1950, a new era in the use of presidential power began. The constitutional rationale for the President's action was spelled out by the Department of State soon after issuance of the order to intervene. Observing that there was "a traditional power of the President to use the armed forces ... without consulting Congress,"[5] administration spokesmen emphasized: "The President, as Commander in Chief of the Armed Forces of the United States, has full control over the use thereof. He also has authority to conduct the foreign relations of the United States. Since the beginning of United States history, he has, on numerous occasions, utilized these powers in sending armed forces abroad."[6]   While secondary reliance was placed on the United Nations' Charter and the Security Council's resolution requesting support for those resisting North Korean aggression, primary reliance was on plenary presidential power and its exercise independent of other agencies, including Congress.[7] In effect, our entry into Korea was an act of independent presidential power.

It is generally agreed[8] that there were two constitutional legacies of the Korean conflict. On the one hand, there was the greater caution in the use of troops and the request for "area resolutions"[9] by the Eisenhower Administration; on the other hand, there was the legacy that said that Truman had established—as firmly as did Lincoln almost a century earlier—a clear precedent for later presidential initiatives. Consequently, when the United States became deeply involved in Vietnam beginning in the mid-1960s there was no firm grounding, in either post World War II precedent or practice, for the proposition that Congress needed to "authorize" the use of troops abroad if their use was to be constitutional. On the contrary, the presidential position was that while any formal support that Congress might wish to extend in a given instance would be welcomed, the *independent power* of the chief executive was sufficient.[10]

The Gulf of Tonkin Resolution,[11] which preceded by several months the massive buildup of American combat forces in Vietnam by President Lyndon Johnson in 1965, in specific terms authorized nothing, but supported a great deal.[12] So did subsequent appropriations for the war. In the resolution, Congress approved "the determination of the President as Commander in Chief, to take all necessary measures to repel any armed attack against the forces of the United States and to prevent further aggression."[13]   Congress then went on to say: "[T]he United States is ... prepared, as the President determines, to take all necessary steps, including the use of armed force, to assist any member or protocol state of the Southeast Asia Collective Defense Treaty requesting assistance in defense of its freedom."[14] The operative phrases were "as the President determines" and "all necessary steps." The language itself negated any presumed limitations on the power of the President to use military force and, in effect, delegated the war powers of Congress to the President without a clear understanding of what the logical consequences of this action might be.[15] Not surprising, the administration—and later the lower federal courts[16]—took the resolution to be the "functional equivalent" of a declaration of war.

Both the Johnson and Nixon Administrations viewed Vietnam from somewhat different perspectives. President Johnson's response to the Tonkin Gulf Resolution was that it was unnecessary, even though the administration requested the resolution and employed it openly as the justification for the use of armed forces in Southeast Asia. The President possessed inherent, and independent, war powers—and it was these powers (in addition to the facts of history, the SEATO Treaty, and the Tonkin Gulf Resolution) that justified his constitutional position.[17] President Nixon, on the other hand, abandoned reliance on the SEATO Treaty and—when the Tonkin Gulf Resolution was repealed by Congress[18]—relied instead on the historical precedent of some two hundred plus instances in which troops had been used abroad by previous Presidents without congressional authorization. In addition, the President argued the "functional equivalence" theory; and when the validity of that argument came to an end, Nixon (like Johnson before him) once again relied on the inherent, independent powers of the President as commander-in-chief over armed forces committed in the field.[19] Unfortunately, the Nixon Administration overstepped its hand, here, by continuing to press the independent powers of the President argument, even after the argument had lost its substance. After the troop withdrawal was completed in March 1973, the President ordered bombing of Cambodia and Laos and still continued to rely on his power as commander-in-chief to repel attacks on American armed forces.[20] But after March 1973, there were none left to be attacked.

Earlier I suggested that the essence of the debate over the President's powers as commander-in-chief outside of declared wars is whether he has independent power to use military forces not only to protect the Nation from attack but to further the Nation's interests—as he perceives those interests. That question, notwithstanding Jackson's concurring opinion in *Youngstown*,[21] has not been answered by any *definitive* Supreme Court decision, but Congress has attempted its own clarification in the War Powers Resolution[22] and the National Emergencies Act.[23] The former was vetoed by President Nixon as an unconstitutional infringement of the President's powers as commander-in-chief. It was enacted over his veto, and may be seen as the making of constitutional law by Congress.[24] The War Powers Resolution (WPR) is a statutory restriction on the President's powers. It is also ambiguous. Even though it limits the President's powers to commit troops into hostilities to instances of (1) a declaration of war; (2) a specific statutory authorization; or (3) a national emergency created by an attack on the United States, its territories or possessions, or its armed forces, the limitations and prohibitions contained in the WPR are more imagined than real. The Resolution continues to recognize that the President can unilaterally use military forces whenever and wherever he wishes to do so.[25] In other words, despite the fire storm of emotion and rhetoric, very little—if anything—has changed.[26]

The National Emergencies Act (NEA), on the other hand, attempts to correct decades of congressional inactivity in the legislative oversight of executive actions. The Act terminated four existing states of emergency, abolished most of the existing 470 emergency statutes, and created new procedures for delegating emergency powers to the President. Under the NEA, the President *can still use* standing emergency legislation to declare a state of emergency, but his authority to act can only remain in effect for one year. The President is required to report to Congress his reasons for declaring the emergency and must indicate in his report the constitutional and statutory bases for all emergency actions.[27] He must also report to Congress every six months while the state of emergency remains in effect. Congress is required to vote at six-month intervals on whether to continue the state of emergency. At the end of the year, the President may ask Congress to renew the state of emergency for another year term. The law also provides that the House and Senate can end the state of emergency by a concurrent resolution not subject to presidential veto.[28]

Like the WPR, the NEA recognizes the authority of the President to declare a state of national emergency, as well as to terminate one. Like the WPR, the NEA says nothing about the exercise of presidential emergency powers in that crucial period between declaration and termination. Is this really a significant structural change in constitutional meaning—and an effective legislative limitation on presidential emergency powers—from the Civil War period when Lincoln invoked the power to declare the existence of the emergency, took all necessary measures to meet the emergency, and determined when the emergency was over?[29] I think not. In fact, it is really the political process, not the positive law, that determines the course of American action, and it is the political process that provides a "precedent" for the use of violence.[30] The essential points to remember, however, are that (1) if you cannot control and limit presidential initiative to take action, you simply cannot control and limit presidential power; and (2) the President, when he takes such actions, labors under the obligation to be successful.[31] Certainly little or nothing has changed since 1968 when Philip Kurland wrote:

We are prepared, according to our loyalties, to back a President that we admire and condemn the one that we dislike, when what we should be doing is to recognize the wisdom of the Constitutional provisions that would preclude the unlimited exercise of power that we have witnessed by each of our recent chief executives and the unalloyed cowardice of the Congress in allowing such arrogation of power to the executive branch.[32]

Since the end of World War II, the United States has been engaged (until recently) in a cold war which constantly threatened to turn hot, as it did in Korea in 1950, Vietnam in the decade of the 1960s and 1970s, and the Persian Gulf in 1991. This protracted period of tension has made necessary an appraisal of the impact which wartime conditions have on the organization and operation of American government itself, for military crises test the basic conceptions of our constitutional system.[33] Which agency, for example, is primarily responsible for determining the existence of an emergency and for taking action to meet it? Are there limits on the powers of government in time of war? What is the scope of judicial review during emergency periods? How does war affect the citizen's constitutionally guaranteed liberties? These questions go to the heart of America's ability to maintain its system of constitutional democratic government while meeting the challenges of an age in which the specter of war—real or imagined—is always present. Next to the issue of war or peace itself, they raise the most serious problems of our time.

The Nation's experience with wartime regimes is relatively limited. Yet during the past century and one-third, the United States has faced five major war emergencies—the Civil War, the two World Wars, Korea, and Vietnam—and from this experience has emerged a number of principles of wartime government involving both the form and the substance of the constitutional system. These principles are:

1. In time of war the power of the national government is expanded to whatever extent the political branches deem necessary for a successful response to the crisis. There are no limits on the power of the government to ensure the Nation's survival.[34]

2. This vast emergency power is largely concentrated in the executive branch of government. War crises require unity, leadership, and action. Only the President can fill these needs, and he is inevitably the focus of any emergency regime. Wartime government is essentially executive government.[35]

3. The expansion and concentration of governmental power under war conditions results in suspension of the Constitution's basic structural principles. Federalism has virtually no effect, for the Nation must act as a single entity in meeting the challenge; the separation of powers is bridged, as Congress must accept the commander-in-chief's determination of the Nation's needs.[36]

4. Judicial review of governmental action is largely nullified in time of war, as the law of necessity supersedes the law of the Constitution. With the Nation's survival at stake, the Supreme Court cannot substitute its judgment of what is permissible for the political branches' determination of what is necessary. As a result, the Court must acquiesce in assertions of power which under normal conditions it could not consider constitutional.[37]

5. With the Constitution suspended and the Court neutralized, individual liberty is subject to restriction by governmental authority. Personal freedom may be circumscribed to whatever extent the war effort demands. The preservation of the Nation, which gives life and meaning to the Constitution, takes precedence over the rights which that Constitution was established to protect.[38]

These principles, of course, apply only to conditions of total war, and, reflecting the limited nature of past American wars (as compared with the experience of other nations), their full effect has never been felt in the United States. But to the extent which the gravity of each particular crisis requires their application, these are the basic rules of governmental organization and operation during periods of grave national emergency.[39] The cases in this textbook confirm that fact. They make clear that wartime government is, in essence and oftentimes in fact, extraconstitutional government. In times of crisis we exist under a wartime constitution. We are required to fight a successful total war and still be a democracy when the war is over. We have rejected Benjamin Franklin's admonition that "[t]hose who would give up essential liberty to purchase a little temporary safety deserve neither liberty nor safety."[40]

In 1948 Clinton Rossiter presented academia with a pioneering work on this topic titled *Constitutional Dictatorship: Crisis Government in Modern Democracies.* His Preface set the basic theme of what was to follow. He suggested that the institutions and methods of dictatorship have been used by free men of the modern democracies during periods of severe national emergency. He then went on to suggest what he believed to be a dangerous but inescapable truth: "No form of government can survive that excludes dictatorship when the life of the nation is at stake."[41] According to Rossiter, the principle of constitutional dictatorship finds its rationale in three fundamental facts:

1. The complex system of government of the democratic, constitutional state is essentially designed to function under normal, peaceful conditions and is oftentimes unequal to the exigencies of a great national crisis.[42]

2. Therefore, in time of crisis a democratic, constitutional government must be temporarily altered to whatever degree is necessary to overcome the peril and restore normal conditions. In effect, government will have more power and the people fewer rights.[43]

3. Finally, this strong government, which in some instances might become an outright dictatorship, can have no other purpose than the preservation of independence of the state, the maintenance of the existing constitutional order, and the defense of the political and social liberties of the people.[44]

Furthermore, Rossiter continues, the duty to be pursued by constitutional dictatorship is exceedingly narrow: to end the crisis and restore normal times. The government "assumes no power and abridges no rights unless plainly indispensable to that end; it extends no further in time than the attainment of that end; and it makes no alteration in the political, social, and economic structure of the nation which cannot be eradicated with the restoration of normal times. In short, the aim of constitutional dictatorship is the complete restoration of the *status quo ante bellum.*"[45]

The fact that the institutions of free government cannot operate normally in abnormal times has always been recognized—though not always openly admitted. Consequently, all institutions and techniques of constitutional dictatorship fall into one of two related categories: emergency action of an executive nature, and emergency action of a legislative nature.[46] The crisis of rebellion is dealt with primarily in an executive fashion and calls for the institution of some form of military dictatorship. The crisis of economic depression is dealt with primarily through emergency laws and calls for lawmaking by the executive branch of government. The crisis of war, at least total war, is dealt with both ways.[47] Whether we end up with martial rule (Abraham Lincoln, FDR) or the complete delegation of legislative power to the executive (Woodrow Wilson, FDR), the end result is constitutional dictatorship. Add to this, of course, the law of necessity doctrine, which is little more than a rationalization of extraconstitutional, illegal emergency measures. I am talking about measures—by Lincoln, Wilson, and FDR—that have no sanction in law, constitution, or custom. In Rousseau's words: "In such a case there is no doubt about the general will, and it is clear that the people's first intention is that the State shall not perish."[48] It is the simple recognition that war and peace are not the same thing.

John Locke could champion the supremacy of the legislature and bespeak the Whig fear of overweening executive power, but even he had to admit that it was the undefined power of this organ—the Crown Prerogative "to act according to discretion for the public good, without the prescription of the law and sometimes even against it"[49]–that was the ultimate repository of the Nation's will and power to survive. It was never so apparent as in time of crisis that the executive is the aboriginal power of government. Justice Grier's opinion in the *Prize Cases*[50] was the modernized restatement of Locke's position on the exercise of prerogative. Prerogative power (constitutional dictatorship may be substituted), of necessity, was to be exercised in response to particular crises rather than specifically at the behest of or pursuant to the authorization of the legislature.[51] If the President exceeded his statutory authority in protecting the Nation, congressional authorization could come later.[52] According to the Court, the President had an obligation to respond to crisis even in the absence of authorization. It is always the executive branch in the government which possesses and wields the extraordinary powers of self-preservation of any democratic, constitutional state. Whether the crisis demands the initiation of martial rule or an enabling act or a full-blown war regime, it will be the executive branch that the extraordinary authority and responsibility for prosecuting the purposes of the constitutional dictatorship will be consigned; he alone must shoulder the burden and deal with the emergency under the law of necessity.[53]

Rossiter recognized three general forms of modern crisis government: executive dictatorship, legislative dictatorship, and war government. But the institutions and techniques of government adopted under each of these forms are remarkably similar in all constitutional democracies. Consequently, it is possible to treat them in composite form and refer simply to the following situations as the possibilities and expectations of constitutional dictatorship: it is reserved for crises of a sudden and violent character and it sanctions the executive to employ arbitrary action in defense of the state. There is also a general or complete delegation of lawmaking power to the executive. Thus, one can expect the suspension of some or all rights of some or all citizens; the use of troops to maintain or restore order; the institution of military courts for the summary trial and punishment, even by execution, of crimes against the public safety and order; the invasion by an expanded administration of the ordinarily bitterly defended areas of free enterprise; the suspension of elections by the elected officials themselves; the imposition of confiscatory taxes, and the conscription of manpower; the general relaxation of popular and legal controls on all public officials; the admission of the military to the high councils of the land in a manner not paralled in peacetime; the relegation of the legislature and judiciary to a very secondary status; and the inflation of executive power through delegation and initiative to permit this arbitrary action of executive, legislative, and judicial character.[54]

Suggesting that some or all of these dictatorial forms were found in the democratic governments during the First and Second World Wars, Rossiter does not forget, even for a single moment, the grave danger inherent in any resort of constitutional dictatorship. He says:

Constitutional dictatorship is a dangerous thing. A declaration of martial law or the passage of an enabling act is a step which must always be feared and sometimes bitterly resisted, for it is at once an admission of the incapacity of democratic institutions to defend the order within which they function and a too conscious employment of powers and methods long ago outlawed as destructive of constitutional government. Executive legislation, state control of popular liberties, military courts, and arbitrary executive action were governmental features attacked by the men who fought for freedom not because they were inefficient or unsuccessful, but because they were dangerous and oppressive. The reinstitution of any of these features is a perilous matter, a step to be taken only when the dangers to a free state will be greater if the dictatorial institution is not adopted.[55]

The facts of history demonstrate conclusively that constitutional dictatorship has served repeatedly as an indispensable factor in the maintenance of constitutional democracy. For all the formidable dangers they present, the accepted institutions of constitutional dictatorship are weapons which the democracies will henceforth renounce at their own peril.[56] Even now that the Cold War is over, the Atomic Age still exists; and the use of constitutional emergency powers may still become the rule and not the exception. That, at least, is what Rossiter suggested throughout his entire volume. Saying this, however, does not supply answers to a great many perplexing questions: How are free people to ensure that emergency powers will preserve and not destroy their liberties and free government? How are they to make their system of government better prepared for the shock of future crisis? In short, how are they to maximize the efficiency and minimize the dangers of constitutional dictatorship?

What follows, then, are the essential criteria of constitutional dictatorship. Rossiter includes here criteria for the initial resort to constitutional dictatorship, its continuation during the crisis, and its final termination.

1. *No general regime or particular institution of constitutional dictatorship should be initiated unless it is necessary or even indispensable to the preservation of the state and its constitutional order.* This is the first and great commandment of constitutional dictatorship. As far as may be feasible, the salvation of a constitutional democracy in crisis should be worked out through its regular methods of government. Only when the benefits to be assured by resort to constitutional dictatorship clearly outweigh the dangers to be expected should emergency powers be called into action.[57] In Rousseau's words: "But only the greatest dangers can outweigh that of changing the public order, and the sacred power of the laws should never be interfered with except when the safety of the country is at stake."[58]

2. *The decision to institute a constitutional dictatorship should never be in the hands of the man or men who will constitute the dictator.* In other words, no constitutional dictator should be self-appointed. That this criterion has not been uniformly observed in modern experiences with emergency powers is obvious.

The greatest of constitutional dictators was self-appointed, but Lincoln had no alternative. The same may be said of Wilson and FDR. Few Americans seem to realize that almost all of the President's lengthy catalogue of emergency powers go into operation upon the declaration of an emergency ascertained and proclaimed by himself alone. This unquestionably leads to an increased frequency in the use of these powers.[59]

3. *No government should initiate a constitutional dictatorship without making specific provision for its termination.* As the American people know only too well, it is far more difficult to end a period of national emergency than it is to declare one.[60]

4. *All uses of emergency powers and all readjustments in the organization of the government should be effected in pursuit of constitutional or legal requirements.* In short, constitutional dictatorship should be legitimate. It is an axiom of constitutional government that no official action should ever be taken without a certain minimum of constitutional or legal sanction. This is a principle no less valid in times of crisis than under normal conditions. The constitutional dictatorship should be instituted according to precise constitutional forms; it should be constituted in no less a spirit of devotion to constitutional provisions and principles. Give a government whatever power it may need to defend the state from its enemies, but ground that power in the constitution or laws and make the dictatorship lawful.[61]

5. *No dictatorial institution should be adopted, no right invaded, no regular procedure altered any more than is absolutely necessary for the conquest of the particular crisis.* Certain it is that no normal institution ought to be declared unsuited to crisis conditions unless the unsuitability be painfully evident. The more dictatorial a government becomes, the more exposed it will be to all the dangers of constitutional dictatorship.[62]

6. *The measures adopted in the prosecution of a constitutional dictatorship should never be permanent in character or effect.* Emergency powers are strictly conditioned by their purpose, and this purpose is the restoration of normal conditions. The actions directed to this end should therefore be provisional. Permanent laws, whether adopted to regular or irregular times, are for parliaments to enact. By this same token, the decisions and sentences of extraordinary courts should be reviewed by the regular courts after the termination of the crisis.[63]

7. *The dictatorship should be carried on by persons representative of every part of the citizenry interested in the defense of the existing constitutional order.* The circumstances of crisis and the fact that constitutional dictatorship is often a one-man affair make this criterion often nothing more than a moral reminder to an emergency regime that it is defending the whole community and maintaining an established order. The old Tory doctrine of virtual representation must be resurrected and twisted to democratic ends.[64]

8. *Ultimate responsibility should be maintained for every action taken under a constitutional dictatorship.* The criterion is directed against one of the chief dangers of constitutional dictatorship: the transient abuses wrought and the needless dictatorial steps adopted by persons charged with extraordinary powers

in times of crisis. It is manifestly impossible and even detrimental to demand that an official entrusted with some unusual duty under martial rule be made to answer in the heat of the crisis for actions taken in pursuit of that duty. It is imperative that he be held responsible for them after its termination. It would seem to be a categorical principle of constitutional democracy that every public act must be a responsible one and have a public explanation. Officials who abuse authority in a constitutional dictatorship—in other words, men who are charged with defending democracy but instead profane it—should be ferreted out and severely punished.[65]

9. *The decision to terminate a constitutional dictatorship, like the decision to institute one, should never be in the hands of the man or men who constitute the dictator.* This is a direct corollary of the second and third criteria. Congress, and not the President, ought to declare the beginning and the end of all emergencies in which the executive is to be given abnormal powers, so far as it is practicable and possible. It is in this respect that the permanent statutes delegating emergency power to the President are to be most heavily criticized.[66]

10. *No constitutional dictatorship should extend beyond the termination of the crisis for which it was instituted.* It is the crisis alone which makes the dictatorship constitutional; the end of the crisis makes its continued existence unconstitutional. If the purpose of constitutional dictatorship is to defend constitutional democracy in time of peril, then it follows that an extension of the dictatorship beyond the cessation of the peril is directed to another purpose and becomes a dangerous display of unwonted power.[67]

11. *The termination of the crisis must be followed by as complete a return as possible to the political and governmental conditions existing prior to the initiation of the constitutional dictatorship.* It is, of course, impossible to reestablish perfectly the scheme of things in practice at the time the crisis first erupted. Every emergency leaves its mark on the pattern of constitutional government and democratic society. Every period of democratic autocracy leaves democracy just a little more autocratic than before. But better to become one-tenth of a permanent dictatorship in a successful attempt to maintain the rest of the constitutional order than to become a whole dictatorship or an enslaved nation by refusing to take a chance on the dangers of lasting change which attend the constitutional use of dictatorial institutions and powers.[68]

Constitutional dictatorship as the method for securing the continuation of constitutional democracy in the United States should no longer be a matter of critical discussion. The cases sustaining oftentimes excessive exercise of presidential prerogative power—*Martin v. Mott, Luther v. Borden,* the *Prize Cases, In re Neagle, In re Debs, Moyer v. Peabody, United States v. Midwest Oil, Ex parte Quirin, Korematsu v. United States*—attest to this fact. Moreover, the few cases which strike down presidential power seem to lack, because of when and how they were handed down, the ability to actually limit presidential initiative. They are, as Edward S. Corwin once referred to the *Youngstown* decision, "judicial brick[s] without straw."[69] To a free people, therefore, the idea that freedom must be *temporarily* given up in order to be able to enjoy it down the road is both distressing and frightening. All of this raises the one question very few Americans want to talk about, much less attempt an answer: what are the practicable alterations that can be made in the Constitution and laws of the United States to make this a government better fitted to meet national emergencies and better guaranteed to preserve constitutional democracy when the crisis is over?

It is obvious, at least for this author, that any overhauling of the U.S. weapons of constitutional dictatorship is only one small part of a larger and more essential whole—the renovation of the entire constitutional structure and the creation of a national government capable of dealing resolutely and effectively with the bewildering problems of this world at the end of the twentieth century.[70] Although it is not the purpose of this textbook to survey or evaluate the general questions of governmental reform, it should certainly be pointed out that any reform which renders any part of the American government a more efficient and accountable unit renders it at the same time a more effective and trustworthy repository of constitutional emergency powers.[71] The principle ends of the particular reform of the government's instruments of constitutional dictator-ship are identical.[72] In short, constitutional dictatorship in the United States must be made more constitutional as well as more dictatorial.[73]

Power does not necessarily mean despotism. Power can be responsible, strong government can be democratic, and dictatorship can be constitutional.[74] A democratic, constitutional government beset by a severe national emergency can be strong enough to maintain its own existence without at the same time being so strong as to subvert the liberties of the people it has been instituted to defend. A President may act dictatorially as did Lincoln, Wilson, and FDR—ideally under the sanction of law in a constitutional dictatorship—without temporary crisis arrangements becoming lasting peacetime institutions.[75] The problem we face in the United States is not whether the government and the President is to be powerful or not but how to make presidential prerogative powers effective and responsible. In solving that, we will take the necessary giant step towards making any future dictatorship a constitutional one. Harold Laski summarized the need for a strong presidency before America's official entry into World War II and the obvious constitutional dictatorship of Franklin Roosevelt. He wrote:

Power is always a dangerous thing; and the temptation to its abuse, as no generation has learned more surely than our own, the subtlest poison to which a many may succumb. Yet power is also opportunity, and to face danger with confidence is the price of its fulfillment. That is why I end with the emphasis that the President of the United States must be given the power commensurate to the function he has to perform. It must be given democratically; it must be exercised democratically; but if he is to be a great [P]resident, let us be clear that it must be given. With all its risks, its conference is the condition upon which the American adventure may continue in that form of which its supreme exponents have most greatly dreamed. To withhold it, or to frustrate its ample operation, is to jeopardize that adventure. For great power alone makes great leadership possible; it provides the unique chance of restoring America to its people.[76]

One final point that must be reiterated because it is part of the core debate that permeates this textbook. If the purpose of Congress in enacting both the War Powers Resolution and the National Emergencies Act was to ensure that the President *could not act as though his war powers were independent, inherent, and require no prior authorization from the legislature,* then the statutes are incorrectly drawn and neither will accomplish that goal because both lack a trigger mechanism to force Congress to enforce its provisions and responsibilities. If, on the other hand, the purpose of the legislation—something the experts and commentators refuse to acknowledge—was to recognize the President's role as a constitutional dictator, then both pieces of legislation become remarkably similar to what Rossiter argued a half-century ago. The point is not to destroy the ability of the President to exercise prerogative powers but rather to ensure that he exercises them democratically and constitutionally.

The President in wartime exercises a tremendous array of powers, whether he acts as a constitutional dictator or not. The cases discussed in previous chapters document the President's violation of separation of powers and checks and balances as well as the rights of citizens in wartime and/or extreme emergencies short of war. Granted, in a constitutional state the war powers are the most potentially dangerous. Granted, too, during an emergency power is concentrated in the executive branch of government. Granted, further, the other coordinated branches of government—Congress and the Supreme Court— generally play a subsidiary role during the period of crisis; and generally support the President by their acquiescence during (and oftentimes even after) the emergency period. In other words, presidential power is not, in and of itself, a bad thing; and neither is congressional and judicial docility if the President acts according to the generalized rules of constitutional dictatorship and constitutional government and normal times—where legislative and judicial roles really do operate—are restored as completely as possible as soon as the emergency is actually over.

NOTES

1. C. Rossiter, THE SUPREME COURT AND THE COMMANDER IN CHIEF 208 (R. Longaker ed. 1976).

2. *Id.*

3. *Id.* at 208-09.

4. C. Pyle & R. Pious, THE PRESIDENT, CONGRESS, AND THE CONSTITUTION 287 (1984).

5. *Authority of the President to Repel the Attack in Korea,* 23 DEP'T ST.BULL. 173, 173-74 (1950). Members of Congress were consulted informally and after the fact.

6. *Id.* at 174.

7. Several months after our entry into the Korean Conflict, Secretary of State Acheson testified before the Senate Comms. on Foreign Relations and Armed Services. He said: "Not only has the President the authority to use the Armed Forces in carrying out the broad foreign policy of the United States and implementing treaties, but it is equally clear that this authority may not be interfered with by the Congress in the exercise of powers which it has under the Constitution." Quoted in *National Commitments,* Senate Comm. on Foerign Relations, S.Rep. No. 797, 90th Cong., 1st Sess. 17 (1967).

8. *See, e.g.,* Note, *Congress, the President and the Power to Commit Forces to Combat,* 81 HARV.L.REV. 1771 (1968); Lofgren, *Mr. Truman's War: A Debate and its Aftermath,* 31 REV.POL. 231 (1969).

9. During the Eisenhower years, Congress passed "area resolutions" covering Formosa (69 Stat. 7 [1955]) and the Middle East (71 Stat. 5 [1957]). Even President Kennedy initially sought, and secured, an area resolution on Cuba (76 Stat. 697 [1962]) before using independent presidential initiative in declaring a blockade. And since a blockade is tantamount to an act of war under international law, the presidential action can be considered an act of prerogative.

10. Was this position, taken by the President in the 1960s, really any different from the one taken by Lincoln in the 1860s? The immediate basis of the Lincolnian dictatorship was the commander-in-chief clause and the insistence on a very strict interpretation of the separation of powers principle. In other words, the constitutional basis for the war powers has been shifted from the doctrine of delegated powers to the doctrine of inherent powers, thus guaranteeing that the full actual power of the Nation is constitutionally available. E. Corwin, THE PRESIDENT: OFFICE AND POWERS 237, 261 (4th ed. 1957).

11. Pub.L. No. 88-408, 78 Stat. 384 (1964).

12. C. Rossiter, *supra* note 1, at 137.

13. 78 Stat. 384.

14. *Id.*

15. C. Rossiter, *supra* note 1, at 138.

16. *See, e.g.,* Berk v. Laird, 317 F.Supp. 715 (E.D.N.Y. 1970); Orlando v. Laird, 317 F.Supp. 1013 (S.D.N.Y. 1970), *aff'd,* 443 F.2d 1039 (2d Cir. 1971); Massachusetts v. Laird, 451 F.2d 26 (1st Cir. 1971); Mitchell v. Laird, 488 F.2d 611 (D.C. Cir. 1973).

17. *See generally* Meeker, *The Legality of the United States Participation in the Defense of Viet Nam,* 54 DEP'T ST.BULL. 474 (1966). *Cf.* Wormuth, *The Nixon Theory of the War Power: A Critique,* 60 CALIF.L.REV. 623 (1972).

18. The resolution was repealed in 1971 by a one-sentence amendment to the Foreign Military Sales Act, 84 Stat. 2055. What remained unanswered, however, was the legal significance of the repeal. Was the amendment to be read as an end-the-war resolution, or simply a return to whatever inherent warmaking powers the President already claimed? C. Pyle & R. Pious, *supra* note 4, at 340.

19. *See generally* Wormuth, *supra* note 17. The independent power was, as it has always been, substantive authority to dispatch and command the armed forces. But Nixon added a unique twist to the notion: now it was viewed much more broadly as the power of the President to use force as a negotiating instrument to assure the independence of Vietnam and to protect American troops during the process of withdrawal from the war. *Id.*

20. C. Rossiter, *supra* note 1, at 142.

21. Youngstown Sheet & Tube Co. v. Sawyer, 343 U.S. 579, 634-55 (1952) (Jackson, J. concurring).

22. Pub.L. No. 93-148, 87 Stat. 555 (1973).

23. Pub.L. No. 94-412, 90 Stat. 1255 (1976).

24. A. Miller, PRESIDENTIAL POWER 191 (1977).

25. *Id.* at 192.

26. *E.g.,* President Ford's action in May 1975, in the so-called *Mayaguez* incident, vividly illustrates the point that the President still has, despite the War Powers Resolution and the requirement of clock-starting under section 4(a)(1), vast if not unlimited powers on the use of violence. The ship, a U.S. merchant vessel carrying part civilian and part military cargo, was seized by Cambodia near the island of Poulo Wai, for intruding in the

territorial water of Cambodia. President Ford immediately sent in naval and marine forces to rescue the crew and retrive the ship. The President did not consult with Congress first; there was no collective judgment as called for by the legislation. The action was justified by administration spokesmen under the President's constitutional war powers to protect the lives and property of Americans. Furthermore, the administration argued that presidential war powers are inherent and the sole question is "the appropriate level of the response." 2 PRESIDENTIAL DOCUMENTS: GERALD R. FORD 515 (1975). In his report to Congress under section 4(a)(1)—after the incident was over—the President cited his "executive power" and "authority as commander-in-chief."

More American lives were lost in the episode than were saved by rescue of the crew. Further, air strikes were continued on Cambodia after all crew members had been rescued. The seizure of the ship was apparently considered to be an opportunity for the United States to display its determination, after the debacle of Vietnam. A. Miller, *supra* note 24, at 193. It was a use of American power to protect American interests—as the President perceived those interests. Violence, in other words, was deliberately employed by the President without regard to statute and without regard to legal niceties because of the perceived gain for American national interests. That is a pure instance of presidential prerogative in action.

The legality of President Ford's action was dubious at best. But the largely uncritical reaction by Congress and the press, applauding the use of troops by the President, was revealing. The War Powers Resolution, in that instance at least, was a paper tiger. It was the political process, not the positive law, that determined the course of American action—and, indeed, provided a precedent for the use of violence in the future. A. Miller, *supra* note 24, at 194. The essential point, however, is clear: the President, when he takes such actions, labors under the obligation to be successful. *Id.*

27. C. Pyle & R. Pious, *supra* note 18, at 151.

28. The question arises concerning the use of the concurrent resolution device—as a legislative "veto"—to terminate a state of national emergency. In Immigration & Naturalization Service v. Chadha, 462 U.S. 919 (1983), the Supreme Court held the one-house legislative veto unconstitutional. Consequently, legal scholars are undecided whether the same fate may await the concurrent resolution.

29. The Prize Cases, 67 U.S. (2 Bl.) 635 (1863) substantiated Lincoln's argument and legitimated his constitutional dictatorship during the period of emergency. Remember, part of Lincoln's argument was that the President (and the President alone) determined the existence of the emergency, took all measures to successfully meet that emergency, and determined when the emergency was over.

30. A. Miller, *supra* note 24, at 194.

31. *Id.*

32. Kurland, *The Impotence of Reticence,* 1968 DUKE L.J. 619, 624.

33. R. Hirschfield, THE CONSTITUTION AND THE COURT 132 (1962).

34. *Id.* at 133.

35. *Id.* Hamilton argued this point initially in *The Federalist*, No. 70: "Energy in the executive is a leading character in the definition of good government. It is essential to the protection of the community against foreign attacks; it is not less essential to the steady administration of the laws; to the protection of property against those irregular and high-handed combinations which sometimes interrupt the ordinary course of justice; to the security of liberty against the enterprise and assaults of ambition, of faction, and of anarchy....Taking it for granted, therefore, that all men of sense will agree in the necessity of an energetic executive, it will only remain to inquire, what are the ingredients which constitute this energy?...The ingredients which constitute energy in the executive are unity; duration; and adequate provision for its support; and competent

powers." *The Federalist,* No. 70, 423-24 (Hamilton) (C. Rossiter ed. 1961).

36. R. Hirschfield, *supra* note 33, at 133.

37. *Id.*

38. *Id.* at 133-34.

39. *Id.* at 134.

40. Quoted in Commager, *Is Democracy Dying in America?,* 34 LOOK MAG. 16 (July 14, 1970).

41. C. Rossiter, CONSTITUTIONAL DICTATORSHIP viii (1948).

42. *Id.* at 8.

43. *Id.*

44. *Id.* at 7.

45. *Id.*

46. *Id.* at 8-9.

47. *Id.* at 9. If a situation can be dealt with judicially, it is probably not a crisis (at least in the sense of this study). *Id.*

48. J. Rousseau, THE SOCIAL CONTRACT, bk. 4, ch. 6, 131 (L. Crocker ed. 1967).

49. J. Locke, TWO TREATISES OF CIVIL GOVERNMENT, ch. 14, sec. 160, 422 (P. Laslett ed. 1960).

50. 67 U.S. (2 Bl.) 635 (1863). To the charge that Congress's permission was inappropriately issued after the fact, the Court responded: "Without admitting that such an act [the recognition that a state of insurrection existed] was necessary under the circumstances it is plain that if the President had in any manner assumed powers which it was necessary should have the authority or sanction of Congress, then on the well known principle of law, *onmis ratihabitio retrotrahitur et mandato equiparatur* [the retroactive forgiveness for past action at the express command of the sovereign power], this ratification has operated to perfectly cure the defect." *Id.* at 671.

51. D. Franklin, EXTRAORDINARY MEASURES 50 (1991).

52. *Id.*

53. C. Rossiter, *supra* note 41, at 12.

54. *See* the basic ideas in *id.* at 290-94. Is all of this so very different from Justice Sutherland's arguments in United States v. Macintosh, 283 U.S. 605, 622 (1931): "To the end that war may not result in defeat, freedom of speech may, by act of Congress, be curtailed or denied so that the morals of the people and the spirit of the army may not be broken by seditious utterances; freedom of the press curtailed to preserve our military plans and movements from the knowledge of the enemy; deserters and spies put to death without indictment or trial by jury; ships and supplies requisitioned; property of alien enemies, theretofore under the protection of the Constitution, seized without process and converted to public use without compensation and without due process of law in the ordinary sense of that term; prices of food and other necessities of life fixed or regulated; railway's taken over and operated by the government; *and other drastic power, wholly inadmissible in time of peace, exercised to meet the emergencies of war"* (emphasis added).

55. *Id.* at 294. While Rossiter sees obvious danger in constitutional dicta-torship, at the same time he argues for its employment during a grave crisis of a sudden and violent character—rebellion, insurrection, economic depression, and armed attack. "The most obvious danger of constitutional dictatorship, or of any of its institutions, is the un-pleasant possibility that such dictatorship will abandon its qualifying adjective and become permanent and unconstitutional. Too often in a struggling constitutional state have the institutions of emergency power served as efficient weapons for the coup d'etat....The institutions of constitutional dictatorship are not only uniquely available as instruments for a coup d'etat; they are also ideal for the purposes of reactionary forces

not so much interested in subverting the constitutional order as they are in thwarting all legal and electoral attempts to dislodge them from their entrenched positions of power....A third risk inherent in the constitutional employment of dictatorial institutions is the simple fact that changes less than revolutionary, but nonetheless changes, will be worked in the permanent structure of government and society. No constitutional government ever passed through a period in which emergency powers were used without undergoing some degree of permanent alteration, always in the direction of an aggrandizement of the power of the state....A further danger to democracy is inherent in the implicit and even positive acknowledgment that the regular institutions of constitutional government do not have the virility to protect the state from the dangers of war, rebellion, or economic collapse....Finally, it is obvious that individual abuses of public power are more likely to occur under conditions of crisis and in the prosecution of extraordinary duties than in normal times and in pursuit of normal duties. Even the best of public officials charged with a task under a state of martial law may not be able to avoid needless injury to the rights and lives and property of loyal citizens, while the worst will make use of their unwonted authority in such a manner as to defeat the very purposes for which this institution of constitutional dictatorship is called into action....Once a constitutional dictatorship is initiated, it is inevitable that the men charged with its success will seek more extraordinary powers and demand more procedural readjustments than are necessary or even expedient. Unwarranted suspensions of rights and unnecessary alterations of governmental procedure, as well as individual abuses of emergency power, are dangers that must be constantly opposed by public opinion." *Id.* at 294-97.

56. *Id.* at 297.

57. *Id.* at 298. *See, e.g.,* Sheffer, *Presidential Power to Suspend Habeas Corpus: The Taney-Bates Dialogue and Ex Parte Merryman,* 11 OKLA.CITY U.L.REV. 1 (Spring 1986).

58. J. Rousseau, *supra* note 48, at 131.

59. C. Rossiter, *supra* note 41, at 299.

60. *Id.* at 300. The decisions in the Emergency Rent Cases, 256 U.S. 170 (1921), Woods v. Miller, 333 U.S. 138 (1948), and Ludecke v. Watkins, 335 U.S. 160 (1948), confirm this point. Congress eventually made the attempt to assume some responsibility here when it enacted the National Emergencies Act of 1976 (90 Stat. 1255). Unfortunately, like the War Powers Resolution, it does not operate as intended.

61. *Id.*

62. *Id.* at 302.

63. *Id.* at 303.

64. *Id.* at 304.

65. *Id.* at 305.

66. *Id.* at 305-06. Here, once again, Congress has great difficulty getting it right. Under the National Emergencies Act only one of the three methods of termination is granted to Congress; the other two leave it within the President's discretion.

67. *Id.* at 306.

68. *Id.*

69. Corwin, The Steel Seizure Case: A Judicial Brick without Straw, 53 COLUM.L.REV. 53 (1953); *cf.* Kauper, *The Steel Seizure Case,* 51 MICH.L.REV. 141 (1952).

70. C. Rossiter, *supra* note 41, at 307.

71. *Id.* at 307-08.

72. *Id.* at 308. Most important, if reform is to accomplish its purpose, it is for Congress to play a salutary part in future emergency governments in this country—and along those lines the congressional power of legislation, investigation, and control (real

legislative oversight) must be streamlined and strengthened. Rossiter argued: "If it is the President's duty to make emergency government more effective and dictatorial, it is Congress' to make it more responsible and constitutional. If some future strong-minded President is not to run wild in his choice of extraordinary ways and means of exercising his vast powers as constitutional dictator, then Congress is going to have to turn out legislation which will define without constricting and codify without emasculating some of the President's constitutional and statutory powers for emergency action." *Id.* at 309.

73. *Id.* A half-century ago, Rossiter included the following six specific pro-posals for reform: "First, the entire catalogue of the President's statutory emergency powers could well be scrutinized and over-hauled. These laws are for the most part left-overs from former major or minor national emergencies; as such they are in no sense the products of a reflective congressional judgment that the nation's welfare calls for such a panoply of presidential emergency powers....Second, a more precise means of declaring and ending national emergencies should be established by law....Third, the Office of Emergency Management should be established as a permanent adjunct of the Executive Office of the President....Fourth, the possibilities of an American version of the British Emergency Powers Act should be thoughtfully considered by Congress....Fifth, in conjunction with the above statute it seems unfortunately imperative that the President ... be given an undoubted peacetime power to seize strike-bound industries of such importance as the coal mines, telephones, and railroads....Sixth, the codification of martial law at the national level. That the President has the power of martial law is obvious; that martial law is an uncertain institution is equally obvious. If the federal power of martial law can be left as forceful and effective as ever, while at the same time some of its effects can be more precisely defined,... then such a law would be an asset to constitutional dictatorship and thus to constitutional government. The definition of power by no means signifies that it will be any less effective; it does signify that it will be more responsible." *Id.* at 310-13.

74. *Id.* at 314.

75. Not a great deal of literature exists on this point, even after all these years: *e.g.,* S. Fisher, THE TRIAL OF THE CONSTITUTION (1862); W. Whiting, WAR POWERS UNDER THE CONSTITUTION (43d ed. 1871); Rogers, *Presidential Dictatorship in the United States,* 231 Q.REV. 136 (1919) and *Legislative and Executive in Wartime,* 19 FOREIGN AFF. 717 (1941); Hayes, *Emergencies and the Power of the United States Government to Meet Them,* 16 TEMPLE U.L.REV. 173 (1941); Radin, *Martial Law and the State of Siege,* 30 CALIF.L.REV. 634 (1942); C. Fairman, THE LAW OF MARTIAL RULE (2d ed. 1943); Gilmore, *War Powers—Executive Power and the Constitution,* 29 IOWA L. REV. 463 (1944); C. Friedrich, CONSTITUTIONAL DICTATORSHIP AND DEMOCRACY, ch. 25 (1948); D. Franklin, *supra* note 51.

76. H. Laski, THE AMERICAN PRESIDENCY 277-78 (1940).

Conclusion

Are there circumstances under which the rule of law must give way to the judgment of the ruler? The rule of law is, of course, at the very foundation of our political and constitutional order. It is among the oldest principles of political science. Nevertheless, while the law is to be served in the great majority of cases, it may be wise to accept as legitimate a power, inherent in the executive, to overstep the law when the welfare of the Nation requires it. This power, defended by the ancient principle *salus populi suprema lex* (the welfare of the people is the supreme law),[1] is traditionally called the prerogative, which John Locke defined as follows:

This power to act according to discretion, for the public good, without the prescription of the law, and sometimes even against it, is that which is called prerogative. For since in some governments the law-making power is not always in being, and is usually too numerous, and so too slow, for the dispatch requisite to execution; and because also it is impossible to foresee, and so by laws to provide for all accidents and necessities that may concern the public, or make such laws as will do no harm if they are executed with an inflexible rigour on all occasions and upon all persons that may come in their way, therefore there is a latitude left to the executive power, to do many things of choice which the laws do not prescribe.[2]

The basic function of American government is the preservation of the United States. It is reasonable to assume, therefore, that an impending emergency (crisis) might demand actions that exceed the grant of power under the Constitution,[3] in other words, actions that exceed the scope of law. It should also be evident that the President, not burdened by the unwieldiness of the legislature or the narrow constitutional restraints of the judiciary, is most able to provide (as Hamilton initially argued in *The Federalist*, No. 23) the rapid and decisive actions which are the essence of prerogative. Precisely because the

Framers of the Constitution left the powers of the presidency relatively vague, historical practice, precedent, and decisions of courts have contributed as much to the development of presidential prerogative powers as has the ambiguous and cryptic written constitution.

The presidency, because of its structural advantages, is uniquely situated for the exercise of emergency powers. Because of its hierarchical organization and administrative responsibilities, the presidency has an advantage in acting with dispatch and secrecy. Even Locke, who was a great proponent of the sovereignty of the legislature, recognized that the executive had a special responsibility for the exercise of prerogative powers.[4] As a practical matter, he believed the executive must be free to respond to crisis.[5] Yet, unfettered power, even if exercised in what is perceived to be the best interests of the Nation, is dangerous to the continuation of limited government. If the cure is to remain less harmful than the disease, prerogative must be narrowly and specifically circumscribed. The executive must know that the exercise of prerogative is subject to strict review and that while the President may have the power to perform acts which are per se unconstitutional, such acts may be taken only in response to a dire emergency and then only subject to certain specific limitations.

As a practical matter it was impossible to plan in advance for all the extraordinary situations in which the exercise of prerogative powers might be necessary. Consequently, the limits of prerogative were inevitably linked to the office in government through which those powers were exercised. The king, by virtue of his divine sanction, was "limited" in his exercise of prerogatives by the Supreme Being. In a republic, on the other hand, the exercise of prerogative powers is delimited by notions of proper representation. The representatives in a constitutional regime have a duty to wield extraordinary powers in a "responsible" manner. What is responsible or irresponsible in a republic is, in part, a function of law and, in part, a function of consensus. The courts and the legislature determine the law. An examination of precedent and historical text establishes the boundaries of consensus. Inasmuch as the most prominent framers of the Constitution subscribed to what later became known as the principle of Burkean representation,[6] prerogative powers came to have a fairly broad sanction in American government. This notion of representation opened the floodgates for the exercise of prerogative powers in a republic. Indeed, for the presidency the crucial turning point in the establishment of prerogative powers came with the recognition of the President as Burkean "trustee" rather than "delegate."[7]

Given the ambiguity of our founding period and the debate that still rages surrounding the Framers' intentions respecting the office of the presidency,[8] one can at least safely say that they envisioned the need for emergency government. This can be seen in the provisions for martial law[9] and for the suspension of the writ of habeas corpus.[10] But the extent to which a President can act independent of Congress in an emergency remained—and still remains—an unsettled question. Did the Framers feel that there were, in effect, two Constitutions, one for peacetime and one for wartime—and if the Constitution for war overrides provisions of the Constitution for peace, actions under one rubric are no less constitutional than actions under the other. Or, they may well have intended that inherent in the entire fabric of the social contract is the implication that express provisions of the Constitution can be superseded to meet a crisis that threatens national sovereignty,[11] and that the grant of power under the Constitution, taken as a whole, allows the exercise of a prerogative.[12]

In times of dire national emergency the President must exercise prerogative power. Both Lincoln and FDR enunciated and initiated prerogative based on the same doctrine of paramount necessity: the preservation of the Nation supersedes adherence to the Constitution. Given our history over the past two centuries, is this notion really open to question? One must never forget that implicit in the theory underlying prerogative is the argument that Presidents, elected in accordance with the Constitution, possess a power in reserve to violate the Constitution in order to insure the preservation of the Nation. Free government is not only consistent with prerogative, but is also dependent upon strong and effective government[13]—of which prerogative is a part. If we, as a people, desire—even demand—dynamic, forceful leadership from our President,[14] why would we possibly wish to reject the extra-ordinary[15] use of prerogative power and risk destruction of our system of constitutional democracy?

If the doctrine of prerogative is to be compatible with the genius of republican government, it must be seen as an extraordinary measure, a measure that does not set permanent precedents. It must be kept separate from the President's store of constitutional powers. Unfortunately, as the cases have too often suggested, this has not always been the case. Prerogative is—and must always be—a temporary power to be relinquished when the crisis has passed or, if possible, when Congress can act to sanction the President's actions. As such, the dislocation to constitutional democracy caused by prerogative would be fleeting and its impact of limited duration.[16] I believe, in spite of some of the scholarly criticism, that the doctrine of separation of powers and checks and balances and the Constitution are hardy (as well as flexible) enough to absorb the temporary shock which prerogative might deliver.

There is no doubt that the doctrine of prerogative, applied over an extended period of time, can be destructive to our notion of constitutional democracy. It is occasioned by extraordinary crisis and the extended use of the doctrine might very well lead to the realization of James Madison's fear that war or emergency does irreparable damage to the liberties of republican government.[17] It is submitted, however, that the danger is not mitigated by prohibiting the invocation of the doctrine; but it can be mitigated by circumscribing it. Precise guidelines concerning exercise of prerogative and public accountability for use of the doctrine are the best and perhaps only insurance we can hope to have against mischief and misuse.

The general conclusions that may be drawn directly from the cases discussed and analyzed in the preceding pages are relatively simple: (1) courts are powerless to prevent a President from invoking, and using, his powers of martial rule; (2) courts are likewise powerless to prevent him (or his subordinates) from carrying their plans through to conclusion; (3) courts generally will not, even when the necessity has clearly passed, presume to substitute their judgment for that of the military (or civilians) acting under presidential orders. The more specific conclusions, on the other hand, are a little more complicated. The cases presented here give to the President an independent discretion not subject to prior congressional activity, a virtually dictatorial power to successfully meet the emergency, an inherent power applicable to domestic situations, and great discretion and freedom to act in the foreign affairs field. The commander-in-chief clause even gives the President full martial powers. There is a basic distinction between those constitutional principles applicable in time of war and those applicable in time of peace. In other words, we possess what might be called a wartime constitution.

More important, several basic structural principles of crisis government were established in these cases—and have been grafted on to the Constitution. First, to meet the challenge of a major emergency, the barriers against omnipotent government established by the Constitution must oftentimes be transcended. Preservation of the American system of constitutional rule is the ultimate purpose of a crisis regime, but it acknowledges no restrictions in assuming the authority needed to achieve that goal. The power of crisis government has no definable limits because its operational standard is necessity rather than constitutionality; to whatever extent the situation demands, governmental authority will be expanded and concentrated and individual liberty will be circumscribed in time of emergency. Second, the presidency must always be the dominant organ of crisis government. Only the President can satisfy the crisis demand for unity, action, and leadership, for he is "the sole representative of all the people" and the only agent capable of responding quickly and decisively. Elevated to a position of extraordinary power as a result of both necessity and the tribunate character of his office, the President is constitutionally, politically, and psychologically the focus of any emergency regime. Third, and last, the overriding lesson learned from these cases is that the Supreme Court, whenever possible, will look for any evidence (no matter how insignificant) of congressional participation in the actions taken by the commander-in-chief. The result of such an approach enables the Court to speak about the "war powers of the United States" or "the war powers of Congress and the President" rather than having to legitimize the reality starkly before the Justices: that oftentimes unconstitutional actions had taken place and the President—and the President alone—was responsible. This is what happened with Lincoln during the Civil War period, and the Supreme Court has justified all succeeding exercises of emergency power in executive-legislative terms rather than attributing such extraordinary power to the President alone.

In the Introduction to this volume I raised an issue that goes as far back as the debate between Hamilton and Madison in *The Federalist* over the inability of the national government to meet a sudden emergency. That debate, unresolved by the Framers, remained dormant until Lincoln and the Civil War experience. Sidney G. Fisher reopened the issue in 1888 when he wrote:

There are few things in American history more worthy of discussion than the power exercised by Lincoln in [the years 1861 to 1865]. It was absolute and arbitrary and, if unauthorized, its exercise was a tremendous violation of the Constitution. Whether it was justifiable and necessary is another matter. If its use was unconstitutional and yet necessary to preserve the Union, it shows that the Constitution is defective in not allowing the government the proper means of protecting itself.[18]

We have, to an extent, finally answered Fisher's pointed inquiry. By the creation of a wartime constitution this Nation may (in the extreme) become dictatorial and still remain constitutional. What is not granted by one constitution is granted by the other. That, after all, was what Rossiter's argument was all about.[19] Our myth about constitutional government and power refer to *Milligan* and *Duncan* and *Youngstown* and the ideal that the Constitution is equally applicable in peace as well as war. The reality, on the other hand, demonstrates that war and peace are not the same thing, and constitutional provisions applicable in time of peace may not be equally applicable in time of war.

What role does the Supreme Court play in all this? What role should it play? Can the ideal logic of theory and the harsh reality of war ever combine neatly enough to find a proper role for the Court to play? I raise these questions only because I have become convinced that what the Court has done when confronted with the exercise of presidential war or emergency power since the beginning of the Republic has not worked well, resulting all too often with the Constitution (and constitutional law) full of inconsistencies and errors that lead us to an imperial presidency without the democratic constraints necessary to keep a dictatorship constitutional. Giving the President everything he wants (and sometimes even more than he wanted) during the crisis and then saying no after the crisis has run its course simply causes confusion and worse. It is not a proper role for the Supreme Court to play.

Perhaps the answer lies in the Court accepting the uncontested fact that war and peace are not the same thing and that the institutions of free government cannot operate normally in abnormal times—no matter how much legerdemain the judiciary indulges in. Perhaps Robert H. Jackson's extraordinary dissenting opinion in *Korematsu*[20] is the answer we seek after all. And it was Jackson who wrote in his Godkin Lectures (six years after his return from Nuremberg) what should have been the standard for judicial perception and logic:

If an organized society wants the kind of justice that an independent, professional judicial establishment is qualified to administer, our judiciary is certainly a most effective instrument for applying law and justice to individual cases and for cultivating public attitudes which rely upon law and seek justice. *But I know of no modern instance in which any judiciary has saved a whole people from the great currents of intolerance, passion, usurpation, and tyranny which have threatened liberty and free institutions. The Dred Scott decision did not settle the question of the power to end slavery, and I very much doubt that had Mr. Justice McLean not dissented in that case it would have done any more to avoid war. No court can support a reactionary regime and no court can innovate or implement a new one. I doubt that any court, whatever its powers, could have saved Louis XVI or Marie Antoinette. None could have avoided the French Revolution, none could have stopped its excesses, and none could have prevented its culmination in the dictatorship of Napoleon. In Germany a courageous court refused to convict those whom the Nazi government sought to make the scapegoats for the Reichstag fire, clandestinely set by the Nazis themselves, and other courts decreed both the Nazi and the*

*Communist parties to be illegal under German law. Those judgments fell on deaf ears
and became dead letters because the political forces at the time were against them.*
    It is not idle speculation to inquire which comes first either in time or importance, an
independent and enlightened judiciary or a free and tolerant society. Must we first
maintain a system of free political government to assure a free society, or can we rely on
an aggressive, activist judiciary to guarantee free government? While each undoubtedly
is a support for the other, and the two are frequently found together, it is my belief that
the attitude of a society and of its organized political forces, rather than its legal
machinery, is the controlling force in the character of free institutions.[21]

    When the Framers chose to give the Congress the power to "declare" war
rather than "make" war,[22] they thought that they were giving the President the
power to repel sudden attacks. They did not pause to consider whether the
President could, in the course of responding to an attack, declare the existence of
a state of war and thereby alter the legal rights and obligations of citizens and
foreigners alike.[23] Nor did they discuss the possibility that a President might
provoke an attack (or even manufacture an attack) and then recognize the
existence of a state of war in the legal, as well as military, sense.[24]
    The Constitution does not define all hostile military actions against the
government of the United States as acts of war. In fact, most military actions do
not create a state of war with all of its adverse legal consequences to the liberty
and property of the belligerents and those who do business with them.[25] The
constitutional text speaks of war, rebellion, and invasion[26] and implicitly
acknowledges imperfect war by the clause governing letters of marque and
reprisal.[27] Thus, there is no textual impediment to treating each of these circumstances differently as a matter of constitutional law.[28]
    Conversely, if one conceives of the war power in monolithic terms, it is not
difficult to accept the notion that, in times of dire emergency, the war powers of
the Nation must be entrusted to the President as commander-in-chief. By
looking at a comprehensive war power, however, one is able to shift the
definitional referents from the Constitution (and its allocation of powers) to
international law (and its lack of concern for constitutional theories regarding
the locus of sovereignty).[29] This was the view taken by Lincoln[30] and FDR and
all other prerogative exercising Presidents during periods of dire emergency. It
is, ultimately, the view taken whenever this Nation has faced such an emergency
and requires the leadership and direction of a constitutional dictator.
    In his <u>Democracy in America</u>, Alexis de Tocqueville warned his readers that
"foreign politics demand scarcely any of those qualities which are peculiar to a
democracy....[A democracy] cannot combine its measures with secrecy or await
their consequences with patience. These qualities more especially belong to an
individual or an aristocracy."[31] A century and a quarter later, Carl Friedrich
brought the notion up to date when he wrote: "Reason of state is nothing but the
doctrine that whatever is required to insure the survival of the state must be done
by the individuals responsible for it, no matter how repugnant such an act may
be to them in their private capacity as decent and moral men."[32]
    The concept of *raison d'etat* (constitutional reason of state) has always been,
is, and will continue to be, a thread running through the living Constitution—the

Constitution in action.[33] The nation-state is analogized by the President[34] to be a real person; it—the Nation—is thus considered to have an existence separate and apart from the individuals who live within its geographic boundaries. The United States takes on a life of its own, at once separate from and greater than any of its constituent parts,[35] and the President is the spokesman for that entity. The danger, of course, should be obvious. By considering the state a real person, it then must be held to have a real will, and that brings on the danger of making it a Leviathan. When the state's will comes into collision with other wills, it may assert that, being the most important, it must and should prevail; accordingly, its supreme will may be transformed into supreme force.[36] Ultimately, that could mean that the state will become a mere personal power over and above law.[37]

This is what presidential prerogative power and constitutional dictatorship is all about. It is a recognition that war and peace are not the same thing and cannot coexist in the same place at the same time. It is a recognition that the rules always change to accommodate the circumstances during a dire emergency. It is a recognition that presidential power is necessary for the survival of the Nation. And it is a recognition that sometimes the Constitution must be suspended in order for there to even be a Nation—with a Constitution— after the emergency is over. The problem, once again, is how to live with emergency power, for the citizenry are going to have it whatever they may wish and whatever the Constitution implies. It is a grave mistake—as Hamilton argued—to assume that the Constitution is suited for every emergency. Madison was wrong in making such an assumption in *The Federalist,*[38] and the Supreme Court was assuredly wrong in emphasizing such a position in *Ex parte Milligan.*[39] As long as the need continues for rules to govern men, presidential prerogative power will be justified when those rules prove temporarily insufficient to the task.[40] In the face of crisis, the acts that are necessary to preserve the Nation, constitutional or not, are acts that must be undertaken.[41]

As a concluding thought, let me once again return to Rossiter's argument in favor of constitutional dictatorship as the ultimate salvation of the Nation during a period of dire emergency.

The general principle and the particular institutions of constitutional dictatorship are political and social dynamite. No democracy ever went through a period of thorough-going constitutional dictatorship without some permanent and often unfavorable altera- tion in its governmental scheme, and in more than one instance an institution of constitutional dictatorship has been turned against the order it was established to defend. Indeed, it is an inevitable and dangerous thing, and must be thoroughly under- stood and controlled by any free people who are compelled to resort to it in defense of their freedom. That is exactly what makes this problem so critical, for no free state has ever been without some method by which its leaders could take dictatorial action in its defense. If it lacked such method or the will of its leaders to use it, it did not survive its first real crisis. It is in this twentieth century and indeed in these very days that the age- old phenomenon of constitutional dictatorship has reached the peak of its significance. Men are just as willing today as they were in ancient Rome to renounce their freedom for a little while in order to preserve it forever.[42]

Rossiter, in effect, supplied an answer to the question posed by Lincoln on July 4, 1861—"Must a government be too strong for the liberties of its people, or too weak to maintain its own existence?"[43]—by arguing that a democratic, constitutional republic can be strong enough to maintain its own existence without having to subvert the liberties of the people it has been instituted to defend.

And it should be emphasized, again and again and again, that courts cannot save a constitutional democracy from its periodic excesses. Simultaneously, courts should never participate, by legitimizing unconstitutional behavior, in democracy's demise. Yet by the very nature of how constitutional democracy operates in the United States, particularly during an emergency, courts have little choice.

NOTES

1. Hurtgen, *The Case for Presidential Prerogative,* 7 U.TOL.L.REV. 59 (1975).

2. J. Locke, TWO TREATIES OF GOVERNMENT, ch. 14, sec. 160, 422 (P. Laslett ed. 1960). The favoring a prerogative in the hands of the executive authority can be traced back to Plato's STATESMAN, Aristotle's POLITICS, Cicero's DE LEGIBUS, Machiavelli's DISCOURSES ON THE FIRST TEN BOOKS OF TITUS LIVIUS, Bacon's essay OF JUDICIATURE, Hobbes's A DIALOGUE BETWEEN A PHILOSOPHER AND A STUDENT OF THE COMMON LAW, and Blackstone's COMMENTARIES ON THE LAWS OF ENGLAND.

3. Is Locke's argument so different from Hamilton's in THE FEDERALIST, No. 23 at 153: "These [war and emergency] powers ought to exist without limitation, be-cause it is impossible to foresee or to define the extent and variety of national exigencies, and the correspondent extent and variety of the means which may be necessary to satisfy them."

4. "When the legislative and executive power are in distinct hands, (as they are in all moderated monarchies, and well-framed governments) there the good of society requires that several things should be left to the discretion of him that has the executive power; for the legislators not being able to foresee and provide by laws, for all that may be useful to the community, the executor of the laws, having the power in his hands, has by the common law of nature a right to make use of it for the good of the society in many cases, where the municipal law has given no direction, till the legislature can conveniently be assembled to provide for it." J. Locke, *supra* note 2, at 421.

5. Roughly defined, the executive's prerogative is ideally exercised in response to exigencies that impose time constraints on the ability of government, as a whole, to respond. D. Franklin, EXTRAORDINARY MEASURES 42 (1991).

6. "Government is not made in virtue of natural rights, which may and do exist in total independence of it; and exist in much greater clearness, and in a much greater degree of abstract perfection; but their abstract perfection is their practical defect. By having a right to everything they want everything.... Society requires not only that the passions of individuals should be subjected, but that even in the mass and body, as well as in the individuals, the inclinations of men should frequently be thwarted." E. Burke, REFLECTIONS ON THE REVOLUTION IN FRANCE 64 (Prometheus ed. 1967).

7. D. Franklin, *supra* note 5, at 44.

8. *See generally* Sheffer, *Presidential Power and Limited Government,* 21 PRES.STUD.Q. 471 (Spring 1991).

9. U.S. Const. art. I, sec. 8, cl. 15.

10. U.S. Const. art. I, sec. 9, cl. 2.

11. Hurtgen, *supra* note 1, at 64.

12. American history abounds with numerous examples of presidential prerogative. Among the more prominent examples are Jefferson and the purchase of Louisiana, the *Chesapeake* affair, Polk and the Mexican War, Lincoln and the Civil War (particularly his suspension of the writ of habeas corpus and the institution of the blockade), Wilson before our entry into World War I (and during it as well), FDR before and during World War II (but particularly the "destroyer" deal, the threatened suspension of the Constitution, and the internment fiasco), and Truman's commitment of troops to Korea and the seizure of the steel mills.

Justice Grier's majority opinion in the Prize Cases, 67 U.S. (2 Bl.) 635 (1863), was the modernized American version of Locke's position on the exercise of prerogative. *See* ch. 8, note 63, *supra.* In other words, prerogative power (of necessity) was to be exercised in response to particular crises rather than specifically at the behest of or pursuant to the authorization of the legislature. If the President exceeded his authority in protecting the Nation, congressional authorization could come later. According to the Supreme Court majority, the President has an obligation to respond to the crisis even in the absence of authorization.

13. Hurtgen, *supra* note 1, at 73.

14. Hamilton began this argument in THE FEDERALIST, No. 70, at 423: "Energy in the executive is a leading character in the definition of good government. It is essential to the protection of the community against foreign attacks; it is not less essential to the steady administration of the laws; to the protection of property against those irregular and high-handed combinations which sometimes interrupt the ordinary course of justice; to the security of liberty against the enterprises and assaults of ambition, of faction, and of anarchy."

15. Prerogative power should be invoked only when the demands of paramount necessity require it—for example, threat of invasion, dire impositions of war, or threat of civil breakdown exceeding the capacity of civil authorities to maintain order.

16. Hurtgen, *supra* note 1, at 82.

17. *See generally* E. Corwin, THE PRESIDENT'S CONTROL OF FOREIGN RELATIONS, ch. 1 (1917). If narrow constraints are drawn around the exercise of prerogative, the extent to which the doctrine saps the Nation's faith in fundamental jurisprudential notions can be reduced to a minimum. The danger lies in allowing the prerogative to be invoked by Presidents who feel they must act to safeguard the sovereignty of the Nation but who can only premise their actions on a vague and ambiguous concept of the limits and prescriptions of prerogative. And such danger is manifest. FDR promised to return his extraordinary powers to the people, yet we have witnessed in the development of the Cold War presidency that powers, once assumed, are not always laid down. We have witnessed an advisor to a President argue on national television that the extraordinary circumstances of contemporary life warrant breaking and entering as a legitimate safeguard of national security. Hurtgen, *supra* note 1, at 82-83.

18. S. Fisher, *The Suspension of Habeas Corpus during the War of the Rebellion,* 3 POL.SCI.Q. 454, 457 (1888).

19. C. Rossiter, CONSTITUTIONAL DICTATORSHIP (1948).

20. Jackson's dissent can be found at 323 U.S. 242-48. *See* note 50, introduction, *supra.*

21. R. Jackson, THE SUPREME COURT IN THE AMERICAN SYSTEM OF GOVERNMENT 80-81 (1955) (emphasis added).

22. M. Farrand, RECORDS OF THE FEDERAL CONVENTION OF 1787, 318-19 (3d ed. 1966).

23. When the southern states declared their independence of the United States in April 1861, Lincoln refused to treat them as a nation that other nations might recognize and

supply. Nor could he treat them as a mere criminal conspiracy or minor uprising, which would require him to respect their property rights even as he used the military to suppress their violence. So he chose to treat them as nongovernmental belligerents, in the nature of, but not technically, foreign states. Pursuant to this concept, Lincoln ignored laws and constitutional provisions by assembling the militia, enlarging the army and navy beyond their authorized strengths, calling for volunteers for three years' service, spending public money without congressional appropriations, suspended the privilege of the writ of habeas corpus, arresting people on mere suspicion of disloyalty, and instituting a naval blockade of the Confederacy. C. Pyle & R. Pious, THE PRESIDENT, CONGRESS, AND THE CONSTITUTION 322-23 (1984). Eighty years later, FDR's Executive Order 9066 treated the west coast of the United States as "a theater of military operations," thus depriving the citizens of their civil liberties. This is the prerogative presidency at the height of its dictatorial powers.

24. By the deployment of troops near the disputed border with Mexico and positioning of reinforced naval units in the Pacific where they would be able to seize the Mexican province of upper California, Polk sought to make the Mexicans feel militarily insecure. Secret agents encouraged American settlers in the coveted provinces to revolt, while at the same time diplomats offered to purchase California for as much as $40 million. Polk then ordered General Zachary Taylor and his troops into the disputed territory. Mexico then declared "defensive war" and some American troops were killed in the engagement. Polk had already decided to ask for a congressional declaration of war when news of the incident enabled him to claim that Mexico had invaded Texas. Congress then voted to recognize the existence of a state of war and to reinforce General Taylor's forces. L. Fisher, PRESIDENTIAL WAR POWERS 30-34 (1995). Is all this so very different from Lyndon Johnson's message to Congress claiming North Vietnamese torpedo attacks on American naval warships in the Gulf of Tonkin?

25. C. Pyle & R. Pious, *supra* note 23, at 322.

26. U.S. Const. art. I, sec. 8, cl. 11; art. I, sec. 9, cl. 2.

27. U.S. Const. art. I, sec. 8, cl. 11. The notion of imperfect war was legitimized by the Supreme Court, *e.g.,* Bas v. Tingy, 4 U.S. (4 Dall.) 37 (1800); Talbot v. Seeman, 5 U.S. (1 Cr.) 1 (1801); Little v. Barreme, 6 U.S. (2 Cr.) 170 (1804). *See* Preface, note 1, *supra.*

28. C. Pyle & R. Pious, *supra* note 23, at 322.

29. *Id.*

30. In a letter to J. G. Conkling on Aug. 26, 1863, Lincoln wrote: "I think the Constitution invests its commander-in-chief with the law of war, in time of war." 6 COLLECTED WORKS OF ABRAHAM LINCOLN 406 (R. Basler ed. 1953). In a letter to S. P. Chase on Sept. 2, 1863, he wrote: "As commander-in-chief ... I have a right to take any measure which may best subdue the enemy,... including things ... which cannot constitutionally be done by Congress." *Id.* at 428. Earlier, on July 4, 1861, he told Congress: "I have taken it upon myself to call out the war power of the Government and so to resist force employed for its destruction....All of these actions,... whether strictly legal or not, were ventured upon under what appeared to be a popular demand and a public necessity; trusting then as now that Congress would readily ratify them." 4 J. Richardson, MESSAGES AND PAPERS OF THE PRESIDENTS 23 (1900).

31. 1 A. Tocqueville, DEMOCRACY IN AMERICA 234-35 (D. Boorstin ed. 1990).

32. C. Friedrich, CONSTITUTIONAL REASON OF STATE: THE SURVIVAL OF THE CONSTI-TUTIONAL ORDER 4-5 (1957).

33. A. Miller, PRESIDENTIAL POWER 201 (1977). *"Raison d'etat* is the fundamental principle of national conduct, the State's first law of motion. It tells the statesman what he must do to preserve the health and strength of the State. The State is an organic struc-

ture whose full power can only be maintained by allowing it in some way to continue growing; and *raison d'etat* indicates both the path and the goal for such a growth." F. Meinecke, MACHIAVELLISM: THE DOCTRINE OF RAISON D'ETAT AND ITS PLACE IN MODERN HISTORY 1 (D. Scott trans. 1957).

34. See the statement by President Kennedy at his press conference when he answered a question concerning collective bargaining agreements: "These companies are free and the unions are free. All we [the Executive] can try to do is to indicate to them the public interest which is there. After all, the public interest is the sum of the private interests, or perhaps it's even a little more. In fact, it is a little more." N.Y. Times, Mar. 8, 1962, col. 7, at 1 (emphasis added).

35. A. Miller, *supra* note 33, at 203.

36. *Id.*

37. *Id.* at 203-04.

38. *See, e.g.,* THE FEDERALIST, Nos. 14, 37, 40, 44-45, 48, 51, 55 (Madison). The literature on this point is excessive, but of particular interest: Adair, *That Politics May Be Reduced to a Science: David Hume, James Madison, and the Tenth Federalist,* 20 HUNTINGTON LIBR.Q. 343 (1957); Diamond, *Democracy and the Federalist: A Reconstruction of the Framers' Intent,* 53 AMER.POL.SCI.REV. 52 (1959); Mason, *The Federalist: A Split Personality,* 57 AMER.HIST.REV. 625 (1952); Scanlan, *The Federalist and Human Nature,* 21 REV.POL. 657 (1959); Smith, *Reason, Passion, and Political Freedom in The Federalist,* 22 J.POL. 525 (1960); Wright, *The Federalist on the Nature of Man,* 49 ETHICS 1 (1949).

39. 71 U.S. (4 Wall.) 2 (1866). The Court said: "The Constitution of the United States is a law for rulers and people, equally in war and peace, and covers with the shield of its protection all classes of men, at all times, and under all circumstances. No doctrine involving more pernicious consequences was ever invented by the wit of man than that any of its provisions can be suspended during any of the great exigencies of government. Such a doctrine leads directly to anarchy or despotism, but the theory of necessity on which it is based is false; for the government, within the Constitution, has all the powers granted to it which are necessary to preserve its existence; as has been happily proved by the result of the great effort to throw off its just authority." *Id.* at 120-21.

40. Hurtgen, *supra* note 1, at 84.

41. *Id.*

42. C. Rossiter, *supra* note 19, at 13-14. Rossiter later adds the following caveat: "Crisis government in this country has ... been a matter of personalities rather than of institutions. Indeed, the one consistent instrument of emergency government has been the Presidency itself, a fact never more apparent than in the recent war. The study of constitutional dictatorship in the United States is not so much an analysis of institutions like martial law and the delegating statute as it is a history of Abraham Lincoln, Woodrow Wilson, and Franklin Roosevelt." *Id.* at 210.

43. 6 J. Richardson, *supra* note 30, at 78.

Table of Cases

Bibliography

Government Documents

Aggression from the North: The Record of North Viet-Nam's Campaign to Conquer South Viet-Nam, 52 DEP'T ST.BULL. 404 (1965).

Armed Action Taken by the United States Without a Declaration of War, 1789-1967, DEP'T ST.HIST.STUD.DIV. (1967).

Authority of the President to Repel the Attack in Korea, 23 DEP'T ST.BULL. 173 (1950).

Background Information on the Use of United States Armed Forces in Foreign Countries, House Comm. on Foreign Affairs, 91st Cong., 2d Sess. (1970).

Bombing in Cambodia, Hearings before the Senate Comm. on Armed Services, 93d Cong., 1st Sess. (1973).

Congress, the President and the War Powers, Hearings before the Subcomm. on Nat'l Security Policy and Scientific Development of the House Comm. on Foreign Affairs, 91st Cong., 2d Sess. (1970).

Congressional Oversight of Executive Agreements, Report of Subcomm. on Separation of Powers of the Senate Comm. on the Judiciary, 93d Cong., 1st Sess. (1973).

Documents Relating to the War Powers of Congress, the President's Authority as Commander-in-Chief and the War in Indochina, Senate Comm. on Foreign Relations, 91st Cong., 2d Sess. (1970).

Emergency Powers Statutes, Rept. No. 93-549 of the Senate Special Comm. on the Termination of the National Emergency, 93d Cong., 1st Sess. (1973).

Hearings on Separation of Powers before the Subcomm. on Separation of Powers of the Senate Comm. on the Judiciary, 90th Cong., 1st Sess. (1967).

Legal Case for U.S. Action in Cuba, 47 DEP'T ST.BULL. 763 (1962).

Legality of the U.S. Participation in the Defense of Vietnam, 54 DEP'T ST.BULL. 474 (1966).

Powers of the President as Commander-in-Chief of the Army and Navy of the United States, H.R. Doc. No. 445, 84th Cong., 2d Sess. (1956).

Powers of the President to Send Armed Forces outside the United States, Hearings before the Senate Comms. on Foreign Relations and Armed Services, 82d Cong., 1st Sess. (1951).

Transmittal of Executive Agreements to Congress, Hearings on S. 596 before the Senate Comm. on Foreign Relations, 92d Cong., 1st Sess. (1971).

Use of the United States Navy in Nicaragua, Hearings before the Senate Comm. on Foreign Relations, 70th Cong., 1st Sess. (1928).

War Powers after 200 Years: Congress and the President at a Constitutional Impasse, Hearings before the Senate Comm. on Foreign Relations, 100th Cong., 2d Sess. (1988).

War Powers: A Test of Compliance, Hearings before the Subcomm. on International Security and Scientific Affairs of the Senate Comm. on Foreign Relations, 94th Cong., 2d Sess. (1988).

War Powers Legislation, Hearings before the Senate Comm. on Foreign Relations, 92d Cong., 1st Sess. (1971); 93d Cong., 1st Sess. (1973).

War Powers, Libya, and State-Sponsored Terrorism, Hearings before the House Comm. on Foreign Affairs, 99th Cong., 2d Sess. (1986).

War Powers under the Constitution, S. Doc. No. 105, 65th Cong., 1st Sess. (1917).

Primary Sources

Aristotle, POLITICS (E. Baker trans. 1946).

Blackstone, W., COMMENTARIES ON THE LAWS OF ENGLAND (J. Ehrlich ed. 1959).

Elliot, J., DEBATES IN THE SEVERAL STATE CONVENTIONS ON THE ADOPTION OF THE FEDERAL CONSTITUTION (5 vols., 4th ed. 1888).

Farrand, M., THE RECORDS OF THE FEDERAL CONVENTION OF 1784 (4 vols., 3d ed. 1966).

FEDERALIST PAPERS (C. Rossiter ed. 1961).

Grotius, H., ON THE LAW OF WAR AND PEACE (Evans trans. 1682).

Harrington, J., THE COMMONWEALTH OF OCEANA (Peacock ed. 1992).

Hobbes, T., LEVIATHAN (McPherson ed. 1968).

Hume, D., POLITICAL ESSAYS (Hendell ed. 1953).

Locke, J., TWO TREATISES OF GOVERNMENT (P. Laslett ed. 1960).

Machiavelli, N., THE DISCOURSES (Crick ed. 1970).

_____, THE PRINCE (Adams ed. 1972).

Montesquieu, C., THE SPIRIT OF THE LAWS (F. Neuman trans. 1949).

Richardson, J., MESSAGES AND PAPERS OF THE PRESIDENTS (20 vols. 1900).

Rousseau, J., THE SOCIAL CONTRACT (L. Crocker ed. 1967).

Story, J., COMMENTARIES ON THE CONSTITUTION OF THE UNITED STATES (2 vols. 1833).

Thorpe, F., AMERICAN CHARTERS, CONSTITUTIONS AND ORGANIC LAWS (7 vols. 1909).

Tocqueville, A., DEMOCRACY IN AMERICA (2 vols., D. Boorstin, ed. 1990).

Secondary Sources

Acheson, D., PRESENT AT THE CREATION (1969).

Anderson, D., SHADOW ON THE WHITE HOUSE: PRESIDENTS AND THE VIETNAM WAR, 1945-1975 (1993).

Austin, A., THE PRESIDENT'S WAR: THE STORY OF THE TONKIN GULF RESOLUTION AND HOW THE NATION WAS TRAPPED IN VIETNAM (1971).

Bailey, T., A DIPLOMATIC HISTORY OF THE AMERICAN PEOPLE (6th ed. 1958).

Barber, J., PRESIDENTIAL CHARACTER (4th ed. 1992).

Bemis, S., A DIPLOMATIC HISTORY OF THE UNITED STATES (4th ed. 1955).

Berdahl, C., WAR POWERS OF THE EXECUTIVE OF THE UNITED STATES (1920).

Berger, R., EXECUTIVE PRIVILEGE: A CONSTITUTIONAL MYTH (1974).

Bickel, A., THE LEAST DANGEROUS BRANCH (1962).

Binkley, W., THE POWERS OF THE PRESIDENT (1937).

Bishop, J., JUSTICE UNDER FIRE: A STUDY OF MILITARY LAW (1974)

Blechman, B. & Kaplan, S., FORCE WITHOUT WAR: U.S. ARMED FORCES AS A POLITICAL INSTRUMENT (1978).

Bowett, D., SELF-DEFENSE IN INTERNATIONAL LAW (1958).

Caraley, D., THE PRESIDENT'S WAR POWERS (1984).

Chomsky, N., AMERICAN POWER AND THE NEW MANDARINS (1968).

Corwin, E., THE PRESIDENT: OFFICE AND POWERS (4TH ed. 1957).

_____, THE PRESIDENT'S CONTROL OF FOREIGN RELATIONS (1917).

_____, TOTAL WAR AND THE CONSTITUTION (1947).

Crosskey, W., POLITICS AND THE CONSTITUTION IN THE HISTORY OF THE UNITED STATES (2 vols. 1953).

D'Amato, A. & O'Neil, R., THE JUDICIARY AND VIETNAM (1972).

Dunning, W., ESSAYS ON THE CIVIL WAR AND RECONSTRUCTION (1897).

Eagleton, T., WAR AND THE PRESIDENTIAL WAR: A CHRONICLE OF CONGRESSIONAL SUR-RENDER (1974).

Ely, J., WAR AND RESPONSIBILITY: CONSTITUTIONAL LESSONS OF VIETNAM AND ITS AFTERMATH (1993).

Falk, R., LAW, MORALITY, AND WAR (1963).

_____, THE SIX LEGAL DIMENSIONS OF THE VIETNAM WAR (1968).

_____, VIETNAM SETTLEMENT: THE VIEW FROM HANOI (1968).

_____, THE VIETNAM WAR AND INTERNATIONAL LAW (2 vols. 1969).

Fall, B., THE TWO VIET-NAMS (rev. ed. 1964).

_____, VIETNAM WITNESS, 1953-66 (1966).

Fisher, L., PRESIDENTIAL WAR POWER (1995).

Fisher, L. & Devins, N., POLITICAL DYNAMICS OF CONSTITUTIONAL LAW (1992).

Fisher, S., THE TRIAL OF THE CONSTITUTION (1862).

Franklin, D., EXTRAORDINARY MEASURES (1991).

Friedman, L. & Neuborne, B., UNQUESTIONING OBEDIENCE TO THE PRESIDENT: THE ACLU CASE AGAINST THE LEGALITY OF THE WAR IN VIETNAM (1972).

Friedrich, D., CONSTITUTIONAL DICTATORSHIP AND DEMOCRACY (1948).

_____, CONSTITUTIONAL REASON OF STATE: THE SURVIVAL OF THE CONSTITUTION-AL ORDER (1957).

Fulbright, W., THE ARROGANCE OF POWER (1966).

Gibbons, W., THE U.S. GOVERNMENT AND THE VIETNAM WAR: EXECUTIVE AND LEGIS-LATIVE ROLES AND RELATIONSHIPS (3 vols. 1986-89).

Goulden, J., TRUTH IS THE FIRST CASUALTY—THE GULF OF TONKIN AFFAIR (1968).

Grodzins, M., AMERICANS BETRAYED: POLITICS AND THE JAPANESE EVACUATION (1949).

Halberstram, D., THE BEST AND THE BRIGHTEST (1972).

Hart, H. & Wechsler, H., THE FEDERAL COURTS IN THE FEDERAL SYSTEM (1953).

Henkin, L., CONSTITUTIONALISM, DEMOCRACY, AND FOREIGN AFFAIRS (1990).

_____, Foreign Affairs and the Constitution (1975).

Hirschfield, R., THE CONSTITUTION AND THE COURT: THE DEVELOPMENT OF THE BASIC LAW THROUGH JUDICIAL INTERPRETATION (1962).

Hoopes, T., THE LIMITS OF INTERVENTION (1969).

Hyman, H., A MORE PERFECT UNION: THE IMPACT OF THE CIVIL WAR AND RECONSTRUC-TION ON THE CONSTITUTION (1973).

Jackson, R., THE SUPREME COURT IN THE AMERICAN SYSTEM OF GOVERNMENT (1955).

Javits, J., WHO MAKES WAR: THE PRESIDENT VERSUS CONGRESS (1973).

Jessup, P., A MODERN LAW OF NATIONS (1952).

Kennedy, R., THIRTEEN DAYS (1969).

Keynes, E., UNDECLARED WAR: THE TWILIGHT ZONE OF CONSTITUTIONAL POWER (1982).

Kirkendall, R., HARRY S. TRUMAN, KOREA, AND THE IMPERIAL PRESIDENCY (1975)

Koenig, L., THE PRESIDENCY AND THE CRISIS: POWERS OF THE OFFICE FROM THE INVASION OF POLAND TO PEARL HARBOR (1944).

Koh, H., THE NATIONAL CONSTITUTION: SHARING POWER AFTER THE IRAN-CONTRA AFFAIR (1990).

Lacouture, J., VIETNAM: BETWEEN TWO TRUCES (1966).

Laski, H., THE AMERICAN PRESIDENCY (1940).

Lawyers' Comm. on American Policy Towards Vietnam and International Law, AN ANALYSIS OF THE LEGALITY OF THE UNITED STATES MILITARY INVOLVEMENT (1968).

Leckie, R., THE WARS OF AMERICA (1968).

Leham, J., MAKING WAR: THE 200-YEAR-OLD BATTLE BETWEEN THE PRESIDENT AND CONGRESS OVER HOW AMERICA GOES TO WAR (1992).

Levy, L., ORIGINAL INTENT AND THE FRAMERS' CONSTITUTION (1988).

Longaker, R., THE PRESIDENT AND INDIVIDUAL LIBERTIES (1961).

Marcus, M., TRUMAN AND THE STEEL SEIZURE CASE: THE LIMITS OF PRESIDENTIAL POWER (1977).

Maurice, J., HOSTILITIES WITHOUT DECLARATION OF WAR (1883).

May, C., IN THE NAME OF WAR: JUDICIAL REVIEW AND THE WAR POWER SINCE 1918 (1989).

May, E., THE ULTIMATE DECISION: THE PRESIDENT AS COMMANDER IN CHIEF (1960).

McClure, W., INTERNATIONAL EXECUTIVE AGREEMENTS (1941).

McDonald, F., NOVUS ORDO SECLORIUM (1985).

McIllwain, C., CONSTITUTIONALISM: ANCIENT AND MODERN (1947).

McKenna, G., A Guide to the Constitution: That Delicate Balance (1984).

Meinecke, F., MACHIAVELLISM: THE DOCTRINE OF RAISON d'ETAT AND ITS PLACE IN MODERN HISTORY (D. Scott trans. 1957).

Miller, A., DEMOCRATIC DICTATORSHIP: THE EMERGENCY CONSTITUTION OF CONTROL (1981).

_____, PRESIDENTIAL POWER (1977).

_____, SOCIAL CHANGE AND FUNDAMENTAL LAW (1979).

Moore, J., A DIGEST OF INTERNATIONAL LAW (7 vols. 1906).

Morrison, S., OXFORD HISTORY OF THE AMERICAN PEOPLE (1965).

Neustadt, R., Presidential Power (1960).

Offutt, M., THE PROTECTION OF CITIZENS ABROAD BY THE ARMED FORCES OF THE UNITED STATES (1928).

Pomeroy, J., AN INTRODUCTION TO THE CONSTITUTIONAL LAW OF THE UNITED STATES (1879).

Popper, K., THE OPEN SOCIETY AND ITS ENEMIES (2 vols., 5th ed. 1966).

Pusey, M., THE WAY WE GO TO WAR (1969).

Pyle, C. & Pious, R., THE PRESIDENT, CONGRESS, AND THE CONSTITUTION (1984).

Randall, J., CONSTITUTIONAL PROBLEMS UNDER LINCOLN (rev. ed. 1951).

Rankin, R., WHEN CIVIL LAW FAILS: MARTIAL LAW AND ITS LEGAL BASIS IN THE UNITED STATES (1939).

Rankin, R. & Dallmayr, W., FREEDOM AND EMERGENCY POWERS IN THE COLD WAR (1974).

Reedy, G., THE TWILIGHT OF THE PRESIDENCY (1970).

Reel, A., THE CASE OF GENERAL YAMASHITA (1949).

Relyea, H., A BRIEF HISTORY OF EMERGENCY POWERS IN THE UNITED STATES (1974).

Reveley, W., WAR POWERS OF THE PRESIDENT AND CONGRESS: WHO HOLDS THE ARROWS AND OLIVE BRANCH? (1981).

Rogers, J., WORLD POLICING AND THE CONSTITUTION (1945).

Rossiter, C., THE AMERICAN PRESIDENCY (3d ed. 1987).

_____, CONSTITUTIONAL DICTATORSHIP: CRISIS GOVERNMENT IN THE MODERN DEMOCRACIES (1948).

_____, THE SUPREME COURT AND THE COMMANDER IN CHIEF (R. Longaker ed. 1976)

Schlesinger, A., THE BITTER HERITAGE (1967).

_____, THE IMPERIAL PRESIDENCY (1973).

Schlesinger, A. & de Grazia, A., CONGRESS AND THE PRESIDENCY (1967).

Schwartz, B., THE POWERS OF GOVERNMENT (1963).

Scigliano, R., THE SUPREME COURT AND THE PRESIDENCY (1971).

Sheffer, M., PRESIDENTIAL POWER (1991).

Small, N., SOME PRESIDENTIAL INTERPRETATIONS OF THE PRESIDENCY (1932).

Smith, J. & Cotter, C., POWERS OF THE PRESIDENT DURING CRISIS (1960).

Smyrl, M., CONFLICT OR CODETERMINATION?: CONGRESS, THE PRESIDENT, AND THE POWER TO MAKE WAR (1988).

Stern, G. & Halpern, M., THE U.S. CONSTITUTION AND THE POWER TO GO TO WAR (1994).

Stone, J., AGGRESSION AND WORLD ORDER (1958).

Sutherland, A., CONSTITUTIONALISM IN AMERICA (1965).

Taylor, T., NUREMBERG AND VIETNAM: AN AMERICAN TRAGEDY (1970).

Thomas, A. & Thomas, A.J., THE WAR-MAKING POWERS OF THE PRESIDENT: CONSTITUTIONAL AND INTERNATIONAL LAW ASPECTS (1982).

Tiefer, C., THE SEMI-SOVEREIGN PRESIDENCY: THE BUSH ADMINISTRATION'S STRATEGY FOR GOVERNING WITHOUT CONGRESS (1994).

Tourtellot, A., THE PRESIDENTS ON THE PRESIDENCY (1964).

Turner, R., REPEALING THE WAR POWERS RESOLUTION: RESTORING THE RULE OF LAW IN U.S. FOREIGN POLICY (1991).

_____, THE WAR POWERS RESOLUTION: ITS IMPLEMENTATION IN THEORY AND PRACTICE (1983).

Velvel, L., UNDECLARED WAR AND CIVIL DISOBEDIENCE: THE AMERICAN SYSTEM IN CRISIS (1970).

Walzer, M., JUST AND UNJUST WARS (1977).

Wechsler, H., PRINCIPLES, POLITICS AND FUNDAMENTAL LAW (1962).

Whiting, W., WAR POWERS UNDER THE CONSTITUTION (43d ed. 1871).

Willoughby, W., THE CONSTITUTIONAL LAW OF THE UNITED STATES (2 vols., 2d ed. 1929).

Wilson, W., CONGRESSIONAL GOVERNMENT (1887).

_____, CONSTITUTIONAL GOVERNMENT IN THE UNITED STATES (1908).

Wormuth, F., THE ORIGINS OF MODERN CONSTITUTIONALISM (1948).

_____, THE VIETNAM WAR: THE PRESIDENT VERSUS THE CONSTITUTION (1968).

Wormuth, F. & Firmage, E., TO CHAIN THE DOG OF WAR (2d ed. 1989).

Wright, Q., THE CONTROL OF AMERICAN FOREIGN RELATIONS (1922).

Zagoria, D., VIETNAM TRIANGLE: MOSCOW, PEKING AND HANOI (1967).

Zinn, H., VIETNAM: THE LOGIC OF WITHDRAWAL (1969).

Articles

Acheson, *The Eclipse of the State Department,* 49 FOREIGN AFF. 593 (1971).

Adams, *Machiavelli Now and Here,* 44 AMER.SCHOLAR 365 (1975).

Adler, D., *The Constitution and Presidential Warmaking: The Enduring Debate,* 103 POL.SCI.Q. 1 (1988).

Adler, E., *Executive Command and Control of Foreign Policy: The CIA's Covert Activities*, 23 ORBIS 671 (1979).

Anderson, *The Ambiguities of Defeat*, 114 CURRENT 6 (1970).

Berlin, *The Originality of Machiavelli*, in STUDIES ON MACHIAVELLI (Gillmore ed. 1972).

Bickel, *The Constitution and the War*, COMMENTARY (July 1972).

Bostdorff, *The Presidency and Promoted Crisis: Reagan, Grenada, and Issue Management*, 21 PRES.STUD.Q. 737 (1991).

Burgin, *Congress, the War Power Resolution, and the Invasion of Panama*, 25 POLITY 217 (1992).

Carver, *The Faceless Viet Cong*, 44 FOREIGN AFF. 347 (1966).

Chayes, *Law and the Quarantine of Cuba*, 41 FOREIGN AFF. 550 (1963).

Clifford, *A Viet Nam Reappraisal*, 47 FOREIGN AFF. 601 (1969).

Commager, *Is Democracy Dying in America?*, 34 LOOK MAG. 16 (July 14, 1970).

_____, *Presidential Power: The Issue Analyzed*, N.Y. Times Mag. (Jan. 14, 1951).

Corwin, *The President's Power*, THE NEW REPUBLIC (Jan. 29, 1951).

_____, *Who Has the Power to Make War?*, N.Y. Times Mag. (July 31, 1949).

Davidson, *Congress and the Presidency: Invitation to Struggle*, 499 THE ANNALS (1944).

Fisher, S., *The Suspension of Habeas Corpus during the War of Rebellion*, 3 POL.SCI.Q. 454 (1888).

Ford, *Congress, the Presidency, and National Security Policy*, 16 PRES.STUD.Q. 200 (1986).

Glennon, *The Gulf War and the Constitution*, 70 FOREIGN AFF. 84 (1991).

Halpern, *Lawful Wars*, 72 FOREIGN AFF. 173 (1988).

Harrington, *Getting Out of Vietnam*, 17 DISSENT 5 (1970).

Hoopes, *Legacy of the Cold War in Indochina*, 48 FOREIGN AFF. 601 (1970).

Hoxie, *The Office of Commander in Chief: An Historical and Projective View*, 6 PRES. STUD.Q. 10 (1976).

Kissinger, *The Viet Nam Negotiations*, 47 FOREIGN AFF. 211 (1969)

Lacouture, *From the Vietnam War to an Indochina War*, 48 FOREIGN AFF. 617 (1969).

Lansdale, *Viet Nam: Do We Understand Revolution?*, 43 FOREIGN AFF. 75 (1964).

Lawrence, *Is a Declaration of a State of War Needed?*, U.S. NEWS & WORLD REPT. (July 26, 1965).

Lofgren, *Mr. Truman's War: A Debate and its Aftermath*, 31 REV.POL. 231 (1969).

Longaker, *Emergency Detention: The Generation Gap, 1950-1971*, 27 W. POL.Q. 395 (1974).

Moore, J.B., *Treaties and Executive Agreements*, 20 POL.SCI.Q. 385 (1905).

Moore, J.N., *The National Executive and the Use of the Armed Forces Abroad*, 21 NAV. WAR COL.REV. 28 (1969).

Robertson, *South America and the Monroe Doctrine, 1824-28*, 30 POL.SCI.Q. 89 (1915).

Rogers, C., *Legislative and Executive in Wartime*, 19 FOREIGN AFF. 717 (1941).

_____, *Presidential Dictatorship in the United States*, 231 Q.REV. 136 (1919).

Rossiter, *Constitutional Dictatorship in the Atomic Age*, 11 REV.POL. 395 (1951).

_____, *The Legacy of John Adams*, 46 THE YALE REV. 540 (1957).

Schlesinger, *Presidential War*, N.Y. Times Mag. (Jan. 7, 1973).

Sheffer, *The Attorney General and Presidential Power: Robert H. Jackson, Franklin Roosevelt, and the Prerogative Presidency*, 12 PRES.STUD. Q. 54 (1982).

_____, *Presidential Power and Limited Government*, 21 PRES.STUD.Q. 471 (1991).

Stone, *Presidential First Use is Unlawful*, 56 FOREIGN AFF. 94 (1984).

Tanenhaus, *The Supreme Court and Presidential Power*, 307 THE ANNALS 106 (1956).

Timbers, *The Supreme Court and the President as Commander in Chief*, 16 PRES.STUD. Q. 224 (1986).

Watkins, *War by Executive Order*, 4 W.POL.Q. 539 (1951).
Weissman, *CIA Covert Action in Zaire and Angola: Patterns and Consequences*, 94 POL.SCI.Q. 263 (1979).
Wilmerding, *The President and the Law*, 67 POL.SCI.Q. 329 (1952).
Zeiderstein, *The Reassertion of Congressional Power: New Curbs on the President*, 93 POL.SCI.Q. 393 (1978).

Law Review Articles

Aldrich, *Comments on Legality of United States Action in Cambodia*, 65 AM.J.INT'L.L. 76 (1971).
Alford, *The Legality of American Military Involvement in Viet Nam: A BroaderPerspective*, 75 YALE L.J. 1109 (1966).
Allison, *Making War: The President and Congress*, 40 LAW & CONTEMP. PROBS. 86 (1976).
Andonian, *Law and Vietnam*, 54 A.B.A.J. 457 (1960).
Baldwin, *The Share of the President of the United States in a Declaration of War*, 12 AM.J.INT'L L. 1 (1918).
Banks, *Steel, Sawyer, and Executive Power*, 14 U.PITTS.L.REV. 467 (1953).
Beck, *International Law and the Decision to Invade Grenada: A Ten-Year Retrospective*, 33 VA.J.INT'L L. 765 (1993).
Berger, M., *Implementing a United Nations Security Council Resolution: The President's Power to Use Force Without the Authorization of Congress*, 15 HASTINGS INT'L & COMP.L.REV. 83 (1991).
Berger, R., *Executive Privilege v. Congressional Inquiry*, 12 U.C.L.A.L.REV. 1288 (1965).
_____, *The President's Monopoly on Foreign Relations*, 71 MICH.L.REV. 1 (1972).
_____, *The Protection of American's Abroad*, 44 U.CINN.L.REV. 741 (1975).
_____, *War, Foreign Affairs, and Executive Privilege*, 72 NW.U.L.REV. 309 (1977).
_____, *War Making by the President*, 121 U.PA.L.REV. 29 (1972).
Bestor, *Separation of Powers in the Domain of Foreign Affairs: The Intent of the Constitution Historically Examined*, 5 SETON HALL L.REV. 527 (1974).
Bickel, *Congress, the President, and the Power to Wage War*, 48 CHI.-KENT L.REV. 131 (1971).
Biden & Ritch, *The War Power at a Constitutional Impasse: A Joint Decision Solution*, 77 GEO.L.REV. 367 (1988).
Borchard, *The Attorney General's Opinion on the Exchange of Destroyers for Naval Bases*, 34 AM.J.INT'L L. 690 (1940).
_____, *The Charter and the Constitution*, 39 AM.J.INT'L L. 767 (1945).
Bork, *Comments on the Articles on the Legality of the United States Action in Cambodia*, 65 AM.J.INT'L L. 79 (1971).
Briggs, *Neglected Aspects of the Destroyer Deal*, 34 AM.J.INT'L L. 569 (1940).
Buchanan, *In Defense of the War Powers Resolution: Chadha Does Not Apply*, 22 HOUS.L.REV. 1155 (1985).
Carter, *The Constitutionality of the War Powers Resolution*, 70 VA.L.REV. 101 (1984)
Casper, Constitutional Constraints on the Conduct of Foreign and Defense Policy: A Non-Judicial Model, 43 U.CHI.L.REV. 463 (1976).
Chayes, *The International Issues: Opposition Position*, 45 N.Y.U.L.REV. 658 (1970).
Comment, *The President, the Congress, and the Power to Declare War*, 16 KAN.L.REV. 82 (1967).
Corwin, *The Steel Seizure Case: A Judicial Brick without Straw*, 54 COLUM.L.REV. 53

(1953).

Crudin, *The War Making Process,* 49 MIL.L.REV. 35 (1975).

D'Angelo, *Resort to Force by States to Protect Nationals: The U.S. Rescue Mission to Iran and its Legality under International Law,* 21 VA.J. INT'L L. 485 (1981).

Demato, et al., *War Crimes and Vietnam: The Nuremberg Defense and the Military Register,* 57 CALIF.L.REV. 1055 (1969).

Dembitz, *Racial Duiscrimination and the Military Judgment: The Supreme Court's Korematsu and Endo Decisions,* 45 COLUM.L.REV. 175 (1945).

Deutsch, *The Legality of the United States Position in Vietnam,* 52 A.B.A.J. 436 (1966).

———, *Legality of the War in Vietnam,* 7 WASHBURN L.J. 153 (1968).

Eagleton, C., *The Form and Function of the Declaration of War,* 33 AM.J.INT'L L. 19 (1938).

Eagleton, T., *The August 15 Compromise and the War Powers of Congress,* 18 ST.LOUIS U.L.REV. 1 (1973).

Edgar, *United States Use of Armed Forces under the United Nations,* 10 J.L.&POL. 299 (1984).

Ely, *Suppose Congress Wanted a War Powers Act That Worked,* 88 COLUM.L.REV. 1379 (1988).

Emerson, *Making War without a Declaration,* 17 J.LEG. 23 (1990).

———, *War Powers: An Invasion of Presidential Prerogative,* 58 A.B.A.J. 809 (1972).

———, *War Powers Legislation,* 74 W.VA.L.REV. 53 (1972).

———, *War Powers Resolution Tested: The President's Independent Dfense Powers,* 51 NOTRE DAME LAW. 187 (1975).

Falk, *The Cambodian Operation and International Law,* 65 AM.J.INT'L L. 1 (1971).

———, *International Law and the United States Role in the Viet Nam War,* 75 YALE L.J. 1122 (1966).

Faulkner, *The War in Vietnam: Is It Constitutional?,* 56 GEO.L.J. 1132 (1968).

Fenwick, *War Without a Declaration,* 31 AM.J.INT'L L. 694 (1937).

Ferencz, *War Crimes and the Vietnam War,* 17 AM.U.L.REV. 403 (1968).

Finman & Maculay, *Freedom to Dissent: The Vietnam Protests and the Words of Public Officials,* 1969 WISC.L.REV. 632.

Firmage, *The War Powers and the Political Question Doctrine,* 49 U.COL.L.REV. 65 (1977).

Fisher, L., *Confidential Spending and Governmental Accountability,* 47 GEO. WASH.L. REV. 347 (1979).

Franck, *After the Fall: The New Procedural Framework for Congressional Control over the War Power,* 71 AM.J.INT'L L. 605 (1977).

Franck & Patel, *UN Police Action in Lieu of War: The Old Order Changeth,* 85 AM.J. INT'L L. 74 (1991).

Friedman, *Law and Politics in the Vietnamese War,* 61 AM.J.INT'L L. 776 (1967).

———, *Waging War against Checks and Balances—The Claim of an Unlimited Presidential War Power,* 57 ST.JOHN'S L.REV. 213 (1983).

Fulbright, *The Role of Congress in Internaitonal Affairs,* 47 CORNELL L.Q. 1 (1961).

Gilmore, *War Powers—Executive Power and the Constitution,* 29 IOWA L.REV. 463 (1944).

Glennon, *Strengthening the War Powers Resolution,* 60 MINN.L.REV. 1 (1975).

———, *War Powers Resolution Ten Years Later: More Politics Than Law,* 78 AM.J. INT'L L. 571 (1984).

———, *The Constitution and Chapter VII of the United Nations Charter,* 85 AM.J.INT'L L. 75 (1991).

Goldwater, *The President's Ability to Portect America's Freedoms—The Warmaking*

Power, 1971 LAW & SOC.ORD. 423.

_____, *The President's Constitutional Primacy in Foreign Relations and National Defense*, 13 VA.J.INT'L L. 463 (1973).

Graham, *Toward a Jurisprudence of Peace?*, 59 B.U.L.REV. 1 (1970).

Harmon, *Presidential Power to Use the Armed Forces Abroad Without Statutory Authority*, 41 U.S.OP., OFF.LEGAL COUNS. 185 (Feb. 12, 1980).

Hayes, *Emergencies and the Power of the United States Government to Meet Them*, 16 TEMPLE U.L.REV. 634 (1942).

Henkin, *Executive Privilege: Mr. Nixon Loses but the Presidency Largely Prevails*, 22 U.C.L.A.L.REV. 40 (1974).

_____, *The Invasion of Panama under International Law: A Gross Violation*, 29 COLUM.J.TRANSNAT'L L. 293 (1991).

_____, *The Right to Know and the Duty to Withhold: The Case of the Pentagon Papers*, 120 U.PA.L.REV. 271 (1971).

_____, *Viet-Nam in the Courts of the United States: Political Questions*, 63 AM.J.INT'L L. 284 (1969).

Highsmith, *Policy Executive Adventurism: Congressional Oversight of Military and Paramilitary Operations*, 19 HARV.J. ON LEGIS. 333 (1982).

Hopson, *The Executive Agreement in United States Practice*, 12 A.F.JAG L.REV. 252 (1970).

Hoyt, *The United States Reaction to the Korean Attack*, 55 AM.J.INT'L L. 45 (1961).

Hughes, C., *War Powers under the Constitution*, 42 A.B.A.REPTS. 238 (1917).

Hughes, G., *Civil Disobedience and the Political Question Doctrine*, 43 N.Y.U.L.REV. 1 (1968).

Hurtgen, *The Case for Presidential Prerogative*, 7 U.TOL.L.REV. 59 (1975).

Ides, *Constitutional Responsibility and the War Power*, 17 LOY.L.A.L.REV. 599 (1984).

_____, *Constitutional Authority to Regulate the Use of Nuclear Weapons*, 13 HASTINGS CONST.L.Q. 233 (1986).

Jones, *The President, Congress, and Foreign Relations*, 29 CALIF.L.REV. 565 (1941).

Jenkins, *The War Powers Resolution: Statutory Limitation on the Commander in Chief*, 11 HARV.J.ON LEGIS. 181 (1974).

Kalven, *Even When a Nation is at War*, 85 HARV.L.REV. 26 (1971).

Karst & Horowitz, *Presidential Prerogative*, 22 U.C.L.A.L.REV. 67 (1974).

Kauper, *The Steel Seizure Case*, 51 MICH.L.REV. 141 (1952).

Kelley, *The Constitutional Implications of the Mayaguez Incident*, 3 HASTINGS CONST. L.Q. 301 (1976).

Kramer & Marcuse, *Executive Privilege—A Study of the Period 1953-1960*, 29 GEO. WASH.L.REV. 623, 827 (1961).

Kurland, *The Impotence of Reticence*, 1968 DUKE L.J. 619.

Lee, *Congress Steps Out: A Look at Congressional Control of the Executive*, 63 CALIF.L.REV. 983 (1978).

Levitan, *The Foreign Relations Power: An Analysis of Mr. Justice Sutherland's Theory*, 55 YALE L.J. 467 (1946).

Lobel, *Covert War and Congressional Authority: Hidden War and For-gotten Power*, 134 U.PA.L.REV. 1035 (1986).

Lofgren, *United States v. Curtiss-Wright Export Corporation: An Historical Reassessment*, 83 YALE L.J. 1 (1973).

_____, *War-Making under the Constitution: The Original Understanding*, 81 YALE L.J. 672 (1972).

Malawer, *The Vietnam War under the Constitution: Legal Issues Involved in the United States Military Involvement in Vietnam*, 31 U.PITTS.L.REV. 205 (1969).

Mallison, *Limited Naval Blockade or Quarantine Interdiction,* 31 GEO. WASH. L.REV. 335 (1962).

Mathews, *The Constitutional Power of the President to Conclude International Agreements,* 64 YALE L.J. 345 (1955).

McDougal & Lans, *Treaties and Congressional-Executive or Presidential Agreements: Interchangeable Instruments of National Policy,* 54 YALE L.J. 181, 306 (1945).

McGowan, *The President's Veto Power: An Important Instrument of Conflict in our Constitutional System,* 23 SAN DIEGO L.REV. 791 (1986).

McKay, *The Constitutional Issues: Opposition Position,* 45 N.Y.U.L.REV. 640 (1970).

McLaughlin, *The Scope of the Treaty Power in the United States,* 42 MINN.L.REV. 709 (1958).

Meeker, *Defensive Quarantine and the Law,* 57 AM.J.INT'L L. 515 (1963).

_____, *The Legality of the United States Participation in the Defense of Viet Nam,* 75 YALE L.J. 1085 (1966).

Meeks, *Illegal Law Enforcement: Aiding Civil Authorities in Violation of the Posse Comitatus Act,* 70 MIL.L.J. 132 (1975).

Milva & Neuman, *The Hostage Crisis and the Hostage Act,* 49 U.CHI.L.REV. 292 (1982).

Monaghan, *Presidential War-Making,* 50 B.U.L.REV. 19 (1970).

Moore, J., *International Law and the United States' Role in Viet Nam,* 76 YALE L.J. 1051 (1967).

_____, *Legal Dimensions of the Decision to Intercede in Cambodia,* 65 AM.J.INT'L L. 38 (1971).

Murphy, *Vietnam: A Study of Law and Politics,* 36 FORDHAM L.REV. 453 (1968).

Note, *American Action in Vietnam: Justifiable in International Law?,* 19 STAN.L.REV. 1307 (1967).

____, *Congress, the President, and the Power to Commit Forces to Combat,* 81 HARV.L. REV. 1771 (1968).

____, *Executive Privilege and the Congressional Right of Inquiry,* 10 HARV.J. ON LEGIS. 621 (1973).

____, *The Future of the War Powers Resolution,* 36 STAN.L.REV. 1407 (1984).

____, *Geneva Convention and the Treatment of Prisoners of War in Vietnam,* 80 HARV.L. REV. 851 (1967).

____, *The Legality of the National Bank Moratorium,* 27 ILL.L.REV. 923 (1933).

____, *1973 War Powers Legislation: Congress Reasserts its Warmaking Power,* 5 LOY.U.CHI.L.J. 83 (1974).

____, *Presidential Impounding of Funds: The Judicial Response,* 40 U.CHI. L.REV. 328 (1973).

____, *Presidential Impoundment: Constitutional Theories and Political Realities,* 61 GEO.L.J. 1295 (1973).

____, *Riot Control and the Use of Federal Troops,* 81 HARV.L.REV. 638 (1968).

____, *The Supreme Court as Arbitrator in the Conflict between Presidential and Congressional War-Making Power,* 50 B.U.L.REV. 78 (1970).

____, *United States in Vietnam: A Case Study in the Law of Intervention,* 50 CALIF.L. REV. 137 (1962).

____, *The War in Southeast Asia: A Legal Position Paper,* 45 N.Y.U.L.REV. 695 (1970).

____, *The War-Making Powers: The Intentions of the Framers in the Light of Parliamentary History,* 50 B.U.L.REV. 5 (1970).

____, *The War Powers Resolution: Statutory Limitation on the Commander-in-Chief,* 11 HARV.J. ON LEGIS. 181 (1974).

Putney, *Executive Assumptions on the War-Making Power,* 7 NAT.L.REV. 1 (1927).

Pye, *The Legal Status of the Korea Hostilities*, 45 GEO.L.J. 45 (1956).

Ratner, *The Coordinated Warmaking Power—Legislative, Executive, and Judicial Roles*, 44 S.CAL.L.REV. 461 (1971).

Reven-Hansen & Banks, *Pulling the Purse Strings of the Commander in Chief*, 80 VA.L. REV. 833 (1994).

Rehnquist, *The Constitutional Issues: Administrative Position*, 45 N.Y.U. L.REV. 629 (1970).

Reveley, *Constitutional Allocation of the War Powers Between the President and Congress*, 15 VA.J.INT'L L. 73 (1974).

———, *Presidential War-Making: Constitutional Prerogative or Usurpation?*, 55 VA. L.REV. 1243 (1969).

Richberg, *The Steel Seizure Case*, 38 VA.L.REV. 713 (1952).

Robbins, *The War Powers Resolution after Fifteen Years: A Reassessment*, 38 AM.U.L. REV. 141 (1988).

Robertson, *The Debate among American International Lawyers about the Vietnam War*, 46 TEX.L.REV. 898 (1968).

Rogers, W., *Congress, the President, and the War Powers*, 59 CALIF.L.REV. 1194 (1971).

———, *The Constitutionality of the Cambodian Incursion*, 65 AM.J.INT'L L. 26 (1971).

Rostow, *Great Cases Make Bad Law: The War Powers Act*, 50 TEX.L.REV. 833 (1972).

———, *The Japanese American Cases—A Disaster*, 54 YALE L.J. 489 (1945).

———, *Once More unto the Breach: The War Powers Act*, 21 VAL.U.L.REV. 1 (1986).

Rushkoff, *A Defense of the War Powers Resolution*, 93 YALE L.J. 1330 (1984).

Scharpf, *Judicial Review and the Political Question: A Functional Analysis*, 75 YALE L.J. 517 (1966).

Schick, *Some Reflections on the Legal Controversies Concerning America's Involvement in Vietnam*, 17 INT'L & COMP.L.Q. 953 (1968).

Schwartz & McCormick, *The Justiciability of Legal Objections in the American Involvement in Vietnam*, 46 TEX.L.REV. 1033 (1968).

Sheffer, *Presidential Power to Suspend Habeas Corpus: The Taney-Bates Dialogue and Ex Parte Merryman*, 21 OKLA.CITY U.L.REV. 1 (1986).

Silverberg, *The Separation of Powers and Control of the CIA's Covert Operations*, 68 TEX.L.REV. 575 (1990).

Sofaer, *The Legality of the United States Action in Panama*, 29 COLUM.J.TRANSNAT'L L. 281 (1991).

———, *The Presidency, War, and Foreign Affairs: Practice under the Framers*, 40 LAW & CONTEMP.PROBS. 12 (1976).

Spong, *The War Powers Resolution Revisited: Historic Accomplishment or Surrender*, 16 WM. & MARY L.REV. 823 (1975).

Sponsler, *Universality Principle of Jurisdiction and the Threatened Trials of American Airmen*, 15 LOY.L.REV. 43 (1968).

Standard, *United States Intervention in Vietnam Is Not Legal*, 52 A.B.A.J. 627 (1966).

Steele, *Covert Action and the War Powers Resolution: Preserving the Constitutional Balance*, 39 SYRACUSE L.REV. 1139 (1988).

Stevenson, *The International Law Issues: Administration Position*, 45 N.Y.U.L.REV. 658 (1970).

Stromseth, *Rethinking War Powers: Congress, the President, and the United Nations*, 81 GEO.L.J. 579 (1993).

Symposium, *The President's Power as Commander-in-Chief versus Congress' War Power and Appropriations Power*, 43 U.MIAMI L.REV. 17 (1988).

Tigar, *Judicial Power, the Political Question Doctrine, and Foreign Relations,* 17 U.C.L.A.L.REV. 1135 (1970).

Van Alstyne, *Congress, the President, and the Power to Declare War: A Requiem for Vietnam,* 121 U.PA.L.REV. 1 (1972).

Vance, *Striking the Balance: Congress and the President Under the War Powers Resolution,* 133 U.PA.L.REV. 79 (1984).

Velvel, *The War in Viet Nam: Unconstitutional, Justiciable, and Jurisdictionally Attackable,* 16 KAN.L.REV. 449 (1968).

Wiener, *Martial Law Today,* 55 A.B.A.J. 723 (1969).

William, *Vietnam and Riots in America,* 38 OKLA.B.J. 1677 (1967).

Wolkman, *Demands of Congressional Committees for Executive Papers,* 10 FED.B.J. 103 (1949).

Wormuth, *The Nixon Theory of the War Powers: A Critique,* 60 CALIF.L.REV. 623 (1972).

Wright, *Beyond Discretionary Justice,* 81 YALE L.J. 575 (1972).

————, *Legal Aspects of the Vietnam Situation,* 60 AM.J.INT'L L. 750 (1966).

————, *Subversive Intervention,* 54 AM.J.INT'L L. 521 (1960).

————, *The Transfer of Destroyers to Great Britain,* 34 AM.J.INT'L L. 680 (1940).

Zutz, *The Recapture of the Mayaguez: Failure of the Consultation Clause of the War Powers Resolution,* 8 N.Y.U.J.INT'L L. & POL. 457 (1976).

Index

About the Author

MARTIN S. SHEFFER taught for 29 years at Old Dominion University and Tuskegee University. Professor Sheffer's major areas of teaching and research are the American presidency, constitutional law and theory, and American political thought. He has published extensively in academic journals and law reviews, and he is the author of *Presidential Power* (1991) and *God Versus Caesar* (forthcoming).

ISBN 0-275-96435-3

90000>

EAN

9 780275 964351

HARDCOVER BAR CODE